beneath the waves

EDWARD F. FINCH

beneath the waves

The Life and Navy of

CAPT. EDWARD L. BEACH JR.

Naval Institute Press | Annapolis, Maryland

Naval Institute Press
291 Wood Road
Annapolis, MD 21402

Library of Congress Cataloging-in-Publication Data
Finch, Edward F.
  Beneath the waves : the life and navy of Captain Edward L. Beach Jr. / Edward
F. Finch.
    p. cm.
  Includes bibliographical references and index.
  ISBN 978-1-59114-266-9 (acid-free paper) 1. Beach, Edward L. (Edward
Latimer), 1918-2002. 2. United States. Navy—Officers—Biography. 3. United
States. Navy—Submarine forces—Biography. I. Title.
  V63.B43F56 2010
  359.0092—dc22
  [B]
                                        2010004220

Printed in the United States of America on acid-free paper

14 13 12 11 10   9 8 7 6 5 4 3 2
First printing

All photographs are from the collection of Mrs. Ingrid Beach.

To the women and men who,
whether as professionals or reservists,
for generations have "gone down to the sea in ships"
in the protection of our Republic,
in sincere gratitude and respect this book is dedicated.

Contents

List of Photographs ix

List of Abbreviations xi

Preface xiii

Acknowledgments xvii

Prologue xix

Part I: 1918–1941 1

Part II: 1941–1945 20

Part III: 1945–1953 44

Part IV: 1953–1957 59

Part V: *Run Silent, Run Deep* 76

Part VI: 1957–1958 89

Part VII: 1958–1961—*Triton* 99

Part VIII: 1961–1966 135

Part IX: 1966–2002 150

Epilogue 169

Appendix I: A Brief Chronology
    of the Life of Edward L. "Ned" Beach Jr. 173

Appendix II: Chronological Bibliography
    of the Published Writings of Edward L. Beach Jr. .. 177

Appendix III: Brief Biographies of Beach Family Members .. 181

Notes	219
Bibliography	239
Index	251

Photographs

"Admiral Neddie Beach Jr."   2

Ned, age one, with his parents   3

In 1939—Ens. Edward L. Beach Jr.   14

Officers of USS *Trigger*   33

The newlyweds—Ingrid and Ned   37

Ike and Ned   60

Christmas 1954   61

Office of the Naval Aide   62

Meeting the president and first lady   64

As presidential naval aide, in 1953 Ned participated in the
    decommissioning of USS *Williamsburg*, the presidential yacht.   65

In May 1960, Ned poses at the White House   128

At the dedication of Beach Hall   166

In their "Golden Years"—Ingrid and Ned on the island
    of Ljusterö, off Stockholm, Sweden   169

Capt. Edward L. Beach Sr., USN, Ned's father   182

John B. Beach, U.S. Army, Alice Beach, USN, and Edward L.
    Beach Jr., USN, during World War II   208

Abbreviations

7MC	submarine control announcing system
ASC	American Society of Cinematographers (member of)
CNO	Chief of Naval Operations
CO	Commanding Officer
COB	Chief of the Boat
COMSUBLANT	Commander, Submarine Force, U.S. Atlantic Fleet
COMSUBPAC	Commander, Submarine Force, U.S. Pacific Fleet
CRdM	Chief Radarman
EN2	Engineman 2nd Class
EN3	Engineman 3rd Class
GM2	Gunner's Mate 2nd Class
JANAC	Joint Army-Navy Assessment Committee
LLD	Doctor of Laws
MC	Medical Corps
NATO	North Atlantic Treaty Organization
OPSO	Operations Officer
PA	public address
PCO	Prospective Commanding Officer

PN3	Personnelman 3rd Class
PXO	Prospective Executive Officer
QMC	Chief Quartermaster
QM1C	Quartermaster 1st Class
SecNav	Secretary of the Navy
SH2	Ship's Serviceman 2nd Class
SINS	Ship's Inertial Navigation System
SN	Seaman
SO1	Sonarman 1st Class
SRPC	Senate Republican Policy Committee
SubRon	submarine squadron
WAVES	Women Accepted for Volunteer Emergency Service
XO	Executive Officer
YMS	Yard Mine Sweeper
YNC	Yeoman Chief

Preface

There have been family and friends who surmised that my interest in the history of the U.S. Navy, especially its role during World War II, is an outgrowth of my father having served in that branch of the American armed forces during the greatest conflict in the history of the world. Perhaps on some preconscious level there may be a connection, but my father's reluctance to ever talk about his experiences on board a YMS-class minesweeper in the Pacific provided little fodder for what has grown into a lifelong avocation. The roots of my interest actually began on a rainy day in 1959 when my numerous complaints about being bored were answered when my Grandfather Finch tossed me a book and suggested that I might like reading it. It was a novel, and with nothing else to occupy my time I opened it and began to read.

As a twelve-year-old mediocre reader, I had little interest in fiction and even less in history. Before I was aware of what had happened, though, I was completely absorbed in *Run Silent, Run Deep*, Edward L. Beach Jr.'s realistic tale of life on board a U.S. Navy wartime submarine. Later, I was to realize that through *Run Silent, Run Deep* I took my first steps into a lifetime of reading, as well as an abiding interest in the U.S. Navy's role in World War II.

Beach's vivid descriptions—of the heart-pounding tension to which a crew was subjected as their submarine was hammered by enemy depth charges, and the racing action of a night surface attack—were the carrots that drew me into the novel, but it was his portrayal of men who held to a code of honor and duty even in the midst of war that grabbed my long-term interest.

Over thirty years later, Robert Neuleib and I submitted a proposal for a scholarly paper for presentation at the Naval History Symposium, then held biannually at the U.S. Naval Academy. Bob was a fellow high school debate coach at the time, and we soon discovered a mutual interest in naval history. Our proposal was later accepted and we went to Annapolis to present the paper we had written, on the influence of the Roberts Commission

Report on the general public's perception of who was to blame for the lack of American preparedness for the Pearl Harbor attack.

To our mutual surprise, the commentator on our panel was Edward L. Beach Jr.! Not only did I have the unexpected chance to meet the man who had introduced me to naval history and reading, but I shared the same stage with him. Feeling like a bibliophile given a lifetime gift card to Barnes & Noble, the rest of the conference became largely a blur for me after the session with Captain Beach.

That 1991 meeting was only the first of several personal encounters with Captain Beach. Our relationship, however, never grew beyond the casual as we would meet periodically at naval history gatherings. When I began working on a doctorate in history at Illinois State University, I decided to focus part of my dissertation on Beach and his father, also Capt. Edward L. Beach, USN. That doctoral work led to several telephone interviews, and then a chance to meet and have lunch with Captain Beach, his gracious wife Ingrid, and their elder son, Edward A. Beach. The lunch was followed by a long afternoon interview and then driving the captain through parts of southern Wisconsin so he could meet up with his family again.

As I finished my dissertation and the doctoral program, I periodically pondered the possibility of being able to write a full biographical study of Captain Beach. As a full-time secondary English teacher I had little spare time to work on such a book, but it remained a project I longed to undertake. When Captain Beach passed away in 2002, I was positive that someone would immediately begin work on his biography, if he or she hadn't already.

As I neared retirement from full-time teaching in 2004, however, I began making inquiries of people who knew Captain Beach to determine if they had been contacted by a potential biographer. My queries had hardly begun when I found myself talking directly to Ingrid Beach. She had read my dissertation, which I had sent to her husband in 1999, and she expressed interest in my taking on the project. No one had yet contacted her about a biography, so she was willing to provide me with access to her husband's papers, those that were still in her possession.

So, here begins that long-anticipated biography about a person who has held such great power in my imagination for many, many years. But the reader might rightly ask what purpose a biography of Edward Latimer Beach Jr. may serve.

Very few individuals have the inclination to consider their basic philosophy of life. Most of us go through life acting and reacting without giving too much thought to the underlying views of ourselves or our fellow human beings upon which our actions are based. When it comes to our children some of us might modify our behavior or words so as not to set a "bad" example, but such self-modification seldom lasts long and does little to mask the reality of how we view the world and how we treat others.

The degree to which Ned's father, Edward Latimer Beach Sr., engaged in any introspection is something at which we can only guess. Nevertheless, his writings, his conversations with his elder son, and even the story of his career in the U.S. Navy all impressed upon the junior Beach an approach to life that became an unshakable foundation for Ned's own philosophy. (Note that throughout this work Edward Latimer Beach Jr. will be referred to as "Ned," as he was generally called by family and friends.) The historical record shows little upon which to base any strong opinion as to what shaped the approach to life of the senior Beach, but there is ample evidence as to how he expressed that approach, both in his actions and in his writings. Ned's dedication to the Navy, his faith in the innate goodness of his fellow human beings, and the role that his father's novels played in his life form the thesis of this biography.

The several careers of Edward L. Beach Jr.—professional naval officer, fiction writer, naval historian, and congressional staffer—provide a long list of accomplishments that can each justify a study of his life. Commanding the first submarine to circumnavigate the globe submerged, writing three successful novels as well as numerous historical works, in addition to his wartime exploits—each of these achievements could provide their own rationale for such an examination. When taken in total, Ned's life undoubtedly warrants in-depth analysis.

The genesis of this study, however, lies in the faith that Ned held all his life in both the U.S. Navy and in his fellow humans. The words "Honor, Courage, Commitment" that are part of the creed of the U.S. Navy were not just platitudes to Ned. In spite of the disappointing end to his father's naval career, as well as a similar disappointment at the end of his own naval career, Ned never lost his abiding faith in the institution to which he had devoted his life.

That said, the reader should know that this work is neither hagiography nor exposé. What I seek to do within these pages is to tell the life story of a man who possessed an unshakable devotion to both an organization and its ideals. In this opening decade of the twenty-first century, the devotion and loyalty that Ned lived every day of his life sometimes seem out of date—relegated to romanticized views of the past. The personal and professional values that Ned lived by, coupled with his optimistic faith in the inherent goodness of others, gave him the ability to be an effective leader. They permeate his novels and historical writings, and they are rooted in his upbringing and education.

Edward Latimer Beach was a son, a husband, a father, a career naval officer, a naval engineer, a novelist, a historian, and a leader—this is his story. As Hamlet observes, "He was a man, take him for all in all, I shall not look upon his like again."[1]

Acknowledgments

This work owes much to a great many people. In particular, I wish to acknowledge the contributions made by James B. Winker, a colleague for many years, who reviewed the manuscript chapter by chapter. Gratitude is hereby extended to Robert Neuleib, fellow debate coach and avid consumer of naval history, who also read the manuscript. The sine qua non of this project has been my youngest daughter, Remy C. Garard, editor nonpareil, who kept me on the straight and narrow through the process, even though naval history is not one of her favorite topics. Dr. C. Herbert Gilliland, professor of English at the U.S. Naval Academy, made meaningful and substantive suggestions.

A note of special thanks goes to Paul Stillwell, who reviewed the entire manuscript. His insight into naval matters and personalities were of invaluable service.

Ann Finch, copy editor extraordinaire, whose critical eyes caught many an error that had slipped by all the previous sets of eyes probing for errors, provided the most invaluable of services.

To a very large extent, this work would not have been possible without the assistance of Ingrid Beach. Not only did Ingrid provide valuable insights into Ned as a father, husband, and human being, she also has in her possession the bulk of Ned's papers. She most generously allowed me to prowl through those files to my heart's content. Being of the mindset of a historian, Ned seldom, if ever, threw away a piece of paper, resulting in an extensive record of his life. While I was making a systematic search through his files, Ingrid welcomed me and my wife into her home, and proved to be a most cordial and warm hostess.

Others who read parts of the manuscript include Rear Adm. Maurice "Mike" Rindskopf, USN (Ret.), who reviewed several chapters looking for technical transgressions; John B. Beach Jr., who reviewed the material on his grandfather—Edward L. Beach Sr.—and that covering the childhood years of the elder Beach children; Capt. Will Adams, USN (Ret.), and

Cdr. Allen Steele, USN (Ret.), who reviewed the chapter on USS *Triton*; Donald deKieffer, who spotted errors in the section on Ned's time working for the Senate Republican Policy Committee; and finally, my oldest daughter, Sherry A. Cluver, who urged me to find the right "voice" for Ned's story.

Kathleen Mikkelsen, Lisa Johnson, Cheryl Hartford, and Amy Tolu-Honary, all colleagues, contributed speedy translations of letters from the Beach papers originally written in French, Spanish, or German. To librarian LaVonne Slama, many thanks for using the wonders of the interlibrary loan system to acquire for my use numerous articles and books.

The personnel at the Dwight D. Eisenhower Library in Abilene, Kansas, especially archivist James W. Leyerzapf, and archival technicians Chalsea Millner and Michelle Kopfer, were very accommodating to my queries and calls for help. In addition, the staff members who serve the following archives were also of great assistance: the Submarine Force Museum, Groton, Connecticut; the archives in the Nimitz Library, U.S. Naval Academy; the U.S. Naval Institute Library; and the Naval Historical Center, Washington, D.C.

One final, but certainly not the least, acknowledgement, is in order. To my wife Cathy, the self-proclaimed "computer widow," I extend my deepest appreciation for her support.

All of the above assistance having been duly recognized, it is still incumbent on me to state that any and all errors in this monograph are solely my responsibility, whether they are factual or interpretative.

Prologue

"Father," said Ralph Osborn, looking up from the book he had been reading, "I want to go to the Naval Academy."
—Edward L. Beach Sr., *Ralph Osborn, Midshipman at Annapolis*

It was the early years of the Great Depression and Ned lay on his family's living room floor reading the novel *Ralph Osborn: Midshipman at Annapolis*. The story spun out in the novel took Ned to a world about which he had dreamed since he was first old enough to read the novels his father had penned. He had read each of those novels numerous times—so many times, in fact, that the bindings were falling off. The stories of the fictional Ralph Osborn and others had claimed Ned's imagination and he longed for the day when he, too, would be a midshipman. There was no doubt in Ned's mind—even in his early teens—that he would be admitted to the Academy, for he was both highly intelligent and industrious. The only obstacles in his path were his age—so long to wait—and the objections of his parents.

Ironically, Ned's father had attended the Naval Academy and then served as an officer in the U.S. Navy for thirty-eight years. The barrier of parental objection to Ned's dream was more in the nature of his father and mother wanting to ensure that a naval career was indeed what their elder son really wanted. Encouraging the youth to consider becoming a medical doctor or surgeon was their way of testing Ned's true dedication to naval service.

If the senior Beach had serious concerns about his son's ambitions to attend the Academy, he did little to stand in the way of that dream—except for the prodding about becoming a doctor. Not only had Ned grown up idolizing his father, but he had also grown up reading the thirteen novels about Academy and Navy life that his father had written. Those novels are highly autobiographical and served to reinforce everything Ned saw as noble and honorable about his father and the Navy. Reality tests about medicine and medical school could not stand up to the combination created from the determination, idealism, and hero worship that had evolved from the heady mix of his father's novels and the real adventures of his father's life.

The opening words of that first of the Ralph Osborn novels were repeated to Ned's parents many times as he continually pressed his case for attending the Academy. Eventually the tipping point was reached and his parents agreed to assist their son in achieving his dream. In the interim, there were the novels, the tales told at the dinner table, and a steadfast resolve to fulfill the dream. Ned's four years at Annapolis were followed by a stellar career as an officer in the U.S. Navy intermixed with a highly successful vocation as an author of both fiction and nonfiction.

Through all of Ned's life, whether at the Academy, on active duty, or in all other aspects of his life, the guiding forces were the sense of honor and drive fostered in his youth. "Father, I want to go to the Naval Academy" was not just a phrase symbolizing Ned's desire to follow in his father's profession; it was the beginning of a lifelong endorsement of those ideals implicit in the very essence of an officer who wore a uniform of the U.S. Navy. How Ned Beach lived out those ideals was the central theme of his life.

beneath the waves

Part I: 1918–1941

[1]

The story of the life of Ned Beach has its beginnings in May 1884 when his father, Edward Latimer Beach, first stepped onto the grounds of the U.S. Naval Academy in Annapolis, Maryland. (See Appendix III for a brief biographical sketch of Edward Latimer Beach Sr.) Walking through the gates of the Academy, he began a family journey that would encompass the conversion of the U.S. Navy from wooden to steel ships, and from wind to steam to nuclear propulsion. The senior Beach and his elder son, Edward Latimer ("Ned") Beach Jr., would through their naval careers participate in, as well as provide chronicles of, the emergence of the U.S. Navy as the premier naval force in the world.

From the time Congress authorized the construction of the Navy's first truly modern warships in 1883 to the submerged circumnavigation of the globe by the nuclear powered USS *Triton* (SSR[N]-586) in 1960, seventy-seven years would pass and the Beaches, father and son, would be on active duty during all but fifteen of those years. In the midst of the technological, engineering, and professional revolutions that contributed to the growth in power and prestige of the Navy, the Beaches left their imprints in numerous ways and places.

Not only did the father and son participate as officers in some of the most important and thrilling of those episodes, each further enhanced the Navy's public image by writing highly popular fiction and nonfiction books, as well as journal articles on Navy life and history. While father-and-son naval careers are far from unique, the combination of career officers and highly successful authors sets the Beaches apart.

[2]

The ship's giant guns, all twelve of them, represented the height of naval power in 1927, and a nine-year-old Ned Beach was in awe of what he beheld. The bird-cage masts, the heavy lines, and the massive size of the

32,000-ton USS *California* (BB-44) were the most impressive sight ever. As he toured *California* with his father and younger brother, Ned vowed that some day he would serve on board—even command her.[1]

Elements of the U.S. Fleet were making a port visit, called "flower shows" by the sailors, and the Beaches were on board as the special guests of Adm. Henry A. Wiley, the elder Beach's good friend from their days at the Naval Academy.[2] Wiley was commander-in-chief of the U.S. Fleet in 1927 as *California* and a portion of that fleet paid a visit to San Francisco. As the flagship, *California* was not only the jewel in the crown of the fleet, she also offered Ned the opportunity to finally see his dream ship up close.

When Ned's father commanded the Mare Island Navy Yard across the Bay from San Francisco, *California* had been its premier building project. Ned was only three when *California* was completed and delivered to the fleet, but he had later listened to his father extol the virtues of the battleship. The walls of Ned's room were covered with photos of *California*, and as he was led on this VIP tour of the ship, his desire for a life at sea only deepened.

[3]

Edward Latimer Beach Jr. was born on 20 April 1918 in New York City while his father was at sea in command of USS *New York* (BB-34), the flagship of the U.S. Battle Squadron attached to the British Grand Fleet. World War I was raging, leaving Ned's mother Alice to cope with the birth of her first child in a strange city where English was slowly becoming her third language.

"Admiral Neddie Beach Jr." At age three, dressed as a naval officer, Ned participated in a parade at Mare Island Navy Yard in 1921.

Born and raised in Haiti, Alice (Fouché) Beach was a mixture of French and Dominican blood, tracing her ancestry on one side back to Joseph Fouché, an associate of Robespierre, one of the more famous (or perhaps infamous) leaders of the French Revolution. On the other side, she was related to Ulises Heureaux (1845–1899), the president of the Dominican Republic off and on between 1882 and 1899, as well as to Joaquin Balaguer (1907–2002), a future president of the Dominican Republic. Alice was twenty-one years younger than her husband. They met in Haiti while the senior Beach was there as part of an American intervention in 1915. Beach's wife Lucie (Quin) Beach had died of breast cancer some months prior, the couple having been childless during their twenty-year marriage. The senior Beach spoke French as a second language, but sought someone to teach him Spanish. Alice, an orphaned girl raised in a convent school but then living with relatives, spoke French and Spanish, and agreed to fill the role of the needed tutor. Two years later, Beach and Alice reconnected in New York City where Alice had gone to complete her schooling. They were married there in 1917.

When World War I ended, Beach was ordered to command Mare Island Navy Yard on San Francisco Bay. There Beach, his wife, and young Ned settled into a life together. Soon, two more children arrived—John Blair, born in 1919, and Alice Laura, born in 1921. After the birth of daughter Alice, Beach retired from active duty and took up a position teaching naval and military sciences at Stanford University. When his career at Stanford ended, Beach served as city clerk and assessor for Palo Alto. Having moved to Palo Alto, Beach and his wife would remain there for the rest of their lives, and it was in Palo Alto that Ned and his siblings grew up.

During his youth, Ned was known as "Butch," while his sister was nicknamed "Blackie," and his brother was called "Johnnie." (See Appendix III for brief biographical sketches of John Blair

Ned, age one, with his parents: Capt. Edward L. Beach Sr., USN, and Alice Fouché Beach.

Beach and Alice Laura Beach.) During his years at the Naval Academy, and for some years after, Ned would carry the nickname "Frenchie" because of his ability to speak French. The Beach children were raised in a bilingual home, their mother refusing to speak to or answer any of her children unless they spoke to her in French.

Soon after he learned to read, Ned was introduced to his father's novels. Written in the same genre as the Horatio Alger stories, the elder Beach's novels extol the virtues of honesty and hard work while telling of life in the U.S. Navy at the beginning of the twentieth century. Most of Beach's novels were written when he was teaching English at the Naval Academy. Part of the national literary outpouring that produced the original Nancy Drew and Hardy Boys stories, the thirteen published novels of his father that so influenced Ned were written in four-book series, with the thirteenth book being the first of a planned new series that was never completed. The popularity of such novels for young adults was a by-product of child labor and compulsory schooling laws in the early 1900s that created leisure time for many teens and preteens. Without radio or TV, many young adults turned to reading, with publishers quickly discovering that books in series were a guarantee of repeat customers. It was in this genre that Ned's father's novels fell—novels that so captured Ned's imagination that he reread them to the point of memorization.

Life for Ned, however, was not all devoted to reading. For a time, he delivered the *Saturday Evening Post* as a way to make some pocket money, but the year he spent working part-time in a garage on automobile repairs caused him to be bitten by the "car bug," leading to a lifelong interest in all things related to cars, as well as to his future in engineering. Such activities may have provided early experiences in the world of work, but they could not measure up to his dreams of life at sea.

Ned's fascination with all things naval included his efforts to build scale models of the entire U.S. fleet. Many of the models were simple pieces of wood with nails driven in at angles to represent each ship's main armament. With his "fleet," Ned spent long hours on the family front porch re-creating sea battles of World War I as his father directed the action along historical lines. Imaginary battles were also fought, but Ned would later note that his father almost always won any engagement.

Sometime toward the end of his sophomore year at Palo Alto High School, Ned came to the realization that his academic skills had put him on a course to graduate before he would be eligible to seek admission to the Naval Academy. Knowing that his time in high school would cease at the end of what was the traditional junior year, he decided he needed to get more involved in school activities. Ned had an excellent academic record, but he needed—in his own opinion—to do more than go home after classes to read magazines of the "better class."[3] He had been playing the clarinet for many years, but that musical instrument did not lead him into the activities and social situations he felt ought to be part of his secondary school experiences.

As part of Palo Alto High School's English program, all seniors (Ned was a junior when he took "senior" English) were required to write an essay in which they discussed how their high school career had changed them. The essay was written for the composition class of Miss Ruth Preston, Ned's favorite high school teacher. Ned's essay explains his determined efforts to become more active in his school:

> In pursuance of this plan, I became a reporter of the high school paper, the *Campanile*. I began to go out at night. I went out of my way to seek friends. When the time came for elections to school commissionerships, I deliberately put myself forward, not really believing that I would be elected, but intending to put my name before the student body. I went out for swimming, with the intentions, first of building my body, and second of doing something in the way of sports. I was fortunate enough to have a car, so I made a practice of picking up practically everybody I saw, with the intention of making new friends.[4]

Surprisingly for someone in his early teens, Ned recognized that he had a tendency to eschew social situations. Later in the same essay, he commented, "I think I have succeeded with my aim."[5] Several years later he would still admit, "I have experienced difficulty in a general bantering conversation."[6]

Ned was aware, perhaps painfully, that his inability to become involved in the "bantering conversation" was a main reason his contemporaries found him to be "brisk and conceited."[7] Both as a teen and later as an adult, he was often so focused on performing whatever task was at hand in the best manner possible that he came across to some people he encountered casually as uninterested in them. This stands in remarkable contrast to the glowing praise of Ned from people who knew him even on a limited basis.

Later in his life, he would frequently state that of all the writing awards he had won, the ones he received while on the school newspaper staff were the ones of which he was the most proud. He ran for various class offices—generally unsuccessfully—but he pointed out to his sister that his name became known around the school, leading to his being appointed to several "swell jobs."[8] Ned set out to cram four years' worth of high school activities and social life into his last one.

"Cram" is appropriate. Not only did he carry a heavy academic load, and then actively seek extracurricular activities, but at home he was also very busy. Based on his letters home from the Academy, it is clear that even back in high school Ned was heavily involved in managing the Beach family affairs. Mature beyond his years in this sense, Ned—either by default or at the urging of his father—had assumed numerous responsibilities regarding the family finances and similar functions. By the time Ned entered high school, the elder Beach was in his mid-sixties and already slowing down. Keeping up the full-time duties of the city assessor amid the politics of Palo Alto was draining, and having two energetic teens and a preteen at home added even more pressure to the life of the senior Beach. Ned's mother seems to have had little to do with the supervision of her children, at least the two sons, leaving discipline and mentoring to her husband.

Ned managed the family automobiles when it came to maintenance and repairs. In part this had to do with his love of automobiles, as well as his father's lack of desire to be bothered. Ned oversaw negotiations over medical and other bills that he thought were too high. He advised his father on how much rent to charge for the apartments the family owned. In several letters sent while he was at the Academy, Ned lectures his father about the need for the family to adopt a budget and stick to it in order to live within its means.

[4]

As Ned's high school career came to a close, gaining admission to the Naval Academy became his paramount goal. Appointment to the Academy was needed, but even more important was the successful completion of the rigorous entrance exam. To ensure that he had the best possible chance at passing the exam, Ned spent the entire year between high school graduation and taking the entrance exams in rigorous self-managed study. The year of study was a by-product of the fact that Ned had graduated from high school at age sixteen and the Naval Academy required anyone seeking admission to be at least seventeen.

At that time, the Academy published the questions after each year's exam results were released. Working through the Stanford University library, which retained a file of prior exam questions, Ned studied for and then took the previous six years' exams one after the other. The senior Beach then graded each of his son's exam essays and provided a critique and a list of topics for further study. The fact that Ned's father had both attended and taught at the Academy was valuable in this process. This year-long self-developed prep course met with great success. On the Congressional and Senatorial exam, Ned achieved an overall first place with a 94.3 percent, while on the Presidential exam he finished in second place with a 93.0 percent—the first place examinee earning 93.25 percent. Ned's appointment to the Academy came from Hiram Johnson (1866–1945), a five-term member of the U.S. Senate from California.[9]

Having achieved the first major step in his goal of commanding a battleship, "Butch" left the safe haven of his family in 1935 and traveled east to begin the second step—this one as a midshipman.

[5]

Ned believes in doing something, even if it's wrong; and he has the uncanny knack of seldom being wrong. He barges right into a knot of struggling soccer players, and the ball soon emerges in the direction of the opponent's goal. The same drive characterizes his more professional activities. As a Midshipman Officer, Ned displays both loyalty to the naval service and genuine loyalty to his comrades. Knowing Ned "at ease" is quite a pleasure. Association with him reveals numerous mannerisms, expressions, and humorous points of view. His weakness seems to be a desire to make freak inventions, to the alternate delight and consternation of his friends. We shouldn't forget his high-wheeled Pierce-Arrow Second Class summer. Ned loves the Navy. Here's the best of luck to him out in the Fleet.[10]

In these few words, a wag on the staff of the Naval Academy's yearbook, *The Lucky Bag*, summed up Ned's four years as a midshipman, capturing the headlong zest with which he attacked his Academy years. With a remarkable degree of prescience, the author also managed to capture the essence of Ned's approach to almost all of his life's endeavors.

In many respects, Ned's years at the Academy are better documented than those of any other midshipman of his generation. Beginning with his arrival for "Plebe Summer," through his last days before graduation, he regularly sent home correspondence to his father. The letters, some sent as often as twice a week, were written for the expressed purpose of creating a pool of information from which the elder Beach could draw in writing new works of fiction about life at the Academy in the late 1930s. To be fair, the letters do contain a degree of personal information and family matters, which is only natural, but they also contain a rich treasure of details concerning the day-to-day lives of midshipmen during the years Ned was in attendance. Much of what follows in this section is based on the contents of those letters.

In contrast to the picturesque and historical image of the city of Annapolis today, Ned's first impression was summed up as "the worst dump I've seen in years."[11] Fortunately for Ned, once inside the Academy grounds he had to contend with the city of Annapolis on an infrequent basis, while visitors today are grateful for the restoration of the historic sections of the city.

Like his father, Ned did have to contend with the Naval Academy's unofficial hazing. For example, on one occasion Beach and his roommate were awakened at 0300 and forced to take cold showers in their pajamas. In reporting such incidents to his father, Ned insisted that the elder Beach not repeat any of the events lest word get back to some congressman and an investigation ensue.[12]

The Naval Academy developed a love-hate relationship with the practice of hazing. At best, the practice taught nineteen- and twenty-year-olds the restraint they must learn in the exercise of authority. The temptation to abuse power needed to be resisted, and it was better to learn that lesson at the Academy rather than after being assigned a position of authority in the Navy or Marine Corps. This lesson was critical to the creation of leadership skills. At the other end of the spectrum was the fact that any time the public got wind of an abuse of the practice, the Naval Academy suffered another black eye.

Because the practice of hazing did lead to excesses at times, Congress passed strict laws against it, and any midshipman caught hazing was to be immediately dismissed from both the Academy and the Navy. The laws left no room for degrees of punishment based on the seriousness of the offense, so school personnel at times tended to "look the other way." The unwritten code among the midshipmen was that one was never to inform on another midshipman. As a result, only flagrant hazing that was actually observed by an Academy official usually got reported and subsequently punished.

Ned noted that when he was at the Academy, a plebe in the room next to his was beaten across the buttocks by a first-classman (senior) using a piece of one-inch-thick steel cable. The plebe required medical attention, but no one, not even the injured plebe, would reveal the perpetrator, so the Academy was powerless to exact punishment. However, the other first-classmen organized a shunning of the cable wielder. The ostracizing of a person in this instance meant that not a single midshipman would speak to, provide assistance for, or even acknowledge the existence of, the shunned first-classman. By the end of the semester, the offending first-classman had resigned from both the Academy and the Navy. In this instance, the person misusing authority was silently punished by his peers, but outside the official system.[13] There were instances in which excessive hazing went unpunished and newspaper reports or parental complaints to members of Congress usually led to new investigations and stricter laws.

Within the first weeks of his arrival on campus, Ned was befriended by William R. "Bill" Lowndes, a second-classman. The act of friendship, along with its implicit promise of no further hazing from the upperclass-man offering the "spoon," was welcomed by Ned.[14] As Lowndes explained, his father—Maj. Edward R. Lowndes, USMC—had attended the Naval Academy, graduating in 1889, the year after Ned's father, and the two had known each other well.[15]

Ned also suffered through a rite of passage in learning the lexicon unique to the Naval Academy. His letters discuss the "Awkward Squad," those midshipmen identified as needing extra marching drill practice due to deficiencies in their daily drills. "Ye old guess rod" was the moniker for a slide rule. To "bilge" someone meant to score better on an exam. Ned was "papped" (put on report and given extra duty) for being "out of uniform"—in this case he forgot his neckerchief when reporting for inspection.[16]

Plebes, as first-year midshipmen were called, could not walk around the Academy with a girl, so a couple would agree to meet at a predeter-mined location to which each would walk separately. The system did allow for the possibility that an upperclassman might intercept the girl, thus depriving the plebe of her company—at least that was Ned's speculation about the rule's real purpose.[17] A girl on a date was termed a "drag," and going anywhere with a date was called "dragging a girl" or simply "drag-ging." Late in his plebe year, Ned wrote to his father asking for an extra ten dollars because he was "flat broke" from too much dragging.[18]

The academic side of life at the Naval Academy for Ned was heavily focused on the continual pressure to achieve as high a standing in class rank as possible. The Academy used a 4.0 numerical system instead of the traditional grades of other institutions of higher learning, with a midship-man's progress reported as a percentage of the perfect 4.0. Each month, the scores of all midshipmen for each class were calculated and posted for everyone to see. These scores were used to re-section (ability group) the midshipmen for the next month's instruction. Ultimately, class rank at the time of graduation became a very significant factor in the naval career of a graduate.

Men like Ned who had aspirations to high command looked at class rank, even the monthly postings, as the be-all and end-all of their days at the Academy. Ned's letters, for all four years, are filled with constant comments on his class rank, calculations as to how a recent or forthcom-ing exam might impact his status, and his projections for future rankings. To say that Ned was driven with respect to his academic success would be an understatement. An individual who was not the least bit interested in sports, he was as competitive as anyone of his generation when it came to his academic work and his professional advancement.

Ned finished his plebe year first in his class with a standing of 93.25 percent, beating out the next ranking plebe by .03 percent. By the end of his second-class year (equivalent to junior year at university), he stood second in his class with a 91.3 percent cumulative for the three years. The top-ranking midshipman in his class beat out Ned by .09 percent over the three-year accumulation.[19] Upon graduation, Ned would rank second overall, with Louis H. Roddis Jr. at the top of the class and James M. Dunford third.

Course work at the Academy was in a state of flux during Ned's years. In the early 1930s, the Academy's superintendent, Rear Adm. Thomas C. Hart, USN, Class of 1897, instituted a series of curriculum innovations that led to an increase from 21.6 to 31.6 percent in the amount of class time midshipmen spent in courses in the field of the humanities.[20] Such subjects as economics, government, geography, and comparative literature were among those added to the course work for second- and first-class midshipmen under the Hart program. But in 1934, Rear Adm. David F. Sellers, USN, Class of 1894, replaced Hart. Seeking to restore what he saw as the primary mission of the Naval Academy, Sellers pushed the new programs aside stating, "I can say without hesitation that in my opinion success or failure in battle with the fleet is in no way dependent upon a knowledge of biology, geology, ethics, social science, the literature of foreign languages or the fine arts."[21] As Ned's plebe year began, Sellers' retrenchments were being implemented, and by the start of his first-class year (1938–1939), "the humanities' share of the curriculum had shrunk to 17.6 percent."[22] None of the innovations Hart had championed had survived long enough for Ned to partake of them.

As a plebe, Ned began his day with reveille at 0615, followed by formation, inspection, and a march to breakfast. Infantry drills and rifle drills were conducted from 0850 to 0930. Academic classes were attended from 0950 to 1130. 1215 found the midshipmen formed for inspection and then the march to lunch. Classes resumed in the afternoon, followed by a period set aside for some form of physical training. All midshipmen were then, and are still today, required to participate in an organized sports activity, either intercollegiate or intramural. Mandatory evening formation and inspection preceded dinner, followed by required study time. The plebe was left with about thirty minutes per day of unstructured time.

During his plebe and youngster (equivalent to sophomore) years, Ned played on the intramural water polo and swimming teams. Initially, he had tried out for the boxing team, but found the sport not to his taste.[23]

Entering the Academy at 158 pounds, he gained five pounds in his first two weeks on campus, which he attributed to the training for boxing. During his second- and first-class years, he was active on the intramural swimming, soccer, and cross-country teams.[24] Later, he might have regretted not having played football or kept up the boxing, for he had to tackle former All-American footballer Slade Cutter several times during an improvised game on Midway Island during World War II.

Among the highlights of life at the Academy for all the midshipmen were the summer cruises. Midshipmen were sent each summer on Navy ships to learn about life at sea on board active units of the fleet. During his first summer cruise, Ned sailed on the USS *Arkansas* (BB-33), a 26,000-ton battleship that was the flagship of the Navy's Training Squadron. Visiting ports in Europe—the United Kingdom, France, Gibraltar, and Italy—the midshipmen were exposed to foreign cultures as well as the rigors of life at sea. It was while he was in France that Ned's ability to speak French was called upon in numerous situations by his classmates, earning him the nickname "Frenchie"—a nickname he disliked and was eventually successful in dissuading his fellow midshipmen from using.[25] By the time of his graduation, he was generally known as Ned, the name by which most family, friends, and acquaintances would address him the rest of his life.

The cruise's activities in Italy included audiences with Pope Pius XI and with Italian dictator Benito Mussolini. Always thinking ahead, Ned used the visit to England as a chance to acquire some very high quality wool suit cloth at a price very much below its cost in the United States. He had the cloth shipped back for the purpose of having dress uniforms made from it. The uniform he wore at his graduation and commissioning was made from that cloth.[26]

Ned shared his father's empathy for people harmed by war. On a summer cruise on board the USS *Texas* (BB-35), one of the ports visited was in Mexico. The midshipmen were taken on a tour of the site of the Battle of Chapultepec during the Mexican-American War. Moved by the story of *Los Niños*, the one hundred boy cadets of the military school inside the castle of Chapultepec who died defending their school, Ned wanted to place a wreath in their honor as a symbol of his feelings for the lost children. His fellow midshipmen dissuaded him since it might have been interpreted as an official act sanctioned by the U.S. government.[27]

During his plebe summer, Ned was bothered by his old feelings of not being very popular. He noted that he had anticipated the feelings, adding that he was not so much unpopular, but that it seemed no one sought out his company.[28] The situation had completely reversed, however, once academic classes started. By the end of September, he was writing home that his abilities in math and French found many plebes seeking his assistance as a tutor.[29]

By the end of his second-class (junior) year, Ned's leadership abilities were beginning to be recognized by those in charge of the Academy. Standing second academically in his class, he also had demonstrated a high degree of proficiency in military decorum and drill, as well as providing effective leadership. For the first third of the 1938–1939 academic term, Ned was named "Commander of the Regiment of Midshipmen," or the "five-striper"—meaning he was entitled to wear five gold stripes on the sleeves of his uniform.[30] Only one midshipman in the entire regiment was awarded this honor and it meant that whenever the regiment was assembled, whether for marching to the dining hall, or for a formal ceremony, Ned was in command.

A significant highlight of holding the five-striper rank for the first third of the year was to be in command of the regiment at the annual Navy-Army football game. Ned described the event to his father in these terms: "When we began to march on the field, I heard a stentorian voice announce, 'The regiment of Midshipmen is now marching on the field, Midshipman E. L. Beach is the Regimental Commander.' Hot dog! The papers all say that we bilged the Point horribly. Said West Point's idea of a straight line was a half moon. Shirley Povich, a *Washington Post* sportswriter and columnist, said, 'If Hitler could see the Corps of Cadets march on the field he would immediately declare war on us. He would call off the war when the Regiment of Midshipmen marched on.'"[31]

William G. Hawthorne was named to the same post for the second third of Ned's first-class year. The appointment to the position for the final third of the year was to be determined based on the proficiency of all the leaders of the regiment of midshipmen for the first two-thirds of the year. To hold that position at the end of the year, as the Class of 1939 marched to the end of year activities along with the whole of the regiment, was viewed as the ultimate leadership honor for any midshipman. In this case, it was Ned's tendency to "barge" into situations that may have interfered with his earning that additional honor.

On 30 October 1938, the Mercury Theatre on the Air, a production company headed by Orson Welles, broadcast its version of the 1898 science fiction classic by H. G. Wells, *The War of the Worlds*. Script writer Howard Koch had adapted the story for radio such that, for many listeners, it sounded like an actual invasion of earth by creatures from Mars was in progress. What happened next is best expressed in Ned's own words, written to his father within hours of the incident: "We have just been sold! And what I mean! Heard a radio program of a meteorite landing from the planet Mars or somewhere with people in it, etc. Sounded so real I fell for it and rushed down to tell the D.O. [Duty Office] about it. They fell for it too, for a while. Man we really tumbled. I felt pretty foolish. Guess the whole regiment will have a good laugh on me."[32]

What is missing from the account in the letter to his father is the fact that Ned called for the regiment of midshipmen to be formed to help repel the invasion. Others joined him in the call to arms before the truth was discovered and calm restored. As Adm. Harold Shear, USN, a plebe at the time of the broadcast, later recorded, "I don't recall exactly what word was put out, but Beach was convinced that we were being invaded by Martians. I don't know how long it was before it was called back as a false alarm."[33]

The prediction that Ned would provide the regiment with a "good laugh" at his expense quickly came to pass. Just six days after the incident, he wrote to his father, "I've taken quite a ragging and running on account of that 'Martian' episode. There's a cartoon in this week's *Log* about it, too."[34] He goes on to state that a number of articles about the incident were submitted to the *Log,* the Academy's student newspaper, but someone in authority intervened and had all of them cut. In the same letter, Ned admits that the incident had probably ruined his chances of being selected five-striper for the final third of the year.

While Ned seemed to be able to joke about the incident the rest of his life, and there were classmates always willing to retell the story in his presence, he never found it that amusing. Cdr. Paul H. Backus, USN, a third classman in 1938, noted that Ned "has had to live with this story ever since those days." [35] Had the incident not been tied to the coveted position of five-striper for the final third of the year, perhaps Ned would have developed a broader sense of humor over it.

As it turned out, the position of five-striper for the final third was awarded to Corwin G. Mendenhall. As Ned related in letters home, he and Mendenhall and Hawthorne were "tied" for the post of regimental commander, and the Academy administration decided to award the honor to Mendenhall.[36] Whether the "Martian" incident had anything to do with the selection will never be known, but Ned was very disappointed over the selection.

The regimental commander at the time of graduation was supposed to be the midshipman who was rated at the top of his class—a true leader. Academic standing was only a part of the criteria for the honor. Along with the five stripes of regimental commander usually came the Sword of the Class of 1897. This honor was bestowed on the midshipman who was viewed as having contributed the most to "the development of naval spirit and loyalty within the Regiment."[37] Corwin Mendenhall may have worn the five stripes for the final third of the year but, in a rare departure from common practice, Ned was awarded the Sword of the Class of 1897.

In addition to the honor of receiving the Sword of the Class of 1897, he was one of six graduating midshipmen who were given a letter of commendation from the superintendent. These individuals were singled out for having "contributed most by their officer-like qualities and positive characters to the development of naval spirit and loyalty within the Regiment."[38]

As graduation approached, Ned fervently hoped his father could attend the ceremonies. Failing health, however, kept the elder Beach from making the long journey by train from Palo Alto to Annapolis.[39] Ned's mother and his sister Alice did make the trip, renting a house in the town of Annapolis in order to be present for the week-long activities that surrounded graduation itself.

After the graduation and commissioning ceremonies on 1 June 1939 were completed, Ned, his mother, and his sister drove back to Palo Alto in Ned's 1930 Chrysler Roadster "77." The car was one of many "prize" automobiles upon which Ned would lavish attention during his life. The green and black car had green leather upholstery, a tan top, rumble seat, trunk rack, and six wire wheels.[40] Three adults and luggage packed into the roadster with someone stuck in the rumble seat must have made for a very interesting cross-country journey. The pomp and ceremonial traditions of the Academy's commencement exercises behind him, Ned's long trek back to his home must have allowed him time to contemplate his future and the aspirations he had developed and refined over the past four years.

In 1939—Ens. Edward L. Beach Jr.

Like his boyhood's storybook heroes, Ralph Osborn and Robert Drake, Ned had completed the course at the Naval Academy and was now ready to embark on a career in the U.S. Navy. Two important long-term goals echoed in his mind—achieving command of a battleship like his father had and eventually being promoted to flag rank (admiral), something his father had been unable to achieve.

[6]

Along with those of all his classmates, Ned's immediate career plans in 1939 had to consider the threat of war in Europe between Hitler's Nazi armies and what seemed to be the rest of Europe, as well as the looming strife with Japan in the Pacific. Ned's initial goal upon commissioning had been realized as he was ordered to USS *Chester* (CA-27), a 9,200-ton cruiser that was less than ten years old when he reported on board. In a letter to his father in early 1939, he had expressed a desire to be assigned to an "8-inch cruiser" upon graduation.[41] Eight-inch in this case referred to the size of the ship's main guns, *Chester* being armed with nine such guns. With a crew of 621, *Chester* was looked upon by Ned as a large enough ship on which to begin his career, but small enough to allow for future transfers to larger ships. Reporting on board in June 1939 as assistant engineering officer, Ned's tour of duty on board *Chester* lasted only until August.

In September, he reported on board USS *Lea* (DD-118), a World War I-era four-stack, flush-deck destroyer that had been launched in Philadelphia in the same month and year Ned was born—April 1918. Having been decommissioned and then re-commissioned several times in the intervening years, *Lea* was being brought back into the fleet just as Ned was assigned to her. Eventually, he was given the combined duties of the gunnery, torpedo, and communications officers. Holding all three positions for so junior an officer was unusual, but the rapid expansion of the Navy in the period just before the war was leading to a shortage of officers. Those expanded duties provided Ned with experiences he would not have had in an equivalent period in the peacetime Navy. He was one of only five officers on board *Lea*, which had a total crew of over 130. With only five officers on board, Ned found himself having to stand one four-hour watch in every twelve-hour period while under way, and one day out of three while in port.[42] This was in addition to all his other duties.

Assigned to Key West, Florida, *Lea* was one of several U.S. Navy ships that shadowed the 32,000-ton German passenger liner *Columbus* as she left the neutral port of Vera Cruz, Mexico, on her way back to Germany in December 1939. Caught with tourists in the Mexican port when war was declared between Germany and Britain, *Columbus* disembarked her passengers and headed back to Germany. Indirectly, the American ships provided the British with the Germans' location until a Royal Navy destroyer could intercept and attack the German ship once it was outside the American declared "neutrality zone." As the British destroyer closed in to sink the

German ship, *Columbus*'s crew scuttled her. USS *Tuscaloosa* (CA-37) then closed in on the sinking ship to rescue the 576 crew members who had survived the scuttling.[43]

The word "neutrality" was one with which every officer and sailor on America's eastern seaboard became familiar during the fall of 1939. Ships like *Lea* were soon engaged in "neutrality patrols," trying to ensure that no acts of belligerence were committed in American waters. President Franklin Roosevelt kept pushing the boundary of the neutrality patrols farther out into the Atlantic, making the U.S. Navy an unofficial ally of the Royal Navy in its battle with German U-boats. From the time Ned reported on board *Lea* until he was transferred off, the aged destroyer was continuously engaged in one form of neutrality patrol or another.

In July 1940, Ned experienced another element of international law that governed the rules of neutrality. While *Lea* was in port at Key West, Florida, a British cruiser entered the port. This was a violation of neutrality as a ship of a belligerent nation (i.e., one at war) cannot enter the port of a neutral nation. But when it came to the Royal Navy, the Americans were inclined to a laxness in enforcing such rules. To not overemphasize the point that the Americans needed to protest the cruiser's presence, the most junior officer in the port, Ens. Edward L. Beach Jr., USN, was ordered to board the Royal Navy ship and inform its commanding officer that the ship must immediately leave the port. Decked out in his dress white uniform, complete with his father's sword, Ned was transported by motor launch to the British man-of-war.

As an indication of their intent to stay in the port for only a very short period, the British ship lowered only a Jacob's ladder—wooden rungs held in place by ropes on two sides—for Ned's use. After struggling up the ladder, Ned discovered the railing had not been "broken"—again a symbol of the intended short stay. The railing around the deck was left in place so Ned had to climb over the railing, which consisted of steel cables strung between uprights, rather than walking through an opening created for his arrival. Dressed in his finest whites and wearing a sword as well as white gloves, Ned became entangled in the cable railing, flopping face down at the feet of the commanding officer of the British man-of-war.[44]

Regaining as much dignity as the circumstances allowed, Ned came to attention to salute the British skipper only to notice that the man was dressed in shorts and an open shirt, sporting a long red beard—all in contrast to Ned's formal attire. Formalities exchanged, Ned was then allowed to lodge the formal protest he had been sent to deliver. The commanding officer of the cruiser informed Ned that they had a very sick man on board and would leave as soon as the man had been transferred ashore to a hospital. He then invited Ned to his cabin where the two had scotch and soda while the ailing sailor was being disembarked. Ned's dignity smarted for some time after the incident, but he eventually enjoyed retelling the story.

Word soon passed among the crews of the World War I-era American destroyers that had been re-commissioned for the neutrality patrols that the United States had made a deal to swap fifty of the ships with Britain in exchange for naval bases in the Caribbean and on Newfoundland. Britain desperately needed the ships as a stop-gap measure to replace her growing loss of warships to the German U-boats. The swap also further cemented the relationship between the United States and the United Kingdom.[45]

All of the destroyers in *Lea*'s flotilla were scheduled to be part of the deal, but at the last minute *Lea*'s name was removed from the list and another ship's was added. Later, the young lady Ned had been dating informed him that she had prevailed upon her father, a captain in the U.S. Navy, to scratch *Lea* from the list for fear that once the ship had been transferred Ned would be reassigned to a ship home-ported on the West Coast or elsewhere.[46]

Ned did not identify the name of the young lady or her father's name in his oral history interview, but other correspondence from the period indicate he had been dating a Courtney Prettyman for some time before and after he graduated from Annapolis.[*] The story of *Lea*'s reprieve may have been an apocryphal tale told by a young lady as a means of letting Ned know how much she wanted their relationship to continue. The Destroyers for Bases deal was announced in early September 1940, but in a letter home in June of that same year, Ned indicated that he was then dating a young woman in Key West whose father was a local physician.[47]

The tedium of the neutrality patrols was broken in May 1941 when *Lea* received a radio message instructing any U.S. Navy vessel that came into contact with the German battleship *Bismarck* to shadow the dreadnought and report the ship's location and movements. As communications officer, Ned decoded the message and took it to *Lea*'s commanding officer. Pointing out that the *Bismarck* had 15-inch guns compared to *Lea*'s 4-inch guns, and that the German ship was three knots faster than *Lea*, Ned suggested to his skipper that if they encountered the behemoth it might become a question of who was shadowing whom. Unmoved by his young officer's cautionary comments, the skipper replied, "Well, OK, but

[*] Ned and Courtney remained in contact with each other over Ned's lifetime. The E. Barrett Prettyman Jr. Federal Court House in the District of Columbia was named in honor of her father, who served there for many years as a judge.

we'll chase him if we find him."[48] As it turned out, Ned's cautionary comments were unnecessary as the British caught *Bismarck* long before *Lea* could have stumbled across the much-lionized ship of Nazi propaganda.

No sooner had the *Bismarck* scare subsided than *Lea* was assigned to be part of an escort for a convoy of transports carrying U.S. Marines to occupy Iceland. The move was to establish an American presence there so ships of non-Axis nations could be escorted from Iceland to North American ports and back by the U.S. Navy, and from Iceland to their European destinations by the Royal Navy.[49] As Roosevelt gradually expanded the sphere of American "neutrality," the word "neutral" began to have less and less meaning.

Lea's final mission with Ned on board was to serve as one of the four escorts for USS *Augusta* (CA-31), flagship of the Atlantic Fleet, as the American heavy cruiser transported President Franklin D. Roosevelt to a cove on the southeastern coast of Newfoundland. This trip was carried out in complete secrecy. Roosevelt left the public eye on board the presidential yacht USS *Potomac* (AG-25) for a supposed fishing trip. Off Cape Cod, FDR was transferred to *Augusta* and then secreted to Placentia Bay, near the fishing village of Argentia. Dropping anchor there on 7 August 1941, the presidential party awaited the arrival of HMS *Prince of Wales* bearing Winston Churchill, the British prime minister.[50] Beginning on 9 August, the two leaders and their staffs conferred for three days, outlining strategy and agreeing on the wording of a joint statement that became known as the Atlantic Charter.

While *Lea* was again in Iceland after the Placentia Bay duty, Ned received orders to report for a physical exam to see if he was fit for submarine duty. Seeking to avoid imminent transfer, he approached *Lea*'s skipper for advice. While submarine duty was supposed to be voluntary, in this case the "volunteer" had to volunteer to say "no" to the transfer in order to avoid the duty. Always insisting that he was "drafted" into submarines, Ned was surprised when his formal departure from *Lea* led to an encounter with the destroyer's skipper, Clarence Broussard, wearing his dress uniform complete with a submarine pin indicating Broussard's qualification as a submarine officer. Ned later realized why no encouragement had been forthcoming from Broussard in Ned's efforts to thwart the orders to submarine school.[51]

"I hated the idea of leaving the leaning, leaking, lopsided *Lea*, for after two years in her exclusive and demanding service I had grown to love that old four-piper, and felt very likely—as turned out to be the case—that I would never see her again."[52] Ned carried an affection for *Lea* the rest of his life. Among the many custom-made ship models in his collection was a beautiful rendering of *Lea*. It was one of the first acquisitions in his collection and he always looked upon it with great fondness. He also remained in close contact with his old skipper, Broussard, for the rest of his life.

In September 1941, as the United States was on the verge of entering World War II, Ned reported to the Submarine School in Groton, Connecticut. His father's advice to stay in "big ships" because they were the center of power in the Navy reverberated in Ned's mind as he settled into the submarine course of study. Being Edward L. Beach Jr., however, he would give 100 percent to the new endeavor that had been selected for him. Dreams of a battleship command may have been deferred, but regardless of what the Navy asked, he would charge into the task with all the gusto and daring that had characterized his years at the Academy.

Part II: 1941–1945

In the pre-dawn hours of a pitch dark night, the submarine USS *Tirante* deftly threaded her way along the coastline of Quelpart Island off the southwestern tip of the Korean Peninsula. Pushing her way into waters too shallow for her to submerge, and thereby losing her natural protection from the enemy, *Tirante* hugged the coastline to hide from enemy radar. As she nosed her way into the anchorage, the "exec's keen shooting eye" picked out dark shapes lying silently in the gloom. Three torpedoes were fired at the largest shape and "a tremendous beautiful explosion" followed as a 4,000-ton ammunition ship shot flames over two thousand feet into the air.

The instant glare of light from the exploding ship made *Tirante* stand out "like a snowman in a coal pit." Immediately, two enemy frigates turned toward *Tirante*, intending to take revenge. Undaunted by the approaching enemy, *Tirante* calmly fired two torpedoes at the frigate on her left and then one at the frigate on her right. Both ships disappeared in balls of flame and debris. *Tirante*, having only one torpedo left, turned back the way she came, evading other enemy patrol ships as she wended her way to the open waters of the Yellow Sea.[1]

The daring attack on the Quelpart anchorage on the night of 13–14 April 1945 earned *Tirante* (SS-420) a Presidential Unit Citation, her commanding officer, Lt. Cdr. George L. Street III, USN, the Medal of Honor, and her exec (short for executive officer, a ship's second in command), with the "keen shooting eye," the Navy Cross. That exec was Ned Beach, and that war patrol was his eleventh overall of the war.

What the attack represented, moreover, was an example of the highly honed weapon of war that the U.S. Navy's submarine force had become by the end of World War II. When the war started, however, such an outcome did not seem the likely future of the submarine service. In his history of the Navy, titled *The United States Navy: 200 Years*, Ned offered the thesis that World War II was the "Armageddon at sea" for which the United States had created a navy—a fight to the death in protection of America.[2] Ned graduated from submarine school just a few days before the Japanese attack on Pearl Harbor and his entire wartime service was completely in submarines. As such he participated in the process by which the submarine service achieved that high degree of proficiency and success that the attack at Quelpart Island represented.

[2]

The "boats" in which Americans fought World War II beneath the seas were mostly of the *Gato*-class, being mass-produced copies of a single design. Modifications to the design were made throughout the war, with some late-war submarines considered as their own class of ship distinct from the basic *Gato* design. In the most general terms, the American submarines of the war were each slightly over three hundred feet long, and carried a crew of six to ten officers and fifty to seventy enlisted men. They could travel eleven thousand nautical miles at a speed of ten knots on the surface based on power provided by four diesel engines. Submerged, they were capable of speeds of up to nine knots for a very short time, but could travel submerged for forty-eight hours at a speed of two knots. They were rated as "safe" down to a depth of three hundred feet, which increased to four hundred feet for late-war construction.[3]

Before the advent of nuclear power, the capability of submarines while submerged was limited to the storage capacity of their batteries and, to a lesser extent, to the available oxygen within their cramped quarters. On the surface, the four diesel engines could push the sub through the water at speeds approaching twenty-one knots. If, however, one or more diesels had to have their power diverted to recharging the batteries, the surface speed was correspondingly slower.

The principal offensive weapon of the submarine during this era was the torpedo, in essence an underwater missile, twenty-one inches in diameter, which was discharged from the submarine and traveled underwater to an intended target. The business end of the torpedo carried an explosive charge that was designed to blow a hole in the target, thereby sinking it. U.S. submarines carried twenty-four torpedoes, with six torpedo tubes firing from the bow of the boat and four tubes firing astern. Late-war subs had a slightly enlarged capacity to fire torpedoes and consequently carried a few more of the deadly weapons.

When fighting on the surface, American subs were equipped with a single 3-inch gun. Late-war subs were equipped with a 5-inch gun, some with two. These could be used to sink unarmed enemy ships that were not protected by warships or airplanes. Most subs also carried various sizes of machine guns for use on the surface, although submarines in general avoided any surface combat where there was a chance that they could be damaged by the enemy. A submarine's best protection was its ability to submerge, but if its pressure hull was punctured, this advantage was lost and the sub became extremely vulnerable.

The chief weapon employed against submarines was the depth charge. In essence, a depth charge was a barrel-shaped weapon containing explosives that was detonated by a water-pressure sensitive device. The explosion produced by a depth charge was intended to crack the hull of the target submarine, either causing flooding that would sink the sub or forcing it to the surface where it could be sunk by gunfire.

Attacking surface ships would set their charges to explode at the depth they suspected an enemy submarine to be lurking. Dropping the depth charges in a pattern allowed the surface ship to account for last-minute maneuvers on the part of the sub. A surface ship equipped with sonar had the ability to locate a submerged sub, but as that surface ship closed in to drop its depth charges, the sonar contact was lost for a brief period. During that interval, the submarine skipper would change direction and speed in an effort to throw off the aim of the attacking surface ship. This deadly game of cat-and-mouse could go on for hours, testing the wits of the commanding officers on both sides and the endurance of the submarine as batteries, oxygen, and nerves were strained by the constant hammering of underwater explosions.

In one of the most serious breaches of security of the war, Andrew Jackson May, congressman from Kentucky and a member of the House Military Affairs Committee, gave an interview to a newspaper reporter in which he stated that Americans need not worry about the safety of their submarines since the Japanese were setting their depth charges too shallow. The story was printed in many newspapers as it was disseminated by the wire services. After the war, Adm. Charles Lockwood, USN, who commanded U.S. submarine forces in the central Pacific for much of the war, concluded that the congressman's comment, and the further thoughtless way in which so many newspapers printed the story, "cost us ten submarines and 800 officers and men."[4]

[3]

As the war began, Ens. Ned Beach was assigned to USS *Trigger* (SS-237), then under construction at Mare Island Navy Yard. It was New Year's Day 1942 when Ned arrived at Mare Island, and he took the time to stop by the fitting-out dock where *Trigger* lay prior to her commissioning. He would later recall his thoughts as he gazed at the black hull: "There's my new home, wonder if I'm looking at my coffin."[5]

Thirty days after Ned reported for duty, Lt. Cdr. J. H. Lewis, USN, commanding officer of *Trigger*, read the orders that placed the submarine in commission, making her a unit of the U.S. Fleet. Being assigned to the crew at her commissioning made Ned a "plank owner," meaning he was one of the crew at the time the ship was commissioned. Ned began his time on board *Trigger* as assistant engineering officer. By the time he left the submarine, he was the executive officer.

After training and trials, *Trigger* was sent to Pearl Harbor, arriving in early June 1942. Ned and the rest of the crew were shocked into silence at the sight of the devastation that was still evident at the great base—six months after the Japanese attack. Ned would later recall with poignancy the sight of his beloved USS *California* as *Trigger* sailed into Pearl Harbor: "She had been sunk at her berth, water up to her main deck, listing to port. When I saw her she was afloat again, with great wounds visible, her carefully ordered topsides in hopeless disarray."[6]

What was supposed to have been several weeks of training at Pearl Harbor following their arrival was quickly abandoned. The new commander of the Pacific Fleet, Adm. Chester Nimitz, himself a former submariner, was determined to stop the anticipated Japanese invasion of Midway Island. *Trigger* was ordered, along with numerous other submarines, to establish scouting lines around the tiny atoll that would soon lend its name to what many historians have labeled the "turning point" in the war against Japan.

The Battle of Midway took place between the fourth and seventh of June 1942. On the night of 6–7 June, *Trigger* had to race on the surface through the darkness to be in her assigned scouting position by dawn. Shortly after 0500, *Trigger* ran aground on the coral reef surrounding Midway Island. So securely was the submarine aground that she was unable to extricate herself despite the efforts of her crew. Anticipating a gruesome end as they lay exposed on the reef, the crew awaited the arrival of Japanese forces.

What did arrive was a tug from Midway, but it was also unable to free the sub. Rising tide and an increase in the ocean waves, however, soon began rocking *Trigger* and she was finally able to free herself by 0758. With slight damage, *Trigger* proceeded to her assigned duty station, where she remained for several days before being ordered back to Pearl Harbor for repairs.

Ned, now a lieutenant (junior grade), was officer of the deck at the time of the grounding, but the sub's skipper was also on the bridge with him. In the accident report, Lt. Cdr. Lewis noted that "the Officer of the Deck had reported seeing breakers ahead, but he did not feel positive of this at the time."[7] In his own statement about the grounding, Ned wrote, "At 0510 the starboard lookout reported a steady white light dead ahead, slightly on the starboard bow. I called the Captain, and immediately after he came to the bridge I reported that I could see land on the starboard bow where the light was. The Captain said there was no land there, and that I must be mistaken, to which I replied that it looked very much like land to me. At that time I said that I thought I could also see breakers ahead. He made no reply to this."[8]

The Navy's investigation into the accident placed no blame on Lt. Cdr. Lewis or his crew, noting that the speed at which the current in the area around Midway was pushing *Trigger* off course had been underestimated, leading to the grounding. Had the sub been on the course her captain believed her to be on, the presence of land would indeed have been impossible. No further action regarding the accident was deemed necessary by the commander of Submarine Division 101, to which *Trigger* was assigned.[9]

Repairs were completed at Pearl Harbor, and *Trigger* was soon heavily involved in training exercises in preparation for her first patrol of the war. The ignominious beginning of their first combat situation was put behind the crew as they studied and practiced the latest techniques for operations against the Imperial Japanese Navy.

If the foray into combat that ended with the grounding had the potential to dull the spirit of *Trigger*'s crew, her first war patrol did little to raise that morale. Assigned to the waters off Attu and then Kiska islands, Alaska, *Trigger* spent thirty-five days on station in the cold, misty northern Pacific with nothing to show for the effort. Fritz Harlfinger, skipper of USS *S-32* (SS-137) described the hazards of sub duty in Alaskan waters in stark terms: "The conditions those boats endured up there are simply indescribable. It was God awful cold. Dreary. Foggy. Ice glaze. The periscopes froze. The decks and lifelines were caked with ice. Blizzards. You could never get a navigational fix."[10] Weather conditions made it very difficult to find and track enemy ships, even though some of the islands in the Aleutian chain had been occupied by the Japanese and were being resupplied by them on a regular basis. When *Trigger* returned to Pearl Harbor, Lt. Cdr. Lewis was hospitalized with pneumonia and a replacement skipper was assigned.

[4]

The exit of Jack Lewis brought Lt. Cdr. Roy S. Benson to *Trigger* as the new commanding officer. A graduate of the Naval Academy, Class of 1929,

Benson was one of a new breed of submarine skippers that were beginning to make the U.S. submarine force into an aggressive and deadly instrument of war. Benson carried the nickname "Pigboat Benny" from his days teaching at the Naval Academy. The nickname came about because of Benson's constant advocacy for submarines—a "pigboat" being a mildly derogatory term for a submarine.

Among the problems that diluted the effective fighting ability of the U.S. submarine force in the early months of the war was a lack of aggressiveness on the part of some skippers. Peacetime promotions to command demanded men who were good at following regulations and doctrine, conservative with supplies, and generally effective bureaucrats. As Thomas Buell noted in his biography of Adm. Raymond Spruance, "The qualities that make a good peacetime officer are not always the same qualities that make an effective officer in time of war."[11] Combat soon proved the ineffectiveness of many of these peacetime officers. The techniques and "by-the-book" procedures of the pre-war submarine service proved to be totally impotent against an actual enemy in a shooting war.

A second problem was that of training. In the years leading up to the war, the fleet-support mission prescribed for U.S. submarines left little time to devote to training in how to attack a merchant ship, while none of the pre-war submarine skippers had been given training in how to attack on the surface at night.[12] On-the-job training during wartime is costly, but the American submarine force had little choice once the shooting started.

Benson brought to *Trigger* an upbeat, "let-me-at-'em" attitude that soon infected the entire crew. Among the changes Benson initiated was what became known as the Morton-O'Kane technique for conducting an approach to firing torpedoes at an enemy ship.[13] Standard operating procedures for approaching an enemy target for U.S. submarines had been for the skipper to man the periscope while issuing all necessary orders that governed the operations of the sub. The uninitiated might assume that such was the role of the skipper, but the nature of undersea warfare during World War II made such multitasking a mentally demanding job.

The Morton-O'Kane technique was developed by Dudley Walter "Mush" Morton and Richard Hetherington O'Kane on board USS *Wahoo* (SS-238). The method Morton and O'Kane developed involved the exec manning the periscope during a submerged approach or on the bridge during a surfaced approach, while the skipper was in the sub's command center issuing all the operational orders. When a submarine approaches a target numerous factors have to be constantly evaluated. Keeping track of the relative positions of the sub, the target(s), and any possible escort(s) is a difficult enough task without having to be also responsible for giving the orders that would steer the sub and determine its speed and depth, plus those that would arm and aim torpedoes, in addition to the numerous other factors that can enter into an attack equation.

Benson also brought with him the idea of making attacks at night on the surface. Pre-war doctrine held that the submarine was least likely to be spotted by an enemy when making an attack if it remained submerged. Since the limited range of sight afforded by the periscope of a submerged submarine was further diminished at night, daylight submerged approaches were preferred. However, the relative slow speeds at which a submarine must operate while submerged meant that getting into a correct firing position was very difficult. While Benson did not pioneer this technique, he utilized it to great success while in command of *Trigger*.

With Benson in command, *Trigger* put two torpedoes into a 5,900-ton Japanese freighter off the Japanese home island of Kyushu. The crew had tasted its first blood and the effect was electrifying. However, that feeling of elation was short-lived, for the next night *Trigger* was attacked by a Japanese destroyer intent on revenge. During the battle with the Japanese destroyer, *Trigger* fired six torpedoes at the enemy. Two exploded prematurely while the rest missed, some passing directly under the enemy ship without detonating.[14] *Trigger* was then subjected to a terrible depth charging by the Japanese destroyer.

What *Trigger* experienced during her encounter with the Japanese destroyer off Kyushu is illustrative of the problems with American torpedoes in the early years of the war. As Ned would later explain in an article in *American Heritage* magazine, the torpedoes with which American submarines were equipped at the beginning of the war suffered from four major defects. The overlapping of the defects made it difficult to determine the exact cause of the failures. Compounding the problem was the fact that the Navy bureaucracy refused to admit there were any problems with the torpedoes.[15]

The frustration submariners felt over the whole torpedo debacle would become so ingrained in Ned that it partially colored the rest of his career in the Navy. He vowed that he would do everything in his power to never allow U.S. Navy ships to be supplied with weapons and equipment that did not work. Risking lives for the sake of bureaucratic niceties would be one thing Ned would forever have trouble accepting. In an oral history interview conducted by Columbia University many years after the war, Ned stated, "And had we had the good torpedoes at the beginning of the war, I'm positive the war would not have gone the way it did."[16] Ned's assessment echoed an unpublished Navy postwar analysis titled *Submarine Operational History of the United States Navy in the Second World War*, which noted, "Undoubtedly torpedo inferiority added months to the war and thus cost the U.S. thousands of lives and billions of dollars in treasure."[17] It was a lesson Ned would never forget, and the residual anger he felt over the issue would come back to haunt him later in his career.

The number and sizes of enemy ships sunk increased as the war went on, mainly due to the increased effectiveness of the torpedoes and the growing efficiency of the sub commanders. In addition, there was a shift in strategy after the first year of the war. Since the submarine was the only offensive weapon the United States had in the first year of the war that could get at the Japanese, priority was given to sinking ships of the Imperial Japanese Navy. These proved harder to hit than the slower-moving merchant ships, thereby limiting the success of attacks. By the second year of the war, the Navy's priority switched to merchant shipping. Sinkings increased dramatically, as did the impact on Japanese war-making capacity. An island nation with few natural resources, Japan was dependent on importing almost all of its needs to feed its war machine. The U.S. submarine offensive against the Japanese merchant marine produced far greater benefits than simply sinking ships that had to be replaced.

Trigger's third war patrol under Benson was during December 1942 to January 1943, when she was sent against the "Empire of Japan," a phrase that covered patrols in the waters around the Japanese home islands. Carrying nineteen underwater mines to be laid in the shipping lanes near one of the narrow passages that led from the Pacific to Japan's Inland Sea, *Trigger* had the opportunity to observe an 8,400-ton freighter strike one of its mines and sink. As *Trigger* exited the area, her underwater sound gear picked up an additional explosion, which was assumed to have been the sub hunter that had been escorting the freighter. It had apparently hit another mine while picking up survivors.

On the night of Christmas Eve, *Trigger* cruised on the surface into Sagami Nada, an entrance into Tokyo Bay. As her diesel engines throbbed, the sub's record player was attached to her PA system and Christmas carols were heard all over the ship. Ned, standing watch on the bridge, heard the carols through the two speakers near his position. He later recalled getting a lump in his throat "the size of a watermelon" as the familiar holiday refrains brought memories of family and home. While the playing of Christmas carols was a way of bringing some Christmas cheer to the crew, it was also an act of defiance against the Japanese since the music could be heard across the waters, giving away the location of the sub. *Trigger* was showing a new spirit of boldness under the command of Roy Benson.[18]

On New Year's Eve, *Trigger* downed an 8,500-ton freighter with two hits. And later in the patrol, a Japanese destroyer of the *Minekaze*-class was sunk with two torpedoes from a three-torpedo salvo. The crew began to use the expression that they could "pull the *Trigger*" on enemy ships. Down to only five torpedoes in the aft torpedo room and one forward, *Trigger* headed back for a refit and some rest. This time, they were ordered to Midway Island.

While the cramped living quarters coupled with the severe stress of being depth-charged made the lives of submariners miserable, the Navy saw to it that when in port the submariners were treated like royalty. Special refit crews were created so that, when a submarine came in for needed repairs and maintenance, the entire regular crew was freed of any duty.

Whether at Pearl Harbor or in Australia, crews back from patrols were provided with the best accommodations, food, and recreation possible while their subs were undergoing repairs and upgrades. Naval biographer Thomas Buell states: "After the war, Nimitz emphasized to a military audience that his men—especially his aviators and submariners—had been his most important asset. He wanted them to be fresh, alert, and well rested. Rotation and recreation programs were essential."[19] In Honolulu, the luxurious Royal Hawaiian Hotel was leased by the Navy for the duration of the war, and set aside for the exclusive use of submariners. Because of wartime secrecy requirements, submariners were forbidden to discuss anything related to their work with anyone outside the submarine community. As a result, submariners lived in a very close-knit, isolated fraternity.

The least popular place for a post-patrol refit was Midway Island. It lacked all the amenities that made Hawaii so popular, but most submarines under the command of the Pearl Harbor-based Central Pacific Fleet spent some time there between patrols. Ned noted, "There was little to do at Midway, except work on your submarine, watch the Gooney birds (the graceful Laysan Albatross), and drink at the 'Skipper's Bar.'"[20] To relieve tension, alcohol was provided in vast quantities for the submariners and, with the lack of "distractions" on Midway, the combination of alcohol and boredom could lead to some interesting events.

 ‑ During one rest period, *Trigger* was at Midway at the same time as USS *Seahorse* (SS-304), skippered by the former football All-American Slade Cutter, Naval Academy Class of 1935. The two crews, after a period of drinking, decided to play a game of football. There being no football available, a billiard ball was substituted. Ned was assigned the task of a defensive back and got stuck trying to tackle Cutter. As Ned noted, "What I remember most about that game was not who won but the set of bruises I carried for a week afterward in trying to tackle Slade Cutter. One does not lightly tackle an All-American tackle, even in a friendly way."[21]

The "friendly" football game on Midway was not Ned's last time having to tackle the redoubtable Cutter, who would end the war as the second-highest scoring American skipper with nineteen confirmed sinkings totaling 72,000 tons.[*] In an error of judgment, the crews of *Seahorse* and *Trigger* agreed to a joint luau while both subs were being refitted in Hawaii. The combination of alcohol, men back from stressful patrols, and two very competitive crews soon led to boasting and then to a physical confrontation. The military police had to break up the ensuing fight, but Cutter was highly incensed by *Trigger*'s chief of the boat (COB) having insulted one of *Seahorse*'s junior officers. In fact, it was the insult that had touched off the minor riot in the first place.

Trigger's commanding officer at the time, Dusty Dornin, ordered Ned, who was then exec, to smooth over the incident with Cutter. Neither Dornin nor Ned wanted charges brought against the COB, who had proven to be a very skillful navigating quartermaster. Ned spent a considerable amount of time calming Cutter down the day after the riot and had just gotten him to agree not to press formal charges on the promise that Cutter would never have to lay eyes on the COB again, when the door to Cutter's hotel room burst open and the inebriated COB stood there. Ned literally had to tackle Cutter as the enraged skipper charged across the room intent on doing bodily harm to the sailor.[22] In the end, the COB remained on board *Trigger*, but under strict orders to steer clear of Cutter and any of the crew of the *Seahorse*.

From April to June of 1943, *Trigger* was again sent against the Empire of Japan. On the night of 10 June, a Japanese aircraft carrier—the prize of all prizes—was observed coming out of Tokyo Bay. The carrier would later be identified as the *Hiyo* on her first sea trials. Maneuvering into position, *Trigger* fired all six forward torpedoes at the massive ship, scoring two hits, two premature detonations, and two misses. The reprisal for daring to attack His Imperial Japanese Majesty's newest carrier was swift and severe.[†]

---

[*] Statistics quoted in this text regarding sinkings and tonnage are based upon the findings of the Joint Army-Navy Assessment Committee. All JANAC statistics cited in this text are from Clay Blair Jr.'s *Silent Victory*, 984–991.

[†] Much later when Ned's first book, *Submarine!* was published, a copy found its way into the hands of Captain Takeo Yasunobu of the Japanese Self-Defense Forces. Yasunobu was on board *Hiyo* that June day, serving on the staff of the commanding officer of the Imperial Japanese Navy's Second Carrier Division. After reading Ned's account of *Trigger*'s version of the events, Yasunobu wrote to Ned, initiating many years of correspondence between the two. The April 1957 issue of the U.S. Naval Institute *Proceedings* carried an article, "Unlucky in June: Hiyo meets Trigger," co-authored by Ned and Yasunobu.

The two destroyers escorting *Hiyo* rushed to the point where the trail of bubbles indicated the location from which the torpedoes had been launched. Desperately, the *Trigger* crawled for depth, her only protection, but the destroyers were soon dropping depth charges all around. The explosions were so close that the crew could not hear the usual "click" that indicated the detonator on the depth charge had reached its prescribed underwater level. Ned would later describe the experience of being depth-charged as akin to being inside a large steel tub while a giant pounded away on it with a massive sledge hammer.[23]

The intensity of the explosions momentarily flexed the steel of *Trigger*. Men not holding firmly to a solid handhold were thrown around. The glass on gauges shattered, as did the light bulbs. The cork that lined the walls of the sub popped off, filling the air with dust. To ensure total quiet, all air ventilation systems were shut down and the air became stifling as the humidity reached 100 percent. Moisture began to condense on every surface; the deck was running with several inches of water. Men sweated profusely and popped salt tablets like candy to replace their bodies' loss through excess perspiration.

Down and down *Trigger* went, her crew praying that her builders had done their jobs well and that the hull would withstand the growing water pressure. The deck plates began to buckle as the outside pressure constricted the hull. Any weakness in an opening to the sea sprang a leak, adding to the water inside. The bilge pumps could not be run for fear of revealing the sub's location to the deadly enemy above. Men silently bailed water from one part of the sub to another in order to offset flooding. Finally, *Trigger* reached a depth beyond that which had been declared safe by her builders, and began to level off and creep away from her tormentors on the surface.

Once clear of the area, *Trigger* surfaced and the clean, cool air of the night flowed throughout the boat, taking the humidity, odors, stress, and pain with it. In spite of the pounding, the crew was elated. They could not claim to have sunk the carrier, but they knew they had at least inflicted severe damage. Much later they would be informed that two large holes were punched in *Hiyo*'s hull, delaying her entry into the war by almost another year. As Ned noted in his book *Submarine!*, the psychological impact on the Japanese people that must have occurred at seeing their newest carrier being towed back to port after having sent her off with fanfare the day before was worth as much as having sunk her.[24]

[5]

When *Trigger* returned from doing battle with *Hiyo*, she was scheduled for a "Navy yard overhaul," which was accomplished at Pearl Harbor, taking forty-five days to complete. Yard overhauls were planned well in advance, allowing men like Ned to forewarn family and friends of upcoming leave. During the summer of 1943, Ned was tentatively scheduled to be home during such a repair period and he had so notified his parents. Since Ned had recently broken up with a girl he had been dating when he left for the Pacific, his mother was anxious that he find someone to date while home. When Alice Beach made inquiries among members of her Palo Alto French Club, Inga Schenck, wife of a Stanford geology professor, indicated that her daughter Ingrid thought it might be a "blast" to date a naval officer. Ingrid was only seventeen years old and still in high school, her mother noted, but both mothers agreed the relationship would just be a "companionship" type of dating, so, "What could it hurt?"[25]

Alice wrote to her son about Ingrid Schenck and gave him the girl's address. Ingrid wrote to Ned first, mistakenly addressing the letter to Ned in care of USS "*Drigger*," instead of *Trigger*. Alice Beach's handwriting was hard for Ingrid to read, resulting in the transcription error of the name of Ned's submarine. In spite of the error, the letter reached Ned.

In her first letter to Ned, dated 31 May 1943, Ingrid discussed several of the dances to which she was looking forward, as well as the dresses she and her mother had picked out.[26] There might be a tendency to look askance at what appears to be the prattle of teenage trivia in a time of war, but for men like Ned, such letters were important reminders that, somewhere, "normal life" had not been totally erased by the war.

➤ By the time Ned's leave was ready to commence, he and Ingrid had exchanged enough letters that each was eager to meet the other. In the last letter Ned sent Ingrid before he arrived in Palo Alto, he wrote:

> I am luckier than I deserve. Am going home on 30 days leave, and will see you soon. Don't know when I will arrive, but it will be not too long after this letter, and maybe even before. Anyhow, expect me when I call you up. Chase the soldier out the door and lock the Marine up in the closet—I'll be seeing you!! If there are any sailors around, tell 'em to beat it, for a while. 30 days ain't so long, but ain't hay neither. They start counting from the day I show up in the good old USA. Wheeeeee Whew!!! With Love, Neddie.

The letter is completed with a stick figure running across the bottom of the page. The figure is wearing a sailor hat and carrying a banner that reads, "Homeward Bound."[27]

The first time Ned went to pick up Ingrid, he was a bit early and had to wait for her in the Schencks' front hall. As Ingrid came down from upstairs, her mother—on her way up—said to her daughter in Swedish, "He's good-looking," an appraisal with which Ingrid soon agreed.[28]

Toward the end of Ned's leave and after numerous dates, he and Ingrid bicycled up into the foothills near Stanford for a picnic lunch. Here Ingrid picks up the story: "He said, 'You know, I've completely fallen in love with you.' And I said, 'Well, I love you, too.' And then we kissed. I always point out when I tell this story, that that's all one did in those days, is kissed. And then I said, 'Well, I guess this means we're engaged.' And the poor man sort of gulped and he said, 'I guess so.'"[29]

While the proposal lacked the much-romanticized kneel and, "Will you marry me?" query, Ned did the gentlemanly thing and sought out Ingrid's father and asked his permission for the two to marry. With the blessings of Ingrid's parents, the couple planned to wed when Ned next came home on leave. As it turned out, that was almost a year later.

The leave period that saw Ned engaged to Ingrid was also the last time he would see his father alive. Ned's father was seventy-six when his elder son came home on leave in 1943. Ned's younger brother, John, having just graduated from the U.S. Military Academy at West Point, was headed for command of an infantry platoon that would eventually slug its way through the Hürtgen Forest in Europe. Ned's sister, Alice, would also soon be in uniform, a member of the Women Accepted for Volunteer Emergency Service (WAVES), specializing in radio communications. All three would get to see their father in the last months of his life. Though in declining health, the senior Beach refused to be admitted to a Navy medical facility because he did not want to take away from the care of wounded men returning from the war. When the elder Beach fell and broke his hip, he was admitted to the naval medical hospital in Oakland, California, where he died of complications arising from that fracture. Ned received news of his father's passing in a radio message while at sea. Only when he returned on leave in May 1944 did he get to visit his father's grave in the Golden Gate National Cemetery, San Bruno, California.

[6]

During Ned's leave time and his engagement to Ingrid, Roy Benson was transferred off *Trigger* and sent to New London, Connecticut, to teach at the Submarine School. At the same time, Ned was promoted to executive officer. The new skipper of *Trigger* was Robert E. "Dusty" Dornin, Academy Class of 1935. Also schooled in the Morton-O'Kane technique, Dornin gladly accepted Ned as his exec. While Lt. Cdr. Lewis had doubted

Ned's night vision, experience since the incident off Midway in June of 1942 had shown that Ned did indeed have excellent night vision. Benson passed this information on to Dornin, who used it to the max.

Officers of USS Trigger, *1944—(left to right) Front row: Lt. (jg) J. W. "Stinky" Sincavich; Ens. Ronny Smith; Lt. (jg) Bob Kemp; Ens. P. R. "Rodge" Rodgers. Back row: Lt. Ned Beach, executive officer; Cdr. R. E. "Dusty" Dornin, commanding officer; Lt. R. S. "Dick" Garvey; and Lt. William "Willy" Lang*

On the first of September 1943, *Trigger* set off on her sixth war patrol—this time to the East China Sea. With the aggressive Dornin in command and Ned as exec, *Trigger* would turn in a patrol that would eventually rank sixteenth in overall tonnage sunk on a single patrol for the entire war.

Having attacked and sunk a freighter on the fifteenth day of the patrol, *Trigger* hit the jackpot three days later. During daylight, smoke from a convoy was spotted on the horizon, so *Trigger* positioned herself to be able to attack at night. Going in on the surface, with Ned on the bridge and Dornin manning the plotting while commanding the sub from inside, *Trigger* found a six-ship convoy traveling in two columns. The three ships in the nearest column appeared to be tankers, so Dusty and Ned decided to attack that column first.

After firing three torpedoes at the lead tanker (Tanker #1), a big 10,000-ton ship, *Trigger* then fired two torpedoes at the second tanker in line (Tanker #2). Tanker #1, probably carrying aviation fuel, exploded with a horrific blast, lighting up the entire area. Stopping dead in the water as it ripped itself apart, its bright orange fire provided the lighting for the rest of the evening's drama.

Tanker #2 was hit by one torpedo, which started it ablaze, but the ship kept its forward progress as its crew fought to control the fire. One of the torpedoes that had missed either Tanker #1 or Tanker #2 traveled beyond, hitting the middle freighter (Freighter #2) in the far column, breaking that ship in half and sending it to the bottom in minutes.

With the fire from Tanker #1 providing light, the last tanker in the nearest column (Tanker #3) turned toward *Trigger* and began firing away with its deck gun. *Trigger* turned heel away from the pursuing enemy and then fired three torpedoes from her stern tubes at her new nemesis. All three missed, and as Tanker #3 closed in, *Trigger* fired the last stern torpedo she had loaded, hitting the tanker in the bow in what is known as a "down-the-throat" shot (firing a torpedo at an enemy ship's bow as the enemy is closing in on the submarine), blowing most of the bow off the tanker.

Trigger now submerged to get away from any enemy fire so she could steady herself to reload her torpedo tubes. With only six torpedoes left—two forward and four aft—she would have to try to finish off as much of the remaining convoy as possible with less than a full load. Upon resurfacing, the tactical situation facing *Trigger* was as follows: Tanker #1 dead in the water and fully engulfed in flames; Tanker #2 ablaze but moving slowly away from the battle area; Tanker #3 down by the bow, dead in the water; Freighter #1 stopped near Tanker #1 picking up survivors; Freighter #2 sunk; and Freighter #3 moving away from the battle area in the opposite direction of Tanker #2.

Dornin and Ned decided to go after Freighter #3, setting up for a shot from the forward tubes. Both torpedoes were fired and two hits were observed on Freighter #3. At this point, Freighter #3, dead in the water and sinking by the bow, spotted *Trigger* and opened fire with its deck gun, so Dornin decided to "polish him off." After setting up for a stern shot, Ned reported that Tanker #3 was also firing its deck gun, but that it appeared it was firing at Freighter #3, thinking it was a sub. Two torpedoes were fired at Freighter #3, but both failed to explode.

Fearing damage from one of the various deck guns being fired wildly in the battle area, Dornin decided to submerge and approach Freighter #3 using radar. When in position, the last two torpedoes were fired, both being duds. As *Trigger* exited the area, she left one ship sunk, one in total conflagration, three damaged, and one undamaged. The entire action lasted three and a half hours and took place within an area of about eight thousand yards.

Out of torpedoes, *Trigger* returned to Pearl Harbor, ending a patrol that had lasted just twenty-nine days. Of the thirteen hits observed on enemy ships during the patrol, five were duds. The Joint Army-Navy Assessment Committee (JANAC) would eventually credit *Trigger* with having sunk four ships totaling 27,095 tons during this patrol. Given the fact that *Trigger* had torpedoed and observed the sinking of a three-deck passenger/freighter early in the patrol, that meant JANAC gave credit for only three ships sunk out of the six in the convoy.[30]

— With Dusty Dornin in command, *Trigger* made two more war patrols, sinking six more ships. At the end of *Trigger*'s eighth war patrol—Dornin's third as skipper and Ned's third as exec—Dornin was detached from the submarine and sent to Washington as personal aide to Fleet Admiral Ernest King, chief of naval operations. King had specifically requested a submariner as his aide, and Dornin was tabbed for the job.[31]

Dornin's replacement was Frederick Joseph "Fritz" Harlfinger II, Naval Academy Class of 1935. He came to *Trigger* from having skippered the *S-32* (SS-137) one of the World War I boats that had been re-commissioned as a stop-gap measure in the months before the United States entered World War II. Harlfinger decided to continue the skipper/exec split in duties during attacks on surface ships using the Morton-O'Kane technique, so Ned served again as the eyes of *Trigger* while Fritz served as the nerve center of the attack.

As *Trigger* left on her ninth war patrol, January–April 1944, she was sent to the area around Palau Island, but her orders were changed when reports came in of large convoys of Japanese ships moving near the Mariana Islands. There, *Trigger* encountered one of the largest Japanese convoys of the war—over twenty ships in four columns escorted by at least ten destroyers and frigates. Harlfinger ordered all ten torpedo tubes made ready as he planned to fire *Trigger*'s full wad in a daylight attack.

Only the fourth torpedo had been fired when a Japanese destroyer found *Trigger* and began firing machine guns at the periscope as it quickly closed in. Submarines like *Trigger* came up to a depth of about sixty feet in order to use their periscopes. With the charging enemy ship closing in, Ned knew there wasn't time for them to get to a safe depth before a hail of depth charges ripped *Trigger* apart. He recalled thinking, "How long does it take a depth charge to sink fifty feet?"[32] The expected explosions did not materialize. Later, Ned would speculate that the Japanese destroyer had charged to the attack so quickly that her depth charge crews had not manned their launchers before they passed over *Trigger*.

The enemy's revenge for the audacity of the attack, however, was soon exacted in full measure. By the time *Trigger* reached three hundred feet of water, depth charges were pounding her. Then six escorts formed a circle around and above *Trigger*, each taking turns dropping depth charges every half hour or so. While the Japanese would have liked to sink the sub they had trapped, their main goal was to prevent it from surfacing in time to radio the location and course of the convoy to other subs. In that they succeeded.

For eighteen hours, the ring of tormentors pounded away at *Trigger*. Conditions in the boat became unbearable. The temperature reached 135°, water from leaks reached up to the bottoms of the deck plates, and the batteries were beginning to run low. Harlfinger and Ned huddled and decided that, when darkness came again, they would surface with all tubes loaded and try to fight it out. In their minds, it would have been better to go down in such a fight, maybe taking a few of the enemy with them, than to die the slow death of suffocation. As preparations were being made to surface, the Japanese began to relax their guard, and *Trigger* was able to slip through a gap in the circle, escaping to fight another day.[33] The damage inflicted on *Trigger* was so extensive that when she returned to Pearl Harbor, an extensive overhaul was ordered.

Upon his return to Pearl Harbor, Ned was given orders to report to new construction with time granted for leave, and to attend Prospective Commanding Officer School. It was with great reluctance that Ned left *Trigger*. He had made nine war patrols on board, four of them as executive officer, helping the boat tally sixteen enemy ships sunk—in all over 83,000 tons of shipping.

Having risen from a junior engineering officer to executive officer, Ned had been a major player in making *Trigger* the efficient instrument of war she had become. Ned had also earned a reputation within the submarine community. As naval historian Paul Stillwell noted, "Boats prospered when Ned was the exec."[34] His new boss, George Street, would describe Ned as "one of the outstanding young submariners of all time."[35]

By the time Ned received orders to detach from *Trigger* after two and a half years on board, there were only two men left on the sub who were plank owners—Ned and the chief steward's mate, Walter Pye Wilson. Determined to be the last plank owner to leave *Trigger*, in his final act as

The newlyweds—Ingrid and Ned after their wedding and before he left for the Pacific on board Tirante *(1944).*

exec, Ned gave Wilson orders transferring him to a refit crew. Wilson dutifully left the boat, waited until Ned had departed and then came back on board, where the new exec, Ned's Academy classmate Johnny Shepherd, promptly tore up the order. Wilson stayed on board for two more war patrols—finally accepting rotation to shore duty after having become something of a legend in the submarine service for his longevity on board *Trigger*.[36]

Perhaps Walter Wilson had a premonition about the future of *Trigger*, for on the sub's twelfth war patrol, while it was under the command of Cdr. David Rikart Connole, the sub was lost with all hands in March 1945. *Trigger* was patrolling between Okinawa and Kyushu when she disappeared, never to be heard from again. All told, *Trigger* finished her illustrious career seventh in overall tonnage sunk (86,552) and eleventh in the number of ships sunk with eighteen, putting her just fourteen thousand tons and eight ships behind the leading boats of the war.

[7]

Recently promoted to lieutenant commander and now on his way to attend Prospective Commanding Officer School, Ned returned to Palo Alto in May 1944, just a few days before his planned wedding. Ingrid had yet to graduate from high school—the same high school from which Ned had graduated—but the wedding was scheduled for the week before commencement exercises.

After a wedding ceremony held in the chapel at Stanford University, the newlyweds honeymooned in nearby Carmel, where they enjoyed grand vistas of the Pacific. Ingrid had once described her affection for the seaside city in one of her early letters to Ned: "I love Carmel, with the ocean beaches and beautiful beaches [sic], not to speak of the adorable little houses."[37] She was also very fond of the "cute little shops" the city offered. In May of 1943 when she penned those comments to a man she had yet to meet, she could little anticipate that within a year she would be spending her honeymoon there with that man.

As the young couple spent their few precious days in the idyllic atmosphere of Carmel, differences in their personalities began to emerge. While walking along Pebble Beach one afternoon, Ingrid commented on how beautiful the sea was that day. "Yeah. Okay, I want to show you something," Ned said in response as he sat down and began to draw a diagram in the sand of a car engine and its transmission. Ingrid would later admit that she feigned interest in the way that only a newlywed could, but she was thinking to herself how very different their personalities were.[38] In spite of those differences, their love for each other would become the paramount force in their lives.

Ned's unromantic impromptu lecture on the functioning of an automobile did have a practical side, over and above his own predilections as an engineer. The couple would soon be living near the Portsmouth Navy Yard, and while Ned was either in class or once he was back to sea, Ingrid would have to be able to drive—something she did not know how to do when they married. Ever practical, Ned felt that Ingrid should know how a car functioned, not just how to drive one.

The driving lessons began during their brief courtship and continued during their honeymoon and after they reached their first home, an apartment in the small town of Rye Center, near Kittery, Maine. Ingrid would later comment, "The only time I think a husband should teach the wife to drive is when they're newlyweds."[39]

The couple's first home was a very small apartment with a pull-down bed. A housing shortage existed in the towns around the Portsmouth Navy Yard, as was the case with all wartime military bases, so a parsonage across the street from a church in Rye Center had been converted into several very tiny apartments. The walls of the apartments were very thin, and Ingrid recalled that she figured their "neighbor" Ed Spruance must have been a very funny fellow because they constantly heard his wife, Jo, laughing. (Lt. Edward Dean Spruance, a submarine officer, was the son of Adm. Raymond Spruance, USN, commander of the U.S. Fifth Fleet during World War II.)

Wartime marriages usually entail long separations, frequently starting soon after the wedding. Ned and Ingrid were lucky in this regard. The fact that he was assigned as executive officer on a submarine under construction meant the couple had almost six months together before he again shipped out. By that time, Ingrid was pregnant, so her mother traveled to Rye Center—then mother and daughter took the train back across the United

States to Carmel, California, on the assumption that, when the war ended, Ned would arrive back at a West Coast naval base.

[8]

Ned was now faced with having to start over again in training a crew and learning the idiosyncrasies of a new boat. He was elated at the prospect of a brand new submarine—stronger hull, more capacity for torpedoes, newer equipment. Yet leaving *Trigger* was still an emotional letdown. The prospect of several months in Kittery, Maine, where *Tirante* (SS-420) was being built did offer some consolation after the years of continuous combat. Wearing the stripes of a newly promoted lieutenant commander and a wedding ring as a newly married man, Ned reported to *Tirante* as the executive officer of a crew that was getting ready to bring a new submarine into the fleet.

The officer commanding *Tirante* was Lt. Cdr. George L. Street III, Naval Academy Class of 1937. He had been on nine war patrols on board USS *Gar* (SS-206), and was as aggressive a skipper as any crew could want. Ned and George took an instant liking to each other, beginning a lifelong friendship. The third officer on the submarine was Lt. Edward G. Campbell, USNR (or U.S. Navy Reserve), a graduate of the Wharton School of the University of Pennsylvania (1938), who served as engineering and diving officer. Also a member of the crew was Lt. Endicott "Chub" Peabody II, USNR, football All-American from Harvard, Class of 1942. Peabody, who would go on to become governor of Massachusetts (1963–1965), was the officer in charge of *Tirante*'s TDC (torpedo data computer) when the sub was in attack mode. Chub would have his dignity somewhat ruffled when boarding a Korean fishing schooner to secure prisoners for interrogation. As he leaped on board the schooner, he stepped on a pile of fish, lost his footing, and unceremoniously landed on his back amid the catch of the day. Uninjured but for his pride, Chub quickly regained his footing, but his shipmates long remembered the All-American's encounter on a fish-covered running field.[40]

As Street and Ned readied *Tirante* for the long journey to Pearl Harbor and then to combat, Street was asked by the force gunnery officer if he would be willing to volunteer *Tirante* to take on a public relations mission in connection with *Tirante*'s first war patrol. The employees of the Westinghouse Corporation plant at Sharon, Pennsylvania, had donated the funds to purchase one of the torpedoes they built for the Navy as a contribution to the war effort. With torpedoes costing over ten thousand dollars each, the contribution was significant, and the Navy wanted to ensure that the torpedo was used to hit a worthy Japanese ship.

Always one to accept a challenge, Street gladly volunteered for the assignment, knowing that it entailed some risk in terms of all the publicity that had already surrounded the torpedo. With much ceremony, and with the attendance of lots of high-ranking officers and photographers, the VIT (very important torpedo)—as Ned and the crew came to call it—was loaded on board *Tirante* just before she departed for the Pacific.

After months of training exercises and the long journey to Hawaii followed by more training, *Tirante* left on her first war patrol on 3 March 1945. George and Ned were anxious to get *Tirante* "bloodied" (i.e., firing her first shots in combat) and to get rid of the VIT. Their wish was fulfilled on 25 March when the 3,080-ton *Kiyotada Maru* steamed across their path along the southern coast of Kyushu. Twenty minutes after *Tirante* became aware of the ship's presence, it was sunk, having taken the VIT amidships. The *Kiyotada Maru* broke in half and sank in less than two minutes.[41] *Tirante* was able to report that torpedo #58009, in all its brightly painted glory, had accomplished its mission. George and Ned even managed to snap a photo of the sinking ship through the periscope as further proof.

Several days later, *Tirante* was scheduled to rendezvous with *Trigger*, now under the command of David Connole, whom Ned had known for several years. With the production of new submarines having hit a high mark in 1944 that corresponded with the increasing decimation of the Japanese merchant fleet, targets were getting harder and harder to find. In addition, the Imperial Japanese Navy was trying to protect what shipping assets remained by efforts unseen early in the war. As a result, the U.S. Navy was trying new combinations of tactics to get at the remaining enemy shipping. Wolf packs had been tried off and on during the war, but were being utilized to a greater extent in the later years in an effort to maximize kills—hence, the planned meeting with *Trigger* to coordinate efforts.

After three nights without *Trigger* putting in an appearance and no response to *Tirante*'s tireless radio calls, the inevitable had to be accepted: *Trigger* had been lost. Ned was devastated by the news, realizing that many friends and shipmates had gone down with his beloved *Trigger*.

The actions of the war, however, waited for no mourning periods, and soon *Tirante* was ordered to an area off the southern coast of Korea where radio intelligence had learned of a large transport moving along the Korean coastline. American efforts to crack the Japanese operational codes and then utilize information gleaned from intercepted and decoded messages had met with success, and the results had been fed to submarines on patrol through much of the war. The effects were mixed in that, for reasons unknown, Japanese ships, even escorted convoys, tended to not follow the routes prescribed in their sailing orders, causing many U.S. submarines to wait in areas with nothing to show for the effort.

In this instance, however, the radio intelligence was correct. As the war had progressed and U.S. subs developed the practice of attacking at night on the surface where they were harder to spot and air cover was not as effective, Japanese ships had taken to moving at sea only during the daylight hours and then ducking into a guarded harbor or bay at night. Suspecting that this was the case with the large ship toward which *Tirante* was being vectored, Street decided to utilize a tactic developed by skipper Eugene B. Fluckey, nosing into harbors at night to see what was in there. Fluckey, Naval Academy Class of 1935, skipper of USS *Barb* (SS-220), would end the war ranked fourth among American submarine skippers, credited with sinking 16 ships totaling 95,360 tons.

Based on the radio intelligence, *Tirante* stealthily stole into a Quelpart Island anchorage on the night of 13 April, putting torpedoes into a large freighter loaded with ammunition and then sinking two attacking frigates on her way back out of the shallow harbor. The 4,000-ton *Juzan Maru* and two 900-ton frigates sunk in the attack added to the total of six ships sunk for 12,621 tons during *Tirante*'s first war patrol. On the list of single war patrols with the highest number of ships sunk, *Tirante* ranks seventh.

George Street was awarded the Medal of Honor for the patrol and Ned was awarded the Navy Cross, one of the few executive officers to receive that honor.[42] The Navy Cross is the highest award within the Navy and is presented to individuals who display extraordinary heroism in the face of the enemy. The only honor higher than a Navy Cross that a sailor can merit for heroism in combat is the Medal of Honor.

When *Tirante* returned from her first war patrol on 25 April 1945, orders awaited Ned detaching him from the sub and ordering him to his own command. While everyone sensed that the war was winding down, especially given the increasing difficulty for submarines to find suitable targets, Ned was determined to get into the war with his own command before it ended and while there were still targets to go after.

[9]

While Ned was working feverishly to prepare his new command for the sea, the degree of devastation that the U.S. Navy's submarine fleet had inflicted on the Empire of Japan was becoming apparent to the commanders and political leaders of the United States. The story of the "Silent Service" would not be told until after the war, but during the last months of the conflict, the losses sustained by the Japanese became more and more apparent. U.S. submarines accounted for 55 percent of all Japanese vessels lost in the war. That amounted to 1,314 enemy vessels sunk or disabled—totaling 5.3 million tons. This incredible feat of arms was accomplished by about fifty thousand officers and men, or less than 2 percent of the total Navy personnel during the war. The cost to the submariners, however, was high. Fifty-two submarines were lost during the war from all causes (including accidents), resulting in the deaths of 375 officers and 3,131 enlisted men—a casualty rate of almost 22 percent, the highest of all branches of the military. [43]

[10]

Ned may have had an inkling of the magnitude of the submarine victory in the making that summer of 1945, but the war was still raging and he was determined to get back into combat. Since he had been assigned as commanding officer of USS *Piper* (SS-409), his efforts to get the sub ready for a war patrol were frustrated at every turn. *Piper* was still out on a war patrol when Ned received his orders, so he had to wait at Midway for her return. When she came back, it was to Pearl Harbor, not Midway, so he had to be flown there. Once he arrived at Pearl, Ned was informed that *Piper* was to be fitted with a new type of sonar that would allow her to navigate submerged through underwater minefields.

After the new equipment was installed and tested, *Piper* headed for the island of Guam, which was being used as a forward submarine base. Upon arrival, more tests and tuning were ordered for the secret frequency-modulated (FM) sonar set, and it was determined that seven of the ten cylinder liners of number three main engine were cracked and would have to be replaced. Throwing caution to the wind, on 5 August 1945 *Piper* departed Guam, with one engine inoperable but the new sonar up and running. [44]

On 13 August *Piper* began a submerged passage through the Tsushima Strait, a heavily mined entrance to the Sea of Japan. Though a harrowing experience, *Piper* was soon in open water, running on the surface during the daylight and nighttime hours to arrive on time in her assigned patrol area. Patrolling submerged off the Japanese coast, using the radar antenna for the radio, *Piper* picked up a broadcast announcing that Japan had surrendered—the war was over.

An elated crew seemed not to notice their skipper's somber mood. Unable to comprehend his feelings at the time, Ned was hit with survivor's guilt. Why had he survived when so many of the men he knew and respected had perished? Why did *Trigger* go down after he left her? There was Johnnie Moore who had ordered Ned to submarine school back in 1941—he'd gone down on *Grayback* (SS-209) as her skipper.

After dark, *Piper* surfaced, running along the Japanese coast as the crew celebrated. Ned paced the deck alone in the darkness, his thoughts crowded with the images and memories of friends lost. In his 1947 book *Submarine!* Ned describes how his thoughts turned darker and darker that night:

> As I turned about the deck, always it came back to the same thing.
> We had won the war. It was over—finished—and somehow I had had the incredible luck to be spared. But what little divided those of us who were alive to see this day from those who were not? Just a few feet over the side, the long, cool, clean, silent water was the answer. It could claim many secrets—had claimed them for thousands and tens of thousands of years—one of them might as well have been me—could still be me. . . . I shrank from the abyss of lunacy yawning in front of me. The revulsion from four years of tension, and ultimate rejection of the subconscious idea that I might not make it after all, had plumbed its depth. Stinky and Johnnie Shepherd had not taken my place in the *Trigger*; it had simply been their bad luck, and my good. A call from the bridge, with a sort of wild, half chuckle to it: "Captain, Captain. Here's a message for you!" I walked swiftly forward. Jerry Reeves was standing there, holding a piece of paper in his hand. "You old bastard, sir!" he said. "Why didn't you tell anybody?" The message said: FOR PIPER X MESSAGE TO COMMANDING OFFICER FROM MRS BEACH SAYS DAUGHTER BORN AUGUST TENTH X BOTH WELL X CONGRATULATIONS X COMSUBPAC SENDS. The war had come to an end, and life, for some of us, was beginning.[45]

Like his father, Ned returned from war having commanded his own ship in combat and to a child born while he was at sea. Gone forever was the dream of commanding a battleship as Ned was now totally dedicated to the Silent Service.

Part III: 1945–1953

When USS *Piper* returned from her one and only war patrol with Ned in command, the submarine was ordered to Naval Submarine Base New London, in Connecticut, to assume its place in the post-war Atlantic Fleet. As she left the Central Pacific in her wake, *Piper* made for the Panama Canal and eventual respite from her wartime labors. Ned looked forward to reuniting with Ingrid and meeting his daughter Inga-Marie for the first time. Even as *Piper* worked her way through the canal and across the Caribbean, Ingrid flew across the United States with baby Inga-Marie in tow in order to be in Groton when Ned arrived. Ingrid's hope that Ned's submarine would be home-ported at a West Coast base after the war proved to be a false one.

Making efficient use of his time, and to keep from thinking too much about the longed-for family reunion, Ned began using his spare time on that long passage back to Groton (where the New London base is located) to turn submarine war patrol reports into stories—especially those about the lost *Trigger*. In an effort to memorialize shipmates now on "eternal patrol," Ned wanted his first story to be published by the Navy for distribution to the families of those lost on *Trigger*, as well as for those who had served on board the sub and, like Ned, had been transferred off before the sub's final patrol. The Navy rejected the idea, but suggested that he seek commercial publishing.

With that suggestion, he began to create additional stories about other submarines in addition to his continuing work on *Trigger* stories. Mixing facts from the patrol reports with his submarine experiences, and driven by his desire to follow in his father's footsteps as a writer, he soon produced a full series of stories. Initially thinking in terms of a book, Ned searched for a publisher. Dodd, Mead and Company rejected the idea for the book in 1946, citing a lack of interest in "war stories" so soon after the war.[1]

Seeking a more immediate outlet for his work, Ned turned to magazines as a possible consumer. He submitted one of his articles to *Blue Book*, a magazine that featured both fiction and nonfiction works. The effort was quickly rewarded when the magazine's publisher, Donald Kennicott, accepted it. The October 1946 issue carried "The *Trigger* Fights Her War," marking Ned's commercial debut in print. Over the next four years, *Blue Book* carried eight more of Ned's stories in its pulp-paper pages. (See Appendix II for a complete listing of articles and stories written by Ned.)

All the articles had to be cleared with the Navy as a guard against revealing classified information, but Ned was earning between three hundred and four hundred dollars per story from *Blue Book*. On average, the articles ran to thirteen pages in print, with many articles enhanced by line drawings created by various artists employed by the magazine. Since Ned had access to the war patrol reports from all U.S. submarines, most of the eleven articles that he eventually wrote for *Blue Book* dealt with actions by submarines other than those on which he had served—*Trigger*, *Tirante*, and *Piper*.

Once he had sufficient work published to demonstrate the viability of "war stories" in the immediate postwar era, Ned approached another book publisher, Henry Holt and Company, with the idea for the book that eventually became *Submarine!* This time, he found a publisher ready to listen. Using his published stories, as well as others he had penned but that were as yet unpublished, the book quickly took shape. In 1952, Henry Holt and Company released *Submarine!*, which contained a total of eighteen stories. Vice Adm. Charles A. Lockwood, USN, who had commanded America's submarines in the Central Pacific through most of the war, graciously accepted Ned's invitation to write the foreword for the book. With the publication of *Submarine!*, Ned began a long association with Henry Holt and Company, a relationship that proved profitable to both.

Several stories in *Submarine!* soon took on lives of their own. Francis X. Connolly used excerpts from *Submarine!* as an example of good writing for a college textbook that was published with the title *A Rhetoric Casebook*. Much later, an excerpt from the story of *Tirante* that appeared in *Submarine!* was reprinted in *Authors at Sea: Modern American Writers Remember Their Naval Service*.

To tell the exciting tale of USS *Harder* (SS-257) and skipper Sam Dealy's private war on Japanese destroyers, Ned wrote an article that appeared originally in the June 1949 issue of *Blue Book* as "Hit 'em Again, *Harder!*" After the article reappeared in *Submarine!*, it was included in *Battle Stations: True Stories of Men in War*, an anthology of war stories compiled by Margaret C. Scoggin and published in 1953 by Alfred A.

Knopf. In Scoggin's work, *Harder*'s story appears under its original *Blue Book* title. A year later, A. C. Spectorsky compiled stories for *The Book of the Sea: Being a Collection of Writings about the Sea in All its Aspects.* The story of *Harder* was included under the simple title "*Harder.*"

Ned's article "*Tirante*" from *Submarine!* made it to the television screen in an episode of *Silent Service* (1957–1958). Produced in a docu-drama style with actual combat footage intercut with reenacted scenes using professional actors, the series was supported by the Navy, which pro-vided access to a working submarine for filming purposes. The teleplay for "*Tirante* Plays a Hunch" was adapted from Ned's article to the small screen by Beirne Lay Jr., who had made a name for himself as a screen-writer for such famous films as *Twelve O'clock High* (1949), *The Flying Leathernecks* (1951), and *Strategic Air Command* (1955). In a departure from the norm, Ned and George Street played themselves in the episode.[2]

All this was in the future, however, as Ned worked away on articles while *Piper* headed for her new home port. The need to write would be a constant companion for Ned. No matter what "day job" he held, part of his spare time would be devoted to writing—both fiction and nonfiction. Such extracurricular activities on the part of an active duty officer in the U.S. Navy would become controversial for Ned later on.

[2]

The arrival of Ned and *Piper* at Groton began their role in the Navy's demobilization process as men and ships were released from active naval service. With so many men and ships to be demobilized, the process was long and tedious. In the peacetime Navy Ned lacked the seniority to merit command of his own submarine—there were going to be far fewer ships to command, resulting in the jobs of skippers going to more senior officers. As a result, in December 1945, he was detached from *Piper* and ordered to serve as personal aide to Rear Adm. Louis E. "Uncle Louie" Denfeld, USN. A graduate of the Naval Academy, Class of 1912, Denfeld was chief of naval personnel, having been saddled with the bureaucratic nightmare of discharging over a million officers and enlisted men. A qualified sub-mariner, Denfeld was also a master administrator, skillfully managing the Navy's reduction in personnel to the peacetime levels Congress had estab-lished, while successfully installing new personnel policies and procedures that would govern the postwar Navy.[3]

From December 1945 to February 1947, Ned worked closely for Denfeld in all aspects of the reorganization and demobilization processes. When Denfeld was promoted to vice admiral and named commander-in-chief of the Pacific Command—which included all Navy, Army, and Air

Force operations in the area of the Central Pacific—Ned was transferred to Op-36, the Atomic Defense Section, in the Fleet Operations office. Surprised to find himself the only submariner on the staff, Ned was even more amazed to learn that no one on the staff seemed to know what his job description was or would be.[4]

As it turned out, the real purpose of Op-36 had nothing to do with "atomic defense," and everything to do with "Navy defense." The nature of Op-36 had to do with restructuring the United States' military in those postwar years and integrating nuclear weapons into the strategic policies of the nation.

In the years immediately after the war, officers within the U.S. Army Air Corps pushed Congress to establish a separate U.S. Air Force. Believing strongly in the doctrine of strategic bombing—that air power alone could destroy an enemy's ability to make war, and thereby force surrender—the high-profile, energetic Air Corps officers succeeded in making their case. With the creation of a separate air force, an internecine slugging match ensued as the newest branch of the U.S. military attempted to gather under its command umbrella control of all future atomic weapons.

The Navy, realizing atomic weapons were the wave of the future, and therefore the key to all future funding, worked diligently to ensure a place at the atomic weapons table for itself. While naval officers had participated in developing atomic weapons in the Manhattan Project, and had even been in charge of arming the first atomic bombs dropped in war, the Air Force argued that it alone should have control over the delivery of any and all such weapons in the future.

As the fight over control of atomic weapons boiled on, the Air Force sought funding for larger and larger bombers to deliver future generations of atomic weapons. With the tenor of Congress such that cuts in defense spending were in order, funding requests for new strategic bombers ran headlong into funding requests for a new generation of aircraft carriers for the Navy. The new carriers were to be capable of launching and recovering planes that could carry atomic weapons. It should be remembered at this point that the first atomic bombs were so large that there were no planes capable of carrying one and landing on an aircraft carrier. As a result, much of the struggle that ensued was over "future" delivery systems.

To complicate all of this even more, Congress had authorized the consolidation of the Navy Department and the War Department (i.e., the U.S. Army), as well as the Air Force, into the newly created Defense Department. In the process, the once-powerful cabinet-level positions of secretary of the Navy and secretary of war became subordinate to the new secretary of defense. Not only were there now three branches of the armed services—Navy, Army, and Air Force—competing for funding, but the access of the two senior services to the president's ear was henceforth to be channeled through an overall defense secretary.

As Ned discovered when he tried to figure out his role in Op-36, the real role of the organization was to counter Air Force propaganda with Navy propaganda. With Air Force arguments pointing to a future in which nuclear weapons would be the only ones with which wars would be fought, control of those fearsome weapons was the key to all future funding. As a mere lieutenant commander, Ned was the most junior officer in Op-36, and he was generally not conversant with all the technical aspects of the Navy's argument, but he was regularly informed of the efforts of the unit to develop the specifications for a carrier-borne aircraft that could deliver a nuclear weapon, as well as the design requirements for safe storage areas for unarmed nuclear devices on board a ship at sea.[5]

Without a specific set of duties, Ned's innate drive and self-starter personality came to the forefront. He decided he might as well put his own background as a submariner to use and began working on design concepts for a nuclear-powered submarine. Where others might have quietly served out their tour as a "desk skipper," Ned was not content to hide in the bureaucracy and await reassignment to sea duty.

With no technical knowledge of how nuclear reactions worked, or how one might go about constructing a propulsion system for a submarine using nuclear power, Ned set himself to the task of trying to devise a plan for the development of a submarine powered by a nuclear source. Seeking out those within the Navy who knew about such matters, he ended up spending much of his time listening to the man who would one day be known as the "Father of the Nuclear Navy"—Hyman G. Rickover. At Rickover's suggestion, Ned requested permission to attend several training programs on the basic principles of atomic power.

Based on what he had learned, Ned developed a proposal for a nuclear-powered submarine, submitting it to Rear Adm. William S. "Deak" Parsons, USN, who was then Ned's boss at Op-36. Parsons had been part of the Manhattan Project and was the person who had actually armed the atomic bomb that was dropped on Hiroshima. As the Navy's foremost authority on atomic bombs, Parsons was the point man in the Navy's efforts to thwart the Air Force's scheme to gain hegemony over atomic weaponry.

The proposal had no sooner landed on Parsons' desk than Ned was summoned to Parsons' office and literally read the riot act. Ned was told in no uncertain terms, at decibels just below shouting, that he was to have nothing to do with anything even remotely related to a nuclear-powered submarine.[6] Puzzled, hurt, and dismayed that his initiative had caused such a response, Ned could not understand what had prompted the outburst that was so uncharacteristic of the even-tempered Parsons.

While still smarting from the tongue-lashing, Ned was next summoned to the office of Captain Rickover, who was then assigned to the Bureau of Ships. Rickover, whose personality was the antithesis of Parsons', immediately attacked Ned for not having come up with a design for a nuclear submarine.[7] Ned would later come to believe that he had been a pawn in some power game between Parsons and Rickover, but from that day forward Ned found himself the unofficial employee of Rickover while still maintaining his desk and title in Op-36. In the process, Ned also learned much about the internal politics of the Navy's hierarchy and the emerging political structure within the new Department of Defense.

Ned's musings on what it would take to create a nuclear submarine were not wasted. In October 1947, Ned was asked to a meeting with Rickover and Capt. Elton W. Grenfell, USN, who was then serving in Op-31, the office of the assistant chief of naval operations. Grenfell was a submarine veteran of World War II who had the distinction of having sunk the first Japanese warship in the war and who, like Ned, had been awarded a Navy Cross. Rickover ordered Ned and Grenfell to draft a memo outlining a nuclear submarine program for the Navy.[8]

Rickover, who was a master at bypassing Navy bureaucracy when it suited his needs, used these two junior officers as the back doors to get the proposal approved without its having to wend its way through the time-consuming maze normally allotted to new design concepts. Grenfell's boss in the operations section had to endorse any such proposal, and Grenfell offered the quickest means of gaining access to that high-ranking officer. Next, the proposal would need the endorsement of the chief of naval operations (CNO), Adm. Chester Nimitz. Rickover, knowing Nimitz had been a submarine officer, wanted to get the proposal endorsed before Nimitz's term as CNO ended in a few months. Nimitz had been at the Naval Academy when Ned's father had taught there and had been on friendly terms with Ned for some time. Also, since he was on the staff of Op-36, Ned had legitimate access to Nimitz, being able to request a meeting without having to garner the approval of Admiral Parsons.

Once Grenfell's boss endorsed the memo, Ned walked it into Nimitz's office. Just ten days before his term as CNO ended, Nimitz forwarded the memo with his endorsement to Secretary of the Navy John L. Sullivan. Within three days of receipt of the proposal, Sullivan had appointed the Bureau of Ships to head the Navy's nuclear submarine building program and forwarded the proposal, accompanied with his own strong endorsement, to Secretary of Defense James V. Forrestal.[9] Within a time frame that astonished everyone, the Navy bureaucracy had officially committed to a nuclear submarine program. It had also handed the job to Rickover rather than to Parsons.

[3]

Even as Ned was daily working in the labyrinth of the Navy's bureaucracy, the Beach household welcomed a second child in February 1947, when Edward Latimer Beach III was born. While Ingrid had flown across the country with infant Inga-Marie in the fall of 1945 in order to meet Ned in Groton, in the spring of 1947, she, Ned, Inga-Marie, and newly arrived Edward drove to Key West, Florida, when Ned was reassigned there. The role of a Navy wife was never boring and certainly full of challenges. Swapping Groton, Connecticut, for the warm and sunny Florida Keys seemed like a good trade, but the Beaches arrived just as summer set in, and two small children in the heat of high summer did make life even more challenging than usual.

After Ned's stints in Washington, the detailers in the Bureau of Personnel had determined he had attained enough seniority to be given a sea command once more. In May 1948, he was detached from Op-36 to the command of USS *Amberjack* (SS-522). Ned was replaced at Op-36 by Eugene P. "Dennis" Wilkinson, who would go on to command USS *Nautilus* (SSN-571), the world's first nuclear-powered submarine. While working on the memo that helped create the Navy's nuclear submarine program, Ned had mused on the very real possibility that he might be in a position to be the skipper of that submarine when it was commissioned. Later, in welcoming Wilkinson to Op-36, it also occurred to Ned that he might be looking at the man who would beat him out for that command.[10]

[4]

Amberjack was classified as a "Guppy II" submarine—"Guppy" having evolved from the acronym for "Greater Underwater Propulsive Power."[11] In the years immediately following the war, especially as budgets for new construction were heavily restricted, the Navy turned to experimenting with new concepts by modifying some of the last submarines to be built before the war ended. Much of the focus in the postwar years was on gaining greater underwater speed and developing a snorkel that would allow a submarine to run its main engines while submerged.

Increased speed while submerged required the development of larger battery storage facilities on board the submarine, whose design was already so tight that there was little room for more of the space-consuming batteries.

With the space constraints a fixed reality, the pioneering of batteries with larger capacities to hold a charge became the focus. To aid in the quest for speed, exterior modifications to the submarine were also undertaken, eliminating almost everything that protruded from the hull. Through experiments and a rearrangement of the interior of the sub, progress was made along both lines. By 1947, the first conversions to what became known as the Guppy I-type had been completed.[12]

A second redesign initiative undertaken simultaneously was the development of an effect snorkel—a device that allows a submerged submarine to take in fresh air and expel deadly engine gases at the same time. The Germans had been the first to deploy what they called *schnorchels*, and the U.S. Navy sought to replicate their design. The Navy's engineers discovered that, since the German U-boats were generally much smaller than the American submarines, the American subs required larger intake and exhaust tubes than the German-designed snorkel. The German designs had to be adapted and the Navy did not come up with a workable snorkel until 1947.

Combining the new snorkel with the Guppy I-type's increase in underwater speed led to the creation of the Guppy II-type. Beginning with the fiscal year 1948–1950 shipbuilding program, twenty-four Guppy II-types were authorized. These were conversions of late-war fleet submarines along with two that had previously been converted to Guppy Is.[13]

Amberjack had been commissioned in 1946 at the Boston Navy Yard, where she had been built. By January 1948, she had been converted to the Guppy II-type and was stationed at Key West. When Ned took command, he instituted a series of training exercises to develop techniques for a submarine to recover from a steep angle dive that had gone wrong. With the increase in underwater speed came the worry that while in a steep dive—15° to 20° from the horizontal—a submarine might have its diving planes jam and then would be driven below its crush depth before the crew could recover.

Given *Amberjack*'s increased submerged speed, Ned also wanted to pioneer tactics that would allow the submarine to dive to her test depth much more quickly than had previously been allowed and then to return to the surface with greater speeds. Both maneuvers involved what is known as the "steep angle of attack" (i.e., the angle from the horizontal at which the submarine moves through the water). Under Ned's command, *Amberjack* routinely submerged and surfaced at high speed with a 30° angle—remaining horizontal or with only a slight up angle being the standard for the rest of the Navy's submarines at the time. According to Bert Finley, a lieutenant (junior grade) on board *Amberjack* during Ned's tenure as skipper, "This was unheard of as a diving procedure and considered risky. And it did result in some exceptional and exciting dives."[14]

Amberjack performed so many of these procedures that she earned the nickname "Anglejack."[15] The spectacular eruption of a submarine from beneath the ocean's surface while in one of these high-speed moves was captured by a photographer and published in *National Geographic* magazine. The high-speed maneuvers were taken at such steep angles that crew members in key positions in the control room had to have seat belts to keep them in place. Ned was positive that they never exceeded an angle greater than 47°, but Finley states with confidence that in one memorable surfacing maneuver, *Amberjack*'s angle reached 60° as he and another officer were able to measure it by water marks on the forward pump room bulkhead.[16]

The tactical use of steep angle maneuvers was that they permitted a sub to go from the surface to its test depth and back to periscope depth in a minute and a half. Using this procedure, a submarine that was being attacked by a surface warship could dive safely below the warship as it passed overhead and then reach periscope depth in time to fire a torpedo before the enemy ship could turn around for a second attack.[17] The ability to change depth very quickly also aided submarines in their ability to evade the sonar of surface ships.

In one exercise in which *Amberjack* participated while under Ned's command, *Amber*—as she was known to her crew—became the "enemy" trying to disrupt a landing force of a dozen transports carrying Marines, protected by a half-dozen destroyers. Using the new steep angle techniques, plus the speed with which the sub could move underwater, *Amber* "sank" all the surface ships without receiving any "damage." [18] (The "attacks" by *Amberjack* were signified by the firing of green flares over the center of the target ships, while depth charges were simulated by the dropping of specially designed noisemakers.) In another exercise, Ned claimed to have sunk an aircraft carrier, audaciously sending the carrier group commander a photo of the carrier taken through *Amber*'s periscope and signed, "Regards, from *Amberjack*."[19]

As Ned would note in his memoirs, the months he spent on *Amberjack* remained among his top memories at sea. Still honed from his years in the war, he realized that he now possessed a submarine that had the capability to strike an enemy as hard as he had always wanted. Recapturing the adrenaline rushes of the war years, Ned exercised his crew at levels he would later describe as "hard."[20] He often found himself thinking about the "what if" of having had such high-performance submarines during the war.

Ned had anticipated that his tour on board *Amberjack* would last three years, but within a year he received a letter from Capt. Arleigh Burke, one of the rising stars in the Navy, asking Ned if he was interested in coming back to Washington to work for Burke in a position "of high responsibility for the Navy's future." [21] (The program on which Ned was asked to work was an extension of the Op-36 program—countering Air Force and civilian efforts at eliminating any Navy role in nuclear weapons.) So pleased was Ned with what he was doing on board *Amberjack* that he respectfully declined the offer. Within three months, however, came orders—not a request—detaching Ned from *Amberjack* and directing him to report to the chairman of the Joint Chiefs of Staff. [22]

[5]

The thrill of commanding *Amberjack* was leavened with bitterness for Ned and Ingrid while in Key West. Sadly, Inga-Marie was not with them long. On 17 August 1948, just a week after her third birthday party, she died. Ned described Inga-Marie's death in a letter to friends written just a week after the sad event: "We are utterly desolate. The little girl was such a joy to both of us, and had so many cute mannerisms and expressions which only Ingrid and I could know about. She died of an odd intestinal condition, *not* illness. The whole staff of the hospital was gathered around her bedside, and they never knew what was wrong. The doctors *still* don't know exactly what was wrong. We are comforted that her illness lasted only two days, and that she did not suffer much [emphasis in the original]." [23]

Later, Ned and Ingrid would learn that they were both carriers of the cystic fibrosis gene, and they came to suspect that their little Inga-Marie died of some complication of that disease, which the doctors in 1948 could not diagnose. Inga-Marie was buried in a cemetery only a block from their house in Key West.

With "Neddy" still an infant and Ingrid expecting again, both parents had to balance their sorrow with the joys and demands of their other children. The loss of Inga-Marie would remain, however, an overwhelming grief for the rest of their lives. [24]

[6]

"This is no time for 'fancy Dans' who won't hit the line with all they have on every play, unless they can call the signals. Each player on this team—whether he shines in the spotlight of the backfield or eats dirt in the line—must be All-American." [25] Chairman of the Joint Chiefs of Staff Gen. Omar Bradley, USA, delivered these words before the House Armed Services Committee on 19 October 1949. The "fancy Dans" at whom the football analogy was directed were any persons who were not team players in Bradley's estimation, but the remark sparked what came to be called the "Revolt of the Admirals." The issue was the direction of American defense policy—with its attendant budgetary fallout—and Ned found himself in the middle having assumed the position of an aide to General Bradley at the end of August 1949, just a few months before the famous remark was made. Interservice rivalry, bureaucratic infighting, and civilian control of the military were all intermixed in a controversy that raged as Ned tried to establish the role of a Navy aide to the first chairman of the Joint Chiefs. It was soon obvious to Ned that "politics" would be a permanent part of any job in the Pentagon.

U.S. Army Gen. Omar Bradley was the first person to hold what became the top position in the nation's military. While the idea of cooperation among the branches of the services had been discussed, the creation of the Defense Department and then the concept of one overall uniformed commander were steps toward making "unification" a reality.

As Bradley moved into a position for which there were no established patterns, he felt the need to make his office as diverse—as far as the other branches of the military were concerned—as possible. Believing it would be good for the image of the chairman to have staffers from the other branches, Bradley wrote to Louis Denfeld, then chief of naval operations, asking for "a young, capable naval officer in whom you have great confidence."[26] Denfeld responded by recommending his former aide—Ned Beach.

The move back into the bureaucratic maze of the Pentagon also brought Ned back into the interservice battle still raging over the defense budget and which branch would control nuclear weapons. The press used the phrase "Revolt of the Admirals" to refer to a series of public events that should have been limited to skirmishing in the back hallways of the Pentagon. However, the whole affair got out of hand due to the confluence of unique personalities and bad decisions—ingredients for a "perfect storm" in the Pentagon teapot. The whole affair had to do with only a few overzealous officers in both the Navy and the Air Force, and it is clear the vast majority of officers in both branches did not share the more radical opinions of some of their more vocal fellow officers.[27] Added to the volatile situation was CNO Denfeld, who was either unwilling or unable to control his most outspoken officers. A compromiser by nature, Denfeld was forced into retirement by the events, earning praise from some and condemnation from others.

In the controversy's simplest terms, some of those pushing for unification of the services believed everything that flew should be under the control of the Air Force (read: end Navy aviation and carriers), any operation on land should be under the control of the Army (read: abolish the Marine Corps), and anything that could float should be under the control of the Navy—but since airplanes could sink any ship, a very small Navy should suffice. When President Truman's new secretary of defense, Louis Johnson, summarily cancelled the construction of the Navy's first supercarrier—the *United States*—in 1949 in the name of budgetary constraints, some high-ranking naval officers saw the need to go public with their objections. In violation of rules regarding such activities, memos and reports were leaked to the press and some officers wrote articles for popular magazines in which Defense Department policy was criticized and Air Force projects were declared to be incapable of achieving their stated goals.

By the time the dust settled, the body count of men in Navy blue with ended or ruined careers was in disproportion to the outcome. Congress called for hearings, a parade of high-ranking present and former officers— many of the big names from World War II—testified, but little was resolved. The Air Force got its B-36 strategic bomber, but it proved to be a short-lived weapons platform, and the Navy soon got the first of its supercarriers, anyway. What actually put all of the interservice squabbling to an end was the movement of the North Korean army across the 38th parallel, setting off the Korean War. In a swift turnaround, carrier aviation was justified, the Marines were needed, both as ground forces and for amphibious assaults, and everyone was too busy trying to save South Korea to worry about all the infighting.

In the midst of all this, Ned arrived to serve on the staff of General Bradley, who literally was in the eye of the storm. Denfeld and his Air Force and Army counterparts all worked for Bradley, but none of them had the slightest intention of giving up their old prejudices against the other branches. The leaks to the press of internal memos and reports, coupled with articles written by naval officers, led to the congressional hearings. Called to testify before the congressional committee headed by the powerful Carl Vinson, Bradley had worked closely with some of his staff in preparing his remarks. As the newcomer and a Navy man, Ned was kept out of the loop and was not allowed to preview the general's prepared statement, despite his repeated requests to do so.

Bradley's speechwriter, Lt. Col. Chester V. Clifton, USA, told Ned that Bradley did not want to put Ned in a bad position with the Navy, so Ned was to have no part in drafting the testimony, thereby providing him with the ability to deny any involvement. Ned finally got to see the general's prepared remarks as he rode to Capitol Hill from the Pentagon to listen to Bradley's testimony. When Ned came to the "fancy Dans" comment, he told Clifton that Bradley couldn't say that—it would be interpreted by the Navy as a specific reference to it. Clifton assured Ned that it was not Bradley's intent to call the Navy "fancy Dans," but to call anyone who was not a team player such.[28]

As Ned predicted, the press jumped all over the "fancy Dans" comment and the Navy, especially the Marine Corps, took great umbrage at it. The simmering pot of conflict had been turned up several notches by the general's testimony. Bradley lost credibility as being an evenhanded chair of the Joint Chiefs, and everyone opposed to the Navy's position repeated the phrase ad nauseam. In retrospect, Bradley admitted the phrase should not have been used, and he told Ned he regretted not having allowed Ned to review the remarks before they were given.[29] In his own appraisal of the "Revolt," Ned came to believe the nation was better off because of the sacrifices made by Denfeld and other naval officers.[30]

[7]

Ned's sudden and surprising transfer to Washington, D.C., to serve as an aide to Bradley added stress in his family's lives over and above that suffered from the loss of Inga-Marie. A second son, Hugh, was born in June 1949, less than ten months after the passing of Inga-Marie. In August of the same year, Ned was transferred to Bradley's staff, requiring a move back to Washington. The house the Beaches owned outside Washington, however, was rented out and not available for their immediate return. To relieve the housing crisis and to enable Ingrid to work through the emotional roller coaster of losing one child and giving birth to another in less than a year, she and their two boys went to Japan for six months to live with her parents. (See Appendix III for the story of Ingrid's family and the reasons her parents were living in Japan in 1949.) During that time, Ned was able to visit his family once when he accompanied General Bradley on an official tour of U.S. bases in Japan. By the time Ingrid and the children returned to the United States, their house was ready and the family reunited in their own home.

[8]

In some measure, Ned's being tapped for an aide to General Bradley, for whom Ned always held a great deal of respect and affection, had to do with his writing abilities. By mid-1949, Ned already had several articles published, including one in the influential U.S. Naval Institute *Proceedings*. It was Ned's writing abilities that had attracted Arleigh Burke's attention and led to the offer to work in Op-23, the other ill-fated effort of the Navy to out-propagandize the Air Force.[31] The Navy's policy of rotating officers meant that, despite Ned's writing skills, his time on the staff of the chairman of the Joint Chiefs would come to an end. When it did, he was selected in March 1951 to command the new USS *Trigger* (SS-564), then under construction at Groton, Connecticut. (After World War II, the Navy began naming newly commissioned submarines after subs lost during the war.)

If Ned had reveled in the technical abilities of *Amberjack*, he was positively thrilled at the prospects of the ship he came to call *Trigger II*. The first of the newly designed postwar submarines of the *Tang* class to become operational, *Trigger II*, like her five sister submarines, was supposed to incorporate all the lessons learned during the war. She was to be able to "dive deeper; run faster both surfaced and submerged; be more maneuverable underwater; carry better sonar, radar, and fire-control equipment; be more habitable, with a better source of fresh water."[32] Reality would prove to be a letdown.

As the designated PCO (prospective commanding officer, the title given to the officer scheduled to command a ship once it is commmissioned), Ned dove into the process of assembling and training a crew, sending the personnel officer of the Atlantic Submarine Command several letters requesting specific sailors, both officers and enlisted men, who had served with him on *Amberjack*. He also "strongly" requested that Walter Pye Wilson, the one man who had more time on the original *Trigger* than Ned, be assigned to the new *Trigger*.[33] For the most part, Ned got all the men he requested, including Wilson.

Having been launched on 14 June 1951 by Mrs. Roy S. Benson, wife of one of the skippers who had had such success during the war on the first *Trigger*, the new *Trigger* was commissioned on 31 March 1952 with Ned in command. After testing and trial runs, Ned received permission to sail *Trigger II* up the Potomac to show her off to the officials in Washington. That accomplished, *Trigger II* set off on her shakedown cruise to Rio de Janeiro, accompanied by a Navy photographer equipped with an 8-mm movie camera to record the historic event. In time, the Navy came to regret the publicity it lavished on *Trigger II*, as the sub and her sisters of the same class turned out to be utter disasters.

Submarines of the *Tang* class were equipped with new, lightweight diesel engines that turned out to be every skipper's nightmare. As naval historian Michael Isenberg flatly states, "The lightweight diesel engines of the *Tang* class were consistent only in their defects."[34] Ned summarized their problems in more graphic terms: "My new ship, the first to become operational of a new and different submarine design for our navy, must have been designed by a neophyte committee of amateur inventors who did not test their products before installing them. From main engines to periscopes, nothing in her worked the way it should."[35]

One of the *Tang* class, USS *Harder* (SS-568), suffered the ultimate humiliation of having to be towed across the Atlantic from a Royal Navy base all the way back to Groton, all four of her engines broken down beyond the abilities of her crew to repair them. Given the ingenuity for which submariners are famous in their ability to jury-rig a solution to any problem, having all four main engines beyond even a temporary repair was an amazing testament to the engines' poor quality.

Having been seasoned in the utter frustration of equipment that malfunctioned during the war—especially torpedoes—Ned was in no mood to soft-pedal the problems with *Trigger II*. While on the return trip from Rio de Janeiro, Ned fired off a series of official messages via radio reporting all the shortcomings of his new submarine. Ned's missives were so pointed that, when *Trigger II* docked at Groton, Harold Shear, a veteran submariner and longtime friend of Ned's, made a point of being the first person on board. Shear, who went on to achieve flag rank, pulled Ned aside and told him that he had to take it easy, he was getting himself in trouble because of his reports on how bad the design of the new submarine was proving to be.[36]

Ned would later admit that "I should have had the sense to realize that this thing I was saying was a pretty strong thing, and I'd better check with the admiral first, and that's where I wasn't so smart."[37] Being incensed over the shortcomings of *Trigger II* was perhaps a natural response given the sense of betrayal men like Ned felt over the torpedo fiasco during the war, but when Ned declared in his official report that *Trigger II* was not fit to be deployed, while the admiral in command of the submarine force had already reported to his superiors that she was deployable, trouble was soon to crash down on someone's head. "He [the admiral] really went up and down my back for that one," Ned would later admit.[38] Some observers came to suspect that Ned's intemperate handling of the problems on board *Trigger II* were the root of his later obstacles when it came to promotions.

After what the crew came to call the "shake-up" cruise, as opposed to "shakedown" cruise, *Trigger II* was placed in a dry dock for extensive repairs. While in dry dock, the submarine was out of contact via radio and no phone lines had been run to the boat. One day, a crane swung overhead, lowering a ringing telephone. A surprised sailor answered the phone and announced, "For you, Captain." Ned picked up the receiver and was told simply to report to the Navy Department in Washington the next day to meet with the chief of naval operations.

Part IV: 1953–1957

Between the time Ned received the phone call on the deck of *Trigger II* and his arrival at the office of Adm. William M. Fechteler, chief of naval operations, a state of apprehension would perhaps best describe his emotions. While the reactions to Ned's pointed and highly charged criticisms of the new submarine design had quieted, he did not know if this summons was going to be yet another round of someone wearing gold braid going up and down his backside. Much to his surprise, Ned was told that President-elect Dwight D. Eisenhower had asked specifically for him to serve as naval aide to the president.

In a letter dated 14 January 1953, the president-elect asked White House chief of staff Sherman A. Adams to "arrange to assign Cdr. Edward L. Beach as my naval aide, effective January 21, 1953." In a postscript, Eisenhower noted, "I should like it to be understood that Commander Beach is to be assigned as my naval A.D.C. [aide-de-camp] *only* in the event he desires the position [emphasis in the original]."[1] Without hesitation, Ned accepted the post.

Making his way back to Groton to inform his family of the sudden changes that would impact their lives, Ned pondered several points. First was the realization that his days at sea in command of a submarine were probably over forever. By the time he completed the usual three-year tour as naval aide to the president, he would be too senior to again command a submarine. Another thought that passed through his mind, albeit a very pleasant one, concerned how Eisenhower had come to ask for Ned specifically. Assuming that Omar Bradley, Ike's classmate from West Point, had made the recommendation, Ned was surprised to later learn from Eisenhower that the recommendation had come from Capt. Everett "Swede" Hazlett, USN.[2] Hazlett had read *Submarine!* and liked the book so much that he had written to Ike suggesting that Ned would be a great choice for a naval aide. Ike and Swede had been boyhood friends

Ike and Ned: as presidential naval aide, Ned reads a proclamation at the White House awarding P. Pibulsonggram, prime minister of Thailand, the Chief Commander of the Legion of Merit award on 2 May 1955. Onlookers (left to right)—Front row: President Eisenhower, the prime minister, and Mrs. Pibulsonggram; Second row: Col. Robert L. Schulz, USA, presidential Army aide; Secretary of State John Foster Dulles, Vice President Richard M. Nixon, and Col. William G. Draper, USAF, presidential Air Force aide.

back in Abilene, Kansas, and had made plans to attend the Naval Academy together. Swede got an appointment, but when there were not enough appointments to cover Ike, the future supreme commander of Allied forces in Europe had opted for West Point.

A third thought that concerned Ned was his rank. He would be replacing Rear Adm. Robert Lee Dennison, USN, in the naval aide position. As a recently promoted commander, Ned was junior to anyone who had held that position for as far back as anyone could remember.[3] *Time* magazine pointed out in an article on the new administration's staffing that "Harry Truman had two major generals and a rear admiral (average age: 51) as his White House military aides. Ike's aides, named last week, are younger men (average age: 37) of lower rank: a commander, a lieutenant colonel, a major."[4]

The shake-up was due to Ike's negative experiences in dealing with presidential military aides when he was Army chief of staff during the Truman administration. Presidential aides with stars on their shoulders—or sleeves in the case of the Navy—tended to try to influence policy, coming between the president and the heads of the military branches. Having been annoyed by the efforts of Truman's aides to dabble in policy, Ike was determined to preclude his aides from any such activities.

During 1954–1955, a young Navy lieutenant assigned to Ned's White House staff was William J. Crowe Jr. A graduate of the Naval Academy, Class of 1947, he arrived at the White House just off a submarine stationed at Key West. Crowe described his White House job as a "go-for." He would later recall that while he had a tremendous admiration for Ned as a "tireless worker, full of lots of energy," Ned was often so focused on the tasks at hand that he was usually oblivious to many things and people around him.[5] The work day in the Office of the Naval Aide during Ned's tenure was always a full one with Ned bustling about on various tasks, his pipe sometimes clenched in his teeth. To illustrate his point, Crowe told of a particular female civilian secretary who worked in Ned's office. This woman had fallen hopelessly in love with her boss, so much so that everyone in the office could see what had happened even though the secretary told no one of her feelings, especially Ned. So totally focused on his job was Ned that he remained completely unaware of the situation.[6]

Christmas 1954—(left to right) "Ned Jr.," Ingrid, Hugh, Ingie, and Ned (then naval aide to the president of the United States).

Office of the Naval Aide—(left to right) Ned, Katie Findly, and YNC Charles Langello

Ned was aware of his shortcomings, especially as they applied to his knowledge of political matters, always relying on the White House's and the Navy's legislative affairs people to give prior clearance to all his public statements lest he make some political gaffe.[7] He also avoided political gatherings of any sort unless he needed to attend in his official capacity as naval aide to the president. Having been raised in a household where his father was a steadfast Democrat, Ned had become a supporter of Franklin D. Roosevelt when he reached voting age. He would later note that, while he served in the White House, no one ever asked about his party affiliation. By the time he left Eisenhower's service, however, Ned had become a Republican and would remain so the rest of his life.

Ned and his fellow aides—Army Lt. Col. Robert L. Schulz and Air Force Maj. William G. Draper—were told that their loyalty was to the president first and to their branch of the service second. Ike also informed each aide that if he attempted to influence policy-making, he would be outright dismissed from his post.[8] This loyalty to the president being of first priority would cause Ned problems with senior officers in the Navy, as will be seen later.

[2]

Due to report in as Ike's naval aide, Ned faced the more immediate problems of sorting out the logistics of getting himself and Ingrid to Washington for the inauguration and attendant festivities. Their youngest child, Ingrid Alice (known to the family as Ingie), had been born 5 December 1952. As Ned and Ingrid contemplated going to Washington, Ingie was hospitalized suffering from an Rh blood problem that required transfusions. Staying in a hospital in New London, but not in serious medical danger, Ingie was to be looked after by friends while Ned and Ingrid made the trip to Washington and then Ingrid was to quickly journey back to be at their infant daughter's side the next day.

By the time the couple reached Washington, however, Ingrid had become so ill with a flu virus that she had to be admitted to Bethesda Naval Hospital. As soon as she was able to travel, she went back to Groton, having missed all the inaugural activities. Ned, meanwhile, caught Ingrid's virus and had to spend the first week of his tour as naval aide confined to a bunk on board the presidential yacht USS *Williamsburg*. He had been assigned a place to sleep on the yacht pending his finding housing ashore.[9]

In spite of the oncoming illness, Ned did participate in the inaugural parade, riding in a car with Lt. Col. Schulz. The 1953 inaugural parade was not Ned's first; he had marched as a midshipman in the 1937 inaugural parade for Franklin D. Roosevelt. That parade, however, had been hit with heavy rain, making it a miserable affair for all participants.

At the Eisenhower inauguration ceremony, Ned was assigned a seat, several rows up, in the section behind the dais where Eisenhower took the oath of office. Seated next to him was a woman who introduced herself as "Mrs. Griffith Gilmore." Ned kept thinking how attractive the lady was and that she ought to be in motion pictures.[10] Later, he learned that "Mrs. Griffith Gilmore" was Irene Dunne, an actress who had starred in many movies and had received five nominations for Academy Awards. Curiously, Irene Dunne had just completed what would be her final film, having decided to leave acting to devote her time to other causes. An avowed Republican, she would work the rest of her life (she lived until 1990) in supporting political causes, the United Nations being her chief effort. In 1957, Ike appointed her one of five alternative U.S. representatives to the United Nations.[11]

[3]

As Ned described them, the duties of the naval aide to the president were "to keep the conduits open at a lower level, to help handle the innumerable papers and phone calls that flowed across the Potomac River between the Pentagon and the White House."[12] The reality of the position, which was then housed in an office in the East Wing of the White House, was much more than being a conduit for paperwork. The aides were called upon in many social settings, made the arrangements for any presidential visit to military facilities or ships, and even acted as window dressing in some situations—especially when photographers and cameramen were involved. Ike's Air Force aide was also the pilot of *Independence*, the DC-6 that was the predecessor to today's Air Force One. His military aide (i.e., Army), a specialist in transportation organization, was delegated the task of making arrangements for all presidential trips.[13]

Meeting the president and first lady—Ingrid and Ned are greeted at a 1956 White House reception by President and Mrs. Eisenhower. Ned was still serving as Ike's naval aide at the time.

Providing "social aides" for White House events was delegated to Ned. Not only did he get called upon to escort the Eisenhowers to events—his first official duty as naval aide was to escort the president and First Lady to the premiere of a film on the life of Mahatma Gandhi that was being shown by the government of India—but he was also responsible for recruiting, training, and supervising social aides. [14] These were junior officers from all branches of the Armed Forces who were called upon to attend White House receptions and similar functions. They were to provide escort for unaccompanied ladies—such as the daughter of a senator and his wife attending a White House function—and to fill in as needed for any other duties.

Ned maintained a list of lieutenants, captains, majors, and command-ers from the various branches. These were bachelors who had "day jobs" in the Pentagon or some other Washington military facility. They were screened by Ned as he attempted to keep out social climbers or anyone who might try to take advantage of contacts they made at White House functions to form a romantic liaison with the daughter of a senator, cabinet secretary, or other dignitary. To maintain equality of access, the list of social aides was evenly split between Navy, Army, Air Force, and Marine Corps officers. A strict rule that Ned held to was that none of the social aides were permitted to allow their White House duties to in any way interfere with their regular duties.

[4]

A major part of the responsibilities of the naval aide was not shared by the other aides. Assigned to the White House for presidential use was a yacht, USS *Williamsburg* (AGC-369). The 243-foot long, steel-hulled, diesel-powered ship had been built in 1931 for the wood-pulp magnate Hugh J. Chisolm. The Navy acquired the 1,800-ton ship in 1941, converting it to a gunboat. Late in the war, *Williamsburg* was in the process of being con-verted to a flagship for amphibious operations scheduled for the planned invasion of Japan, but when the war ended before the retrofitting was com-pleted, she was then converted to serve as the presidential yacht, relieving USS *Potomac* (AG-25) in that role in November 1945. With a crew of eighty-one, *Williamsburg* was lavishly fitted out to serve as a floating White House, complete with facilities for state dinners, sleeping accommodations for the president and several guests, and communications gear.[15]

While *Williamsburg* had her own skipper, the naval aide was respon-sible for the supervision of anything and everything that went on regarding the ship. As Ned took up his duties in the White House, the one immediate headache he faced was Ike's campaign promise to get rid of the presidential yacht. The average American in 1952 probably did not even know there was a presidential yacht, and most likely could not have cared less. The exis-tence of the ship, however, was a major concern of some in Washington.

President Truman had liked to play poker with his cronies on the yacht, so on many an afternoon *Williamsburg* would leave with the presidential poker party embarked and head down the Potomac at about rush hour, forcing the bridges to be raised. The ensuing traffic jams did not sit well with Washingtonians on their way home from work.[16] When questioned about the existence of the presidential yacht during the campaign, Ike off-handedly stated he'd get rid of it if elected.

Ned enlisted the assistance of Mrs. Eisenhower in an effort to persuade Ike to keep the yacht, but by that time, Ike felt he had to fulfill the campaign pledge to get rid of it. Ike did make one trip on board *Williamsburg* when he traveled to Colonial Williamsburg, Virginia, to visit the restoration program going on there. With the president and Mrs. Eisenhower, some friends, as well as Ned on board, *Williamsburg* made stops in Norfolk, Annapolis, and Jamestown as part of the trip to the ship's namesake city. Mrs. Eisenhower very much enjoyed the facilities of the ship, but she could not convince her husband to keep the yacht.

Before the presidential yacht was relieved of its duties, Ike did authorize it to be used to provide excursions for wounded servicemen. Ned supervised these trips as men from all branches were treated to the luxuries of the presidential yacht while they were recovering at Bethesda or Walter Reed hospitals. Having served two presidents—Truman and Eisenhower—and hosted such dignitaries as British Prime Minister Winston Churchill and Mexican President Miguel Aleman, *Williamsburg* passed out of service.

As presidential naval aide, in 1953 Ned participated in the decommissioning of USS Williamsburg, *the presidential yacht.*

Before the presidential yacht was released from White House duties, it was also used by the Eisenhowers on several occasions for formal dinners. Ned was in charge of these affairs, so he conducted rehearsal dinners a few days before the actual events. He would pay for the food and drinks, invite friends, and have the Navy cooks prepare the exact menu the president had approved. Stewards, cooks, social aides, and anyone else who would have duties to perform on board *Williamsburg* during the formal dinner were run through their paces during these rehearsals.[17] Just as Ned drilled his submarine crews to achieve maximum efficiency, he drilled the "crews" of the various White House functions over which he was given charge.

The elimination of the presidential yacht may have seemed to Ike a simple matter that made him look like someone concerned about costs and image. For Ned, it was a major headache. The reason for Ned's problems with losing the presidential yacht was that the ship served as a line item in the Navy's budget that covered two other significant functions managed by the naval aide to the president—Camp David and the White House Mess.[18]

Called *Shangri-La* by FDR, the presidential retreat in the mountains of Maryland was originally named for the mythical land in the James Hilton novel *Lost Horizon* where everyone lives forever and war is prohibited. Perhaps not as concerned with literary allusions, Eisenhower renamed it after his grandson David. Staffed by Navy stewards and other Navy specialists, Camp David's funding and personnel were funneled through *Williamsburg*. Ned was the manager of Camp David, having responsibilities for the maintenance of the facilities plus the management of any and all activities that went on there. Like the dinners on board *Williamsburg*, Ned ran rehearsals before presidential visits and formal dinners, again paying for the food out of his own pocket and inviting friends to sit in for the dignitaries who would attend the actual events.

The White House Mess was another operation that fell under the management of the naval aide and was tied to *Williamsburg* for staffing purposes. Ned's predecessor, Rear Admiral Dennison, had started the operation. Prior to Dennison's creation of the White House Mess, the only people who were served food in the White House were the president, his family, and any guests they would invite. Employees working at the White House had to bring their own food or leave the building to find a nearby restaurant. Dennison found this unacceptable, and since admirals traditionally had the prerogative to have their own meal service—called a "mess" in Navy lingo—he decided he should have one, too.

Finding an unused, but not very large, room in the White House, Dennison had the White House Mess set up, staffing it with the stewards and cooks from *Williamsburg* and "borrowing" food service equipment from any Navy facility that was not too watchful. The Mess could seat only forty-two to forty-six people and served only one meal a day—lunch in two sittings. Senior staffers were the only White House employees eligible to "join" the Mess, having to pay for their meals; the naval aide served as the treasurer for the operation. By the time Ned took over the operation, it was self-sufficient financially—the prices paid by the diners covering the costs of the whole operation.[19]

Since the Mess did not cost the Navy anything, its budget implications for *Williamsburg* were related only to staffing. The Navy's Bureau of Personnel assigned enlisted sailors as cooks to work in the Mess, as well as at Camp David, by detailing them to *Williamsburg*. Ned's problem then came down to a bureaucratic one of having the Navy create budgetary havens for the Mess and Camp David independent of a presidential yacht. The budget problems related to the presidential yacht were not new to Ned's time in the White House. Rear Adm. Donald J. MacDonald, USN, who commanded *Williamsburg* during the Truman administration, recalled that when someone decided the White House needed repainting and there wasn't money anywhere else, he was suddenly informed that the cost of the paint would be coming out of *Williamsburg*'s budget.[20]

Today, the White House Mess and Camp David are still under the Navy's budget. According to Rear Adm. Mark I. Fox, USN, who served as director of the White House Office of Military Affairs during part of the presidency of George W. Bush, both operations are now managed by that office. There are presidential aides today from all branches of the military—Navy, Marine Corps, Coast Guard, Army, and Air Force—all working under the umbrella of the White House Office of Military Affairs. The Mess is staffed by Navy culinary specialists and is totally self-supporting, according to Fox. No tax dollars are utilized to provide meals for White House employees.[21]

[5]

When it came to duties in the White House, Ned was not shy about stepping forward to volunteer for some new project or responsibility. One result of this was a much more serious duty than the social arrangements for White House functions. While serving as naval aide Ned was appointed to serve as chair of a subcommittee of the National Security Council. That subcommittee was charged with working out White House plans in the event of a nuclear attack. The Eisenhower administration was the first to have to seriously consider the possibility of a nuclear attack on Washington and how to ensure that the government could survive such an event. It is perhaps a testament to the work Ned's committee performed that their plans and reports are still classified.[22]

While the U.S. government had promulgated plans for civilian actions in the event of enemy attack during World War II, the threat of nuclear weapons posed new problems. As the White House point man in such planning, Ned soon became the "authority" on such planning within the federal government. William Crowe noted that before he came to serve on Ned's staff, he knew nothing about civil defense, especially in the nuclear age, but three months later he was giving speeches all over Washington to agencies and groups trying to set up their own contingency plans.[23]

Ned's work in this area called for the development of a plan to physically transport the president out of Washington quickly. A proposal to use helicopters for the evacuation was nixed by the Secret Service, which viewed helicopters as unreliable in the mid-1950s. Realizing that time would be of the essence once the White House was notified that an attack was imminent, Ned decided a water route would be the quickest means of moving the president out of the District.

At his request, the Navy assigned to the White House two motor patrol torpedo (PT) boats.[24] The 80-foot-long, wooden-hulled craft were docked on the Potomac River at a place that could be quickly accessed from the White House, even in the event of traffic jams. Powered by three 12-cylinder Packard gasoline engines, the boats were capable of speeds in excess of forty knots (over 46 mph). They were to be ready at a moment's notice to whisk the president, his family, and some staff down the river and out into Chesapeake Bay, where they would be met by a larger ship.

An additional part of the job description that went along with responsibilities for White House plans was the task of being a liaison with the Federal Civil Defense Administration and the Office of Defense Management. The White House had a bomb shelter that dated back to before World War II, but it was not designed to protect its occupants from radioactive fallout. It is curious to note at this point that Ned and the other planners assumed that a direct hit on Washington could be survived in an underground shelter.

William Crowe recalled an amusing incident from this era when he was serving on Ned's staff. Crowe was telephoned at his home by Ned on a Saturday afternoon and told to report to the White House immediately. When he asked why, all Ned could say over the unsecured phone was "It's the real thing."[25] As he drove to the White House, Crowe realized that, while he had been preaching all over town about being prepared and having a "plan," he did not have such a plan for himself and his wife.

When Crowe arrived at the White House, Ned told him a telephone threat had been received stating that hidden atomic bombs were set to go off at 2000 that night in New York, Baltimore, and Philadelphia. No one else in the White House was taking the threat seriously; the president was on his way to deliver a scheduled speech at a Washington hotel. However, Ned insisted that he and Crowe sit in the White House bomb shelter, noting that they would look pretty silly if the threat were proven to be true and no one was occupying the bomb shelter. Ned and Crowe sat in the bomb shelter watching the clock until after the appointed hour had passed. Crowe said, "It was obvious that Beach took the threat seriously, even if no one else did. A bit like the Martian attack at the Naval Academy."[26]

Ned submitted plans for a combination fallout and bomb shelter that were based on the design concepts of a submarine. According to Ned's reasoning, there needed to be not only shielding from radiation, but also an air purification system, self-generation of electrical power, the ability to be self-sustaining for days or weeks on end, and a sealing system that would provide a slight over-pressure to prevent outside air leaks into the shelter in order to keep out radiation. To be built in a classified location, but not on White House grounds, the shelter was to be used in the event there was not enough time to evacuate the president out of the Washington area.[27] Ned never knew if his actual plans were put into effect, as he left the White House before any decision was made regarding such facilities.

One of the enduring images of the Cold War also traces its roots back to Ned's time as naval aide. As part of his task in planning for the unthinkable, Ned had to consider the method by which a president could order a retaliatory nuclear strike against an attacking enemy. Hence, the famous "Presidential Football"—a briefcase carried by a uniformed officer of the U.S. military—that follows the president wherever he goes. Ned's original concept was to have a series of the cases held in secure locations all over the nation so that, in the event of an emergency, the president would be taken to the nearest location holding the "launch codes." With the increased speed with which intercontinental ballistic missiles could arrive over their targets, eventually the decision was reached that the codes needed to always be within a moment's reach, leading to the concept of the "football" following the president.[28]

[6]

Always on the lookout for times and places to present the Navy in the spotlight that followed the presidency, Ned kept watch for the launching of a ship that would be important enough to warrant White House participation. Traditionally, a ship is launched by a woman swinging a bottle of champagne against her bow. The opportunity finally presented itself as the Navy prepared to launch the world's first nuclear-powered submarine—USS *Nautilus* (SSN-571)—in January 1954.

The launching of a new ship is always an important occasion, but the precedent of the first nuclear-powered ship would draw significant media and public attention. The Navy was pleased with the suggestion that the First Lady have the honor of sending *Nautilus* down the building ways. All that was left was for Ned to work out the myriad details to coordinate the activities at General Dynamic's Groton facilities with the schedule of the First Lady and the large contingent of guests that would accompany her from Washington.

Not the least of the worries that troubled Ned was to ensure that the timing of the smashing of the bottle of champagne coincided exactly with the first slight movement of the ship as it began its slide backward into the waters of the Thames River. Sailors are ever superstitious and nothing can be worse for morale on a ship than the feeling that the ship is cursed with bad luck because of some mishap at her launching. A dozen things can go wrong in the split seconds that mark the point at which the ship begins to move and the bottle is swung, hits the bow, and smashes into a shower of bubbly wine.

Ned made several trips from Washington to Groton to coordinate all the plans, and took the unprecedented act of having Mrs. Eisenhower practice breaking bottles of champagne against a tree on the White House lawn. Since it is not easy to break the thick glass of which champagne bottles are made, Ned wanted to ensure that the First Lady had a feel for how much force she'd have to put into her swing.

All the intense preparation and planning almost came to naught when Ned's precise schedule was abridged by General Dynamic's chief executive officer, John Jay Hopkins. The CEO led Mrs. Eisenhower to the launching platform fifteen minutes before the time the workers far below the platform had been ordered to release the last obstacles to the ship's launch. With Ned whispering to her that they needed to stall, Mamie Eisenhower took the bottle of champagne and struck numerous poses for the photographers, eating up time.

When the precise second came for the 3,500-ton ship to begin its slide into the river, nothing happened. No movement. The First Lady was poised, waiting for Ned's signal, but there was no movement. Ned placed his hand on the bow of *Nautilus*, hoping to be able to feel the first, slight tremor, but—zip, nada, nothing. In mounting tension, Ned leaned hard against the bow, as if he alone could force the mighty ship to move. Seconds passed as visions of a public relations disaster whirled in Ned's mind. Then, suddenly, the ship was moving away, not slowly, but quickly. Ned estimated that the ship had moved over a foot between the time he felt the first motion and he yelled into the First Lady's ear, "Now! Hit it!"[29]

In what some photographers would later call the best shot of a launching they had ever been able to catch, Mrs. Eisenhower hit the bow, champagne sprayed everywhere, and *Nautilus* began her life at sea. The cheering of the crowd on the dock was augmented by the whistles and horns of other ships in the river, all celebrating the christening of a new ship. The First Lady was pleased with her role, the Navy was happy with the added public attention that her presence brought, and the world's first nuclear-powered ship began its career with appropriate fanfare.

The day's activities were such a whirlwind for Ned that he had little time to contemplate his role seven years earlier when he had taken Rickover's proposal into CNO Nimitz's office. That was part of the steps that had begun the process that led to the eventual launching of *Nautilus*. He might have been mindful, however, of his own premonition that his replacement in Op-36 would beat him out for the command of that first nuclear-powered submarine. However, Ned had supported the nomination of Eugene P. Wilkinson as the first commanding officer of *Nautilus*.

When the Navy got around to selecting the first skipper for *Nautilus*, Ned's name was suggested by several as being the man for the job. Getting wind of his name being so mentioned, Ned had quietly notified several people who were in a position to pass the word up the chain of command that he believed Wilkinson was the best man for the job.[30] That probably had little impact on the decision, however. Rickover wanted Wilkinson, and Rickover generally got what he wanted. Ned might have been able to bring some pressure to bear on behalf of his own candidacy, but that was not Ned's way. One last detail related to the launching of *Nautilus* was Ned's consideration of Commander Wilkinson's wife, Janice. When *Trigger II* was launched, as PCO he was on board the submarine along with the crew, standing at attention as she slipped into the water. Ingrid was relegated to a spot within the masses of other spectators. Ned was determined that Janice would not be so marginalized. He made arrangements for Janice to stand on the launching platform behind Mrs. Eisenhower.

[7]

If the participation of the First Lady had earned Ned some kudos with the Navy, overall, there were some top Navy leaders who were doubtful of his loyalty. President Eisenhower was generally not popular with the Navy, his insistence on holding the line on military spending being the chief source of that irritation. It was well known within the Navy that Ike thought bigger aircraft carriers just made bigger targets and that the Marine Corps was redundant, both fiscally and militarily. Having told Congress, "You can't provide security with just a checkbook," Ike cut the defense budget and made the Pentagon stick to that budget. [31]

Another source of irritation was Ike's insistence that the Joint Chiefs of Staff speak with one, unanimous voice. Unification having only recently been enacted, the interservice rivalry always accompanied decreasing budgets, and since the dust from the "Revolt of the Admirals" during the Truman years was barely settled, Ike was constantly at odds with the uniformed heads of the three branches of the Armed Forces. During his presidency, Ike removed the chief of naval operations two times. Usually, CNOs served for two two-year terms, but Ike was so discontented with the first two CNOs of his administration—Adm. William B. Fechteler and Adm. Robert B. Carney—that he finally picked Adm. Arleigh Burke, a World War II hero, over the heads of at least eighty officers with more seniority. [32] Burke's selection was something of a paradox in that he was one of the culprits in the Revolt of the Admirals, but he had managed to evade much of the fallout in its wake. Ike was looking for heads of each of the services who would work within the new system and speak with a unified voice. Ironically, Burke was known as someone who spoke his mind, regardless of the consequences. The hat of CNO worked so well for Burke, however, that he remained in that position for an unprecedented three terms.

As Ike's naval aide, Ned came in for some criticism from within the Navy. While he had no say in policy, he was the "conduit," as he called it. When the message is unpopular, the messenger can come in for a certain amount of blame. Much of that negativity was also linked to the fact that Ned stayed in the position of naval aide for longer than the normal three years. In his own defense (though he never felt he had to defend his decision), Ned stayed on at Ike's request. That request came soon after Ike suffered a heart attack in August 1955, just as Ned's first tour was due to end. Ned felt he owed Ike the loyalty of remaining at his post during the health crisis as a means of providing continuity. [33]

[8]

One incident that occurred while Ned was serving as naval aide to the president was a favorite anecdote Ned enjoyed telling again and again whenever he was asked to autograph something and a pen was offered him for that purpose. When President Eisenhower signed the treaty that created the Council of Twenty-one American States, a pen had not been provided on the desk where the treaty was to be signed. Ever the efficient aide, Ned quickly offered his own fountain pen to the President. Having affixed his signature, Eisenhower laid down the pen, which was later picked up by Assistant Secretary of State for Inter-American Affairs Henry F. Holland (1954–1956), who had negotiated the treaty. After the ceremony, the only pen left on the desk was not the pen Ned had loaned the president, but Ned took it anyway, later determining that it belonged to Holland. When Ned asked if he could have his pen back, Holland stated he wanted to keep the pen used to sign the treaty as a memento of the event, and offered to let Ned keep the solid gold pen that had once belonged to Holland. In acquiescing to the request, Ned noted that he got the better part of the deal since he much preferred the Parker 51 pen he now possessed to the Sheaffer Snorkel pen with which Holland had absconded.[34] Mrs. Holland was not too pleased with the deal, as the pen her husband traded for the treaty-signing pen was one she had given him as a gift. Ned used Holland's Parker 51 pen the rest of his life, delighting in telling people when he would autograph a book that he was "using the pen that was *not* the pen Eisenhower signed the Council of Twenty-one American States treaty with." The puzzled look of the autograph seeker would then provide an opportunity for Ned to retell his "pen story."

[9]

It is curious to note that while Ned was adrift in a sea of politics while working in the Pentagon—regardless of whether it was in Op-36 or as an aide to the chairman of the Joint Chiefs of Staff—during his tenure in the White House, political considerations were beyond his duties and his own predilections.

Beach's replacement as naval aide was Capt. Evan P. Aurand, USN. A naval aviator who flew dive bombers off carriers in the Pacific during World War II, Aurand was serving as an aide to Assistant Secretary of the Navy Albert Pratt when he was tabbed for the White House post.[35]

Upon Ned's leaving his White House post, Eisenhower presented him with a large model ship handcrafted from wood. The model's base bears an engraved plaque noting that the model was a gift from President Eisenhower.[36] In a letter to then-secretary of the Navy Charles S. Thomas, President Eisenhower summed up his evaluation of Ned as naval aide with these comments: "In judgment, leadership qualities, promotion potential, and ability to carry responsibility, I rate him as a superior officer. Captain Beach has performed his duties in a manner to reflect credit on himself and on the Navy Department. While I regret to see him go, I am glad to know he will have a command assignment, which he has well earned, and which I am sure he will discharge with great effectiveness."[37]

When Ned accepted the position of naval aide to the president, he assumed he would be too senior by the time that tour of duty ended to ever again command a ship at sea, especially a submarine. In agreeing to remain longer than the normal rotation of the position, Ned was moving himself further from the possibility of again commanding a submarine. As the evaluation by President Eisenhower notes, however, Ned was leaving for a "command assignment." What Ned knew as he left the White House—well ahead of the end of a second full term as naval aide—was that he would command a surface ship for about a year and then enter nuclear propulsion school in preparation to take command of one of the Navy's new nuclear-powered submarines then in the planning and building stages. Command at sea—and a submarine at that—had not slipped beyond his grasp.

The eager anticipation with which Ned greeted the tours of duty laid out for him after so long a stint in Washington was heightened by other events that came just prior to his notification of his future assignments. Those two events occurred during the last two years Ned was working in the White House. In 1955, his novel *Run Silent, Run Deep* was published to wide acclaim and achieved the *New York Times* best-seller list. A year later, Ned was promoted to the rank of captain. Both were achievements of which Ned was very proud. The first would provide further financial security for his family, and the promotion was one more step up the ladder of his professional career, especially since it was an "early selection" promotion.

As Ned left the White House to assume a command at sea in 1957, he had abandoned his dream of commanding a battleship like his father, but command of a nuclear-powered submarine was the pinnacle career berth for an officer in the submarine service in the late 1950s. His dream of achieving flag rank—a goal that had been denied his father—now seemed to be within Ned's grasp. As for achieving success as a writer like his father, the acclaim and popularity of *Run Silent, Run Deep* far exceeded anything his father had ever published. At age thirty-nine, Ned seemed to be marked to fulfill all the hopes his father and his father's novels had instilled in him.

Part V: *Run Silent, Run Deep*

[1]

The release of *Run Silent, Run Deep* had a profound impact on Ned's life, and many consider it his highest achievement as an author. While it may seem to disrupt the flow of the narrative of Ned's life, a pause to consider the novel will be valuable at this point.

Run Silent, Run Deep is the fictional story of Edward J. "Rich" Richardson, a commander in the U.S. Navy. Told in a first-person narrative, the novel is presented as the transcript of a statement Richardson has provided for the purposes of publicity to help sell Victory Bonds. Richardson is being awarded the Medal of Honor for heroism in rescuing three American airmen whose plane was shot down off Guam. The reader soon learns that Richardson and the thousands of men like him who served in submarines were more heroic in their day-to-day battles against the enemy and the sea than can be summarized in a citation for a single event. The majority of the novel follows Richardson as he battles the Japanese across the vast reaches of the Pacific.

Part of what makes *Run Silent, Run Deep* such compelling reading is that Beach is able to put a face and a name on the "enemy." A particularly effective and ruthless fictional Japanese anti-submarine commander, Tateo Nakame—nicknamed Bungo Pete by the Americans—becomes the focus of Richardson's struggle, making the role of the antagonist more focused than the amorphous "enemy" of some war novels. Stationed in the Bungo Suido, one of only a few entrances to Japan's Inland Sea, Bungo Pete is so effective in hunting down and sinking American submarines that he earns the enmity of all the American submariners.

In setting up the final confrontation with Bungo Pete, Ned allows Richardson's thoughts to weigh in on the role of personal hatred in war:

> War rarely generates personal animosities between members of the oppos-
> ing forces, for it is too big for that. The hate is there, but it is a larger

hatred, a hatred for everything the enemy stands for, for all of his professed ideals, for his very way of life. Individuals stand for nothing in this mammoth hate, and that is why friends—even members of the same family—can at times be on opposite sides, and why, after the fighting is over, it is possible to respect and even like the man who lately wished to kill you. Bungo, however, had done us personal injury, really many-fold times personal injury, and had thereby lost his anonymity. We had learned to know him by his works and by his name; it didn't seem in the least strange to Keith [XO of Rich's sub] and me that this time, this once, we should be consumed with bitter personal enmity toward a certain personality among the enemy. That this individual was only doing his duty as he saw it, as he had a right to see it, made not the slightest difference.[1]

Having surmised Bungo Pete's tricks, Richardson and his submarine, the fictional USS *Eel*, locate and sink Bungo in the midst of a developing typhoon. Since there are survivors in lifeboats from the Japanese ships that *Eel* has just sunk—Bungo Pete probably being among them—and given that the sinking has taken place within fifty miles of shore, Richardson realizes that within a few weeks Bungo Pete could be back in business. While his submarine is running on the surface, Richardson sends all of *Eel*'s personnel below decks while he personally directs the submarine to run down the lifeboats, thereby ensuring the demise of Bungo Pete. In sending all crew members below, Richardson is trying to insulate the rest of the crew from the responsibility of having committed what Richardson later confesses to have been an act of murder. It is in the act of destroying the lifeboats that Richardson comes to view himself as a "pariah" of humanity.

There is a parallel between Richardson's feelings about his actions in killing Bungo Pete and the Mariner in Samuel Taylor Coleridge's *The Rime of the Ancient Mariner*. Just as the Mariner in Coleridge's poem was forced to atone for his sin by retelling the story of his having killed an albatross—the symbol of good luck to sailors—so Richardson feels compelled to tell the story of the death of Bungo Pete at Rich's own hand. While the imagery of Richardson being the Mariner falls apart quickly as *Eel*'s crew does not suffer the depredations that the Mariner's crewmates face, Richardson feels that his actions in running down the lifeboats with their innocent crew members just to get at Bungo Pete have placed a curse on *Eel* and her crew.

The albatross that Richardson feels is hanging around his neck after the demise of Bungo Pete is seemingly removed when, a few days later, Richardson risks his own life to save the lives of three downed American airmen. It is for his actions in that rescue that Rich is being awarded the Medal of Honor. Whether or not Ned had in mind sequels when he wrote *Run Silent, Run Deep*, two more novels with Richardson as the main character were to follow, and the ghost of Bungo Pete haunts Richardson in both of them. While the reader of *Run Silent, Run Deep* does not realize it, the act of saving the downed airmen does not release Richardson from his feelings of guilt. It is only through actions in *Dust on the Sea* that some sense of atonement is ultimately achieved.

[2]

Classifying a novel like *Run Silent, Run Deep* may seem an easy task: it is a war or action-adventure story. Some critics have misclassified the book, such as literary analyst Ruth Pirsig Wood, who puts the novel in the "how-to-become-a-man" genre, but her conclusion is faulty. Somehow, she manages to confuse the characters of Richardson and Jim Bledsoe noting that, "His [Bledsoe's] growth towards responsible leadership parallels his evolution from cocky detached husband to solid, committed one."[2] Bledsoe remained unfaithful to his wife Laura until his death, while it is Richardson who longs for a committed relationship. The elements that make war novels like Tim O'Brien's *The Things They Carried* and Stephen Crane's *The Red Badge of Courage* into what critics term bildungsromans ("novels of education"), are not found in *Run Silent, Run Deep*. Richardson is already the commanding officer of a submarine, and none of his crew is depicted in enough depth for the reader to see any "growth" that could lead to such a classification.

There are passages of the novel that ring like poetry:

> A submarine's natural habitat is the deep, silent depths of the sea. The deeper she can go, the safer she is, and with the comfortable shelter of hundreds of feet of ocean overhead the submariner can relax. Deep in the sea there is no motion, no sound, save that put there by the insane humors of man. The slow, smooth stirring of the deep ocean currents, the high-frequency snapping or popping of ocean life, even the occasional snort or burble of a porpoise are all in low key, subdued, responsive to the primordial quietness of the deep. Of life, there is, of course, plenty, and of death too, for neither are strange in the ocean. But even life and death, though violent, make little or no noise in the deep sea."[3]

Critics recognized Ned's propensity for writing prose that put the reader right in the middle of the action. *Time* magazine noted, "Even when the yarn runs right away with him, Author [*sic*] Beach keeps jamming in the authentic details, the tingling stress, the sweaty crush of the submariners' war."[4] *New York Times* critic Herbert Mitgang agreed: "If ever a book had the ring of reality, this is it." He goes on to note, "The combat passages rank with the most exciting written about any branch of service."[5]

[3]

Released in March 1955, *Run Silent, Run Deep* sold so well that another printing was ordered in April. The novel sold for $3.95 in hardcover, of which Ned received 10 percent for the first 5,000 copies sold (less his $1,500 advance) and 15 percent of the cover price for any copies over 7,500.

By September 1955, Henry Holt was reporting to Ned that over 33,000 copies had been sold and that still another printing had been ordered.[6] When the paperback edition—which sold for 39 cents—was issued by Pocket Books in November 1956, 250,000 copies were printed in the first run; within a month, 150,000 copies had been ordered in a second print run.[7] Foreign rights for the novel further increased the number of copies sold as it was translated into French, Norwegian, Spanish, German, and Finnish.

Ned edited the original 364 pages of the novel down to 127 pages for a condensed version that appeared in the fall of 1955 as part of volume twenty-five of the *Reader's Digest Condensed Books* series. That version was accompanied by dramatic illustrations reproduced from wood carvings done by Bernard Brussel Smith. Other titles appearing in the same volume with *Run Silent, Run Deep* include Herman Wouk's *Marjorie Morningstar*, Fred Bodsworth's *Last of the Curlews*, and Max Ehrlich's *First Train to Babylon*. The American Library Association included Ned's novel in its list of "Notable" Books for 1955—a further inducement to sales.[8]

The exact number of copies sold has yet to be calculated. In 1983, Ned renewed the copyright on the novel, and eventually Henry Holt sold the paperback rights to Zebra Books, which was still selling copies into the 1990s. Cassell of the United Kingdom acquired the paperback rights in 2003, and published the novel as part of its Cassell Military Paperback Series. Within a year, a second printing was ordered. The Naval Institute Press acquired limited rights to the novel in the mid-1980s, and issued it in hardcover as part of its *Classics of Naval Literature* series in 1985; that edition has exceeded fourteen printings.

All of that was in the future as the novel reached the *New York Times* best-seller list in May 1955 and remained there for nineteen weeks, hovering around seventh place for the majority of its time on the list. Its highest point was sixth place and its lowest was sixteenth, which occurred just before dropping off the list. The top-selling novel in 1955 was Wouk's

Marjorie Morningstar, which was on the *New York Times* best-seller list at the same time as Ned's novel.[9]

[4]

The growing popularity of the novel, aided by Henry Holt's publicity campaign, slowed when "the ship hit the sand," to use a nautical euphemism for a common phrase. Holt had played on Ned's position as naval aide to the president in much of its publicity, causing questions to be raised in Washington about the role of an active-duty officer of the U.S. Navy writing for commercial pay.[10] While Ned wrote the novel late at night or on weekends, never during the parts of his day when he was performing duties for the Navy or the White House, the success of the novel coupled with his high-profile position led to questions about the propriety of his actions. As a result, Ned had to cancel scheduled appearances on such television programs as *The Ed Sullivan Show* and *The Steve Allen Show*. Planned radio appearances were also cancelled as Ned was pressured by the Navy to remain in Washington and attend to duties, even though he had ample leave time available.

One of those curious coincidences of time occurred when *Run Silent, Run Deep* was released. Famed novelist C. S. Forester's *The Good Shepherd* was published at almost the same time and was on the *New York Times* best-seller list for much of the same time as Ned's novel. While *Run Silent, Run Deep* tells a story of World War II from the submariner's point of view, Forester's novel tells a similar story from the point of view of an officer in command of a convoy of Allied ships trying to run the gauntlet of German U-boats in the North Atlantic. Ned left no specific record of his opinion of Forester's *The Good Shepherd*, but he was a big fan of Forester in general, especially the Horatio Hornblower novels—tales of a fictional British officer during the Age of Fighting Sail against the forces of Napoleonic France. "I have been a long-time admirer of everything C. S. Forester has written," wrote Ned in 1960.[11]

[5]

The flap that raised questions about an active-duty officer writing for pay caused only slight concern on Ned's part when compared with the turmoil of a German book that accused him of having actually killed Japanese seamen by running down their lifeboats. The change was based on the introduction to *Run Silent, Run Deep*, which he begins with "This is a work of fiction," and ends with, "To that extent, and with these qualifications, this book, though fiction, is true." *Der Fall Laconia: Ein hohes Ied der U-boot-Waffe* by Jochen Brennecke was published in West Germany in 1959. The book discussed the events that followed the sinking of the British troop ship *Laconia*, a converted passenger liner being used to transport about eight hundred Allied troops, 1,800 Italian prisoners of war, and some women and children. *Laconia* was sunk by *U-156*, a German submarine. Once the commander of the German U-boat discovered the nature of the passengers on board the ship he had just sunk, he began to rescue as many survivors as his U-boat could hold and he radioed for help. Broadcasting in plain English on a radio frequency used internationally for emergencies, the U-boat commander said his ship would not fire on any rescue vessel as long as his submarine was not attacked.

Several other German U-boats, an Italian submarine, and some French surface ships from an African French colony joined the rescue effort. A few days into the rescue effort, an American bomber came across a surfaced German U-boat and, failing to recognize the huge white flag with a red cross on it that the submarine was carrying draped over its conning tower, the American plane dropped depth charges. Later, another American plane dropped more depth charges. Under orders from their higher command, the German U-boats then abandoned the rescue mission. In the end, some eight hundred British and Polish troops were saved, but only 450 of the Italians survived. The vast majority of the deaths were a result of water-tight doors on *Laconia* behind which the prisoners were held, not of the botched rescue efforts.[12]

Outraged by the attacks on German ships attempting a humanitarian mission, German Admiral Karl Dönitz, head of the German navy, issued a famous order to all his U-boats directing them to ignore survivors of ships they sunk. The exception was: "Survivors are to be picked up only in cases where their interrogation would be of value to the U-boats." The order went on to conclude: "Be severe. Remember that in his bombing of German cities the enemy has no regard for women and children."[13]

After the war, Dönitz was tried as a war criminal, with what became known as "The *Laconia* Order" being introduced as evidence that he had indirectly ordered his submariners to kill survivors. As Nathan Miller notes, "Dönitz was saved from a certain death sentence, if convicted, by a deposition by Admiral Nimitz, who acknowledged that American submarines made no effort to rescue survivors."[14] While Dönitz was sentenced to ten years in prison for his part in the war, the British convicted and executed a U-boat commander, Heinz-Wilhelm Eck, for machine-gunning survivors of a Greek ship. Eck's defense was in part based on "the *Laconia* Order."

When Ned arrived in Bremen, West Germany, in 1960 as commanding officer of USS *Triton* (SSR[N]-586), he was informed by Harrison Lewis, the American consul general in West Germany, about the accusations in

Brennecke's book.[15] Brennecke's charges regarding Ned do not ignore the fact that *Run Silent, Run Deep* is fiction. Brennecke points out that Ned wrote the following in the introduction to his novel: "With the proviso that there have been some intentional gaps in descriptive information, the motivation, events, and action herein set forth are representative of that brave period between 1941 and 1945 when many of us unwittingly realized our highest purpose in life. To that extent, and with these qualifications, this book, though fiction, is true."[16]

In his own defense, Ned wrote in an official Navy memo: "I have never machine-gunned survivors of any type, nor harmed them in any way other than by doing my best to sink their ship. I know of no instances where a U.S. submarine has deliberately killed survivors. The incident recounted in *Run Silent, Run Deep* is entirely fictional."[17]

According to his oldest son, Ned did send a letter to Brennecke threatening legal action if the Brennecke book was ever published in the United States.[18] To date, Brennecke's work has remained unpublished in America. Regardless of the intense drama that swirled around Ned over Brennecke's charges, *Run Silent, Run Deep* remained a popular work in the United States, with no one assuming that Ned's fiction was an admission of some diabolical act during the war.

[6]

The popularity of the novel and the fact that it was an action-adventure story meant Hollywood quickly took notice. Delmar Daves (1904–1977), veteran screenwriter and director, was assigned the task of appraising *Run Silent, Run Deep* for adaptation to the silver screen. According to Daves' "Notes on *Run Silent, Run Deep*," as quoted in Lawrence Suid's *Sailing the Silver Screen: Hollywood and the U. S. Navy*, the novel was found to be lacking in interaction between the characters. Daves recommended that any film version would have to play up the conflict between the skipper and the executive officer to a much greater extent than the novel.[19]

The desire of Hollywood writers and producers to develop conflict within the submarine's crew to heighten the drama of the story was coupled with the fact that, by the late 1950s, submarine films had become clichés. These two factors served to ensure that the film that carried the same name as Ned's novel would have little to do with the actual plot. Ned would later note that the screenplay totally lost the meaning of his novel.[20]

The first postwar Hollywood submarine film, *Operation Pacific*, began filming on the lot of Warner Brothers in September of 1950. With its release in 1951, Hollywood latched on to the submarine as a perennial sub-genre of war films that could generate a certain degree of dramatic tension just by the nature of their settings. As Suid notes, "Appearing on an average of more than one a year, virtually all of the movies in the 1950s about submarines relived the real, as well as sometimes imagined, heroics of the men who fought the war against Japan under the Pacific Ocean. Not surprisingly, the films became redundant and their plots almost indistinguishable."[21]

When John Gay set out to translate Ned's novel into a screenplay, he was tasked by the producers with the problems of creating tension among the crew and in finding something to depict in submarine action that would make the film version of *Run Silent, Run Deep* stand out from all the other submarine flicks. Gay, who would go on to write uncredited portions of *Mutiny on the Bounty* (1962) and be fully credited for the 1977 made-for-television movie *The Court-Martial of George Armstrong Custer*, decided to use the novel's early conflict between Richardson and Bledsoe as the focus of the film. To enliven the action sequences of the film, Gay selected a little-used and very dangerous submarine tactic known as the "down-the-throat" shot.

World War II submarine skipper Rear Adm. Mike Rindskopf, USN (Ret.) notes that the maneuver was so dangerous that the vast majority of skippers, if they ever fired one, did so only in desperation.[22] In essence, a surfaced submarine turned toward an attacking destroyer, thus quickly closing the distance between the two, the submarine then firing a couple of torpedoes from its bow tubes at the last possible moment before submerging to avoid colliding head on with the destroyer. Such a maneuver required a great deal of luck so that the attacking enemy did not hit the submarine with gunfire before it submerged, and so that the submarine could dive and turn away from the enemy before it exploded just above the submarine—assuming the torpedoes hit the enemy ship. In some instances, the submarine would be submerged, but remain at periscope depth (about ninety feet of water above the sub's keel) as it faced the onrushing enemy ship, firing its torpedoes before pushing itself to depths that would better protect it against enemy depth charges.

Sam Dealey, who commanded USS *Harder* (SS-257) during World War II, is generally credited with using the technique for the first time in combat.[23] Dealey was awarded the Medal of Honor and became known as "The Destroyer Killer." Veteran submarine skipper Slade Cutter considered Dealey a risk-taker because Dealey preferred attacking escorting warships rather than the cargo ships the escorts were supposed to protect.[24] The propensity to seek out escorting warships allowed Dealey to use the down-the-throat technique often. Dealey was lost, along with all the crew of *Harder*, in August 1944, in an encounter with a Japanese minesweeper being used as a submarine hunter.[25]

The focus on the down-the-throat shot in the film not only ignored Ned's submarine attack passages in the novel, but served to disappoint readers who saw the film before reading the novel. Apparently Ned received some criticism, if not good-natured ribbing, from his fellow submariners over the film, causing him to include in his sequel novel *Dust on the Sea* a situation in which the technique was used, accompanied with a long explanation as to the difficulty of the shot and some references to actual skippers who had used it during the war.[26]

In spite of the director's repeated use of the difficult and improbable down-the-throat shot, the film has a very authentic look.[27] A full-scale mock-up of some of the interior spaces of a *Gato*-class submarine was constructed for the filming. The U.S. Navy cooperated in making the film to a degree which it had not previously, especially for films that depicted conflicts between levels of authority.[28] However, the Navy was becoming more reluctant to support the making of World War II films by the late 1950s. Early submarine films, assuming that they did not show the Navy in a bad light, usually received technical assistance from the Navy, but by the late 1950s, the Navy wanted to highlight its new submarines, not the World War II models that were the subject of the Hollywood productions.[29] Nevertheless, according to a press release from Hecht, Hill, and Lancaster—the team that produced the film—the Navy provided over a half-million dollars' worth of actual submarine equipment for use in the interior mock-up of the fictional *Nerka*.[30] (*Eel* of Ned's novel was changed to *Nerka* in the film.)

[7]

Ned had hoped he would be selected as the technical advisor for the film, but instead the studio turned to a retired submarine officer recommended by the Navy, Rear Adm. Rob Roy McGregor, USN, who lived in San Diego, where the exterior scenes were shot. A 1926 graduate of the Naval Academy, McGregor commanded USS *Grouper* (SS-214) early in the war, but his actions during his third war patrol on that submarine came under criticism and he was relieved of command, being assigned to staff duties in Squadrons Eight and then Six.[31] Later, he was assigned to new construction, commanding USS *Sea Cat* (SS-399) at her commissioning. After several war patrols on board *Sea Cat*, McGregor was made commander of Submarine Divisions 22 and then 202. He retired from active duty in 1955.[32] In McGregor, United Artists did have a technical advisor who was not only familiar with the workings of submarines, but who had commanded them during the war. While disappointed in not getting permission from the Navy to serve as technical advisor on the film, Ned was happy with McGregor's role.[33]

The highlight of the film, from the Navy's point of view, was its focus on the technique of attack in submarine operations, and on command decisions.[34] If the conflict between the submarine's skipper and the XO is taken out of the film, it could be viewed as purely a documentary. The film offers a very strong visual sense of what life was like on board a submarine in the 1940s, in part because of the cinematography of Russell Harlan, ASC (1903–1974). The decision to film the story in black and white, while partially based on the economics of color film versus black and white, had the advantage of giving the film that documentary look. Additionally, audiences in the late 1950s still thought World War II movies should be in black and white—the same shades of gray in which they had viewed countless newsreels during the war. Bosley Crowther, who reviewed the film for the *New York Times,* noted, "Somehow, they look more like the real thing in good old black-and-white."[35] Harlan would go on to do the camera work for such films as *Operation Petticoat* (1959), *To Kill a Mockingbird* (1962), and *Tobruk* (1967). The only award that *Run Silent, Run Deep* won was for its black and white cinematography, placing third in the Golden Laurel Awards presented by the Producers Guild of America.[36]

For director of the film, United Artists selected Robert Wise (1914–2005), who would later receive Academy Awards for his direction of *West Side Story* (1962) and *The Sound of Music* (1966). His experience with films in the war genre included *The Desert Rats* (1953) and *Until They Sail* (1957). Among the many films Wise would go on to direct was *The Sand Pebbles* (1966), where he once again depicts a part of American naval history. The tightness of the action in *Run Silent, Run Deep* can be attributed directly to Wise.

[8]

As the popularity of Ned's novel soared and the negotiations for the film version were in process, a young Lt. William J. Crowe Jr., USN, then working under Ned in the office of the naval aide to the president, spent time discussing who might play the lead characters. Sitting around the office, Crowe, Ned, and YNC Charles J. Langello speculated on who might portray Richardson on the silver screen.[37] Their primary candidate was John Wayne.

When it comes to the selection of big-name actors for a film, direc-
tors and producers try to strike a balance between a "name" that will help
sell the film and one with the right looks coupled with the acting talent to
carry the role. Ned's and Crowe's speculations on John Wayne were not
far off, but Wayne had turned down the part, so Wise turned to another
of Hollywood's enduring stars—Clark Gable. A magnetic presence on the
silver screen from as far back as the 1930s, when he won an Oscar for *It
Happened One Night* (1934), by the late 1950s he had lost much of the
looks that had made his career so dynamic. Born in 1901, Gable was in his
mid-fifties when *Run Silent, Run Deep* was filmed. He was smoking three
packs of cigarettes a day and drinking heavily. Some suspect that the two
"seizures" he suffered in the '50s were actually heart attacks, for it was a
heart attack that claimed his life in 1960, less than two years after the film's
release in March of 1958.

Regardless of the star appeal of Gable, most veteran submariners
immediately recognized that he was far too old to depict a World War II
submariner, even a skipper. In a letter written in May 1944, Ned described
the ages of the men on board *Trigger* in these terms: "The average [age]
of the crew is 23. The youngest is 18 and several are 19. The oldest man
on board is 34. Average age of officers is 26.7 years. Four are younger
than I and four are older than I."[38] Gable, at age fifty-seven and showing the effects of heavy alcohol consumption and heart problems, made a
very unbelievable skipper. (In fairness to Gable, Ned's speculative choice
of John Wayne probably would not have fared any better, as Wayne was
only six years younger than Gable.) Close observation of the film will reveal
that Gable's hands are seldom shown unless he is holding onto something.
In the rare instance when his hands are shown empty, there are visible
tremors. In addition, in those scenes where editing could not hide the
fact, Gable's ability to go up and down the submarine's ladders is decidedly slow compared to what was required of the men who actually serve
on submarines—then or now. But despite these limitations, Gable's name
added prestige to the film and undoubtedly increased the box-office take.

Gable's co-star, Burt Lancaster (1913–1994), who was also one of
the partners in the film's production company, comes off as a much more
believable submariner. While Lancaster was in his mid-forties—still consid-
erably older than the average for wartime service—his natural athleticism
compensated for his age. An experienced acrobatic performer in circuses
before his entrance into the film industry, Lancaster had previously been
featured in one film with a military theme—*From Here to Eternity* (1953),
based on James Jones' novel of the same name. Later, he would star in
other films: *Judgment at Nuremberg* (1961), *Seven Days in May* (1964),

The Cassandra Crossing (1977), *Twilight's Last Gleaming* (1977), and *Go Tell the Spartans* (1978).

Lancaster's appearance in the film also brought with it his former circus partner and good friend, Nick Cravat (1912–1994). Cravat portrays the submarine's cook—Russo. His circus career-developed athleticism is displayed when Russo is trapped topside while dumping the submarine's garbage just as the boat begins to submerge. Cravat, following a pratfall, scampers up the submarine's periscopes as he tries to avoid the onrushing waters and in doing so demonstrates the abilities that made him a top acrobat. While Cravat appeared in nine films with Lancaster, he seldom had a speaking role due to his heavy Brooklyn accent. In *Run Silent, Run Deep*, the accent fits perfectly with the character of Russo, so he has a few lines.

[9]

Run Silent, Run Deep is sometimes used as a yardstick for evaluating other submarine films. In a March 1990 review of the film version of Tom Clancy's novel *The Hunt for Red October*, Roger Ebert, writing for the *Chicago Sun-Times*, referred to the film based on Ned's novel. "As one whose basic ideas about submarines come from Cmdr. Edward Beach's classic 'Run Silent, Run Deep,' in which the onboard oxygen supply was a source of constant concern, I kept asking myself if those Russian sailors should be smoking so much, down there in the depths of the ocean."[39]

[10]

Ned's involvement in the film was zilch. In spite of his protests—and the terms of his contract with United Artists—he did not see the film, or even the script, until it opened to the public. In a letter to a United Artists vice president just a few days before the film was scheduled to open, Ned expressed his embarrassment at having to tell friends and colleagues that he had seen neither the script over which he was to have approval, nor the film itself before it was to open.[40] In the same letter, he asked for at least the privilege of a private showing in Washington before the film was released to the general public. Since the film was scheduled for opening on 28 March and Ned was leaving on Navy business on 30 March, the window of opportunity for him to even see the film was very narrow. Ned and Ingrid did attend the film's premiere in Washington, seeing the film for the first time along with the general public. Ned had been invited to the studio to witness some of the film's production, but he was in the Mediterranean serving as skipper of USS *Salamonie* (AO-26) at the time and could not avail himself of the offer.

[11]

According to Ned's literary agent, the film would eventually show a profit and thereby produce some income in the form of royalties, but by January 1960, almost two years after the film was released, United Artists had yet to earn enough off the film to cover the production costs.[41] Ned came to feel that his agent, Annie Laurie Williams (who was advancing in years at the time), had not represented him to his best advantage in the movie deal with United Artists.[42] Several years after the film's release, Ned signed with a different literary agent.

The continuing popularity of the film, especially for late-night television, plus the release of the film on VHS and then DVD, eventually turned it profitable. According to the contract, Ned received 10 percent of the profits once all the expenses of making the film were paid off. Distribution rights for the film eventually passed to MGM, which continues to send annual royalty checks to Ingrid, who has survivor rights to her late husband's royalties.

In a 1999 interview for *All Hands* magazine, Ned answered the following questions about his involvement in the film version of *Run Silent, Run Deep*: "How involved were you in the making of the movie? Did you have any input in that?" His response:

> None whatsoever. I was unhappy with the movie. If you read the book and look at the movie carefully—one right after the other—you'll see that the movie has little resemblance to *Run Silent, Run Deep*. I mean, I think they [United Artists] had the script pretty well written before they even read the book. They only wanted the title—they simply bought the book for the title. Now Ingrid, that's my wife, says I shouldn't talk like this. She thinks I should say, 'Oh, it was a great movie. Go see it!' Because the more they [the general public] see the movie, the more they'll want to buy the book. But I really can't say that, because it's [the movie] not true to the Navy that I saw and tried to describe.[43]

In spite of his dissatisfaction with the film version of his first novel, Ned had achieved a place for himself in the pantheon of writers of naval fiction. If he published nothing else, he would still be a significant figure among the authors of American war literature of the twentieth century. That much success as a first-time novelist made future publishing contracts easier to obtain, as well as generating advances of a more handsome nature. That was the easy part. His ability to fulfill public expectations with subsequent novels, however, would remain to be seen.

Part VI: 1957–1958

It was to command a fleet oiler that Ned was assigned upon completion of his time in the White House. He had been offered by the Navy's Bureau of Personnel the choice of commanding a destroyer division or USS *Salamonie* (AO-26), and he opted for the oiler.[1] While the command was to be both a stop-gap between his release from White House duties and his assuming the mantle of PCO of *Triton*, skippering *Salamonie* would also fulfill the required tour in a surface command that was generally necessary for a submarine officer to be promoted beyond the rank of captain.

Salamonie had been launched in September 1940 as *Esso Columbia* by the Newport News Shipbuilding and Drydock Company. On 28 April 1941, she was commissioned into the U.S. Navy as *Salamonie*, named after a river in Indiana. Navy policy was to name ships after rivers if those ships transported fuels and gasoline for the fleet. Serving first in the Atlantic, "Old Sal," as she was known to the men who served on board her, spent the last years of World War II in the Pacific theater supporting fleet and amphibious operations in the island-hopping campaign toward Japan. In 1948, she was reassigned to the Atlantic fleet and home-ported at Norfolk, Virginia.

Command of a supply ship like *Salamonie* was one of several options for a submarine officer who might be expected to continue to move up in rank. The Navy still clung to the late eighteenth century ideal that an officer should be a generalist, not a specialist.[2] Based on the Navy's view of the broad training of officers, the practice evolved for a submarine officer who had potential for flag rank to gain experience in commanding a surface ship, preferably a "deep draft command." With surface warfare specialists in line for command of destroyers and other surface combat vessels, submariners were oftentimes relegated to tours of duty as commanding officers of the less glamorous elements of the fleet to get their "ticket punched" as having had surface as well as deep-draft command experience.

When Ned took command in March 1957, the 553-foot-long *Salamonie* was beginning to show her age, as well as her many years of hard service. With a crew of 240, Old Sal was one of those seldom-noticed ships that provide the lifeblood of the fleet. Ned assumed command of *Salamonie* at a time when her "physical condition wasn't very good" according to Dave Wood, a radarman 3rd class who served on board under Ned's command. "It was known as a rust bucket," Wood states, and Ned "was determined to clean it up and be [*sic*] the busiest tanker in the fleet." In fact, Old Sal was so busy under Ned's command that, at one point, while refueling two ships at one time, Ned commented that Old Sal looked like an octopus with all the fuel lines running from her to the other ships. At the suggestion of Wood and his brother-in-law, Charles Currie, a radarman 2nd class who was also serving on board, the image of an octopus was painted on each side of Old Sal's flying bridge.[3]

In an effort to get *Salamonie* looking more like the proper U.S. Navy ship Ned envisioned, he pushed the crew to find every bit of rust, scrape the rust away, and apply a coat of lead primer—red in color—prior to a top coat of Navy gray. For a time, the ship's color was mostly red, earning Ned the nickname of "Red Lead Ned" among both his crew and the rest of the Sixth Fleet.

PN3 Michael McAllister, a twenty-year-old from Manhattan, served as Ned's "phone talker" when the ship was at general quarters (battle stations) or conducting underway refueling operations. McAllister's job was to relay orders from the bridge to the rest of the ship during those crucial periods. He recalls that Ned "took excellent care of his crew and kept a well disciplined, clean, 4.0 ship."[4] Wood and McAllister agree that while Ned worked the crew hard, morale improved greatly while he was in command.

John Lichoff, who was a radioman during the time Ned commanded Old Sal, believes Ned was closer to the crew than other commanding officers under whom Lichoff served. He attributed this closeness to Ned's service on submarines, where the lines between enlisted men and officers were less rigidly observed due to the closeness of the quarters on board a submarine.[5] Lichoff considers Ned his mentor and role model. Joseph Felt, an officer on board at the time who eventually retired from the Navy with the rank of captain, notes that Ned "was good with the enlisted men. . . . He was much respected for his fairness and concern for his crew." However, Felt goes on to note, "He [Ned] seemed to be overly trusting of junior personnel."[6]

Felt's observation about Ned being too trusting of junior officers cites as an example the possible compromise of one of the Navy's radio codes. In June 1957, *Salamonie* sent a routine movement report that was only partially encrypted due to a defective encryption machine. Subsequently, the problem was not reported up the chain of command—not even to Ned—but when the problem was later discovered, an investigation was ordered, as well as thorough reviews of the *Salamonie*'s communications and cryptographic procedures. The faulty machine was to blame for the initial error, but the negligence of not following up in a timely manner rested with a very inexperienced junior officer responsible for the ship's communications. As skipper, Ned accepted the complete blame for the lapse, the proper supervision of a junior officer being a responsibility of the commanding officer.[7]

Salamonie deployed with elements of the Sixth Fleet to the Mediterranean during the summer of 1957, and was called upon to assist with an operation in support of the government of Lebanon. As part of the operation, Old Sal was in the process of steaming from one element of the fleet to another, being unescorted but within close proximity of the Lebanese shore, when she was challenged by a high-speed gunboat from an unknown country. The crew of the gunboat, using blinker light, wanted to know where *Salamonie* was headed and what her intentions were. Ned immediately called his crew to "General Quarters—Surface Action Port Side" and then via blinker light using International Morse Code, informed the gunboat that "we are an American man-of-war," and it was none of their . . . business—or words to that effect. While *Salamonie* was armed with four 5-inch deck guns and several machine guns, she was also carrying tons of fuel oil, jet fuel, and high-octane aviation gasoline. Tankers are generally not inclined to make a show of force toward another warship or even a gunboat, but Ned was determined not to be bullied. Before Sixth Fleet planes and destroyers could arrive in response to *Salamonie*'s call for backup, the gunboat turned tail and ran. As McAllister describes the incident, Ned's response to the gunboat's challenge showed the crew that he had "hair on his ass and balls of steel," doing as much for morale as anything else the crew witnessed.[8] A glimpse of the Navy Cross and other combat decorations that Ned wore on his uniform might tell most people that he was a brave man, but the crew of Old Sal had its own proof.

[2]

The tension of life at sea with incidents like the challenge from the gunboat was relieved when the ship put into Palma, Majorca, just off the east coast of Spain, for a liberty call. Having completed operations off Lebanon, *Salamonie*'s crew looked forward to a few days' rest and relaxation ashore on that Mediterranean paradise. Trouble ensued when one of Hollywood's legends took offense at the speed with which the launches hauling liberty-bound sailors traversed the harbor, causing waves that damaged his yacht. Errol Flynn's yacht *Zaca*, docked at the Hotel Club Nautico, suffered scratches to its hull paint and the loss of one line according to a typewritten letter Flynn sent to the commanding officer of *Salamonie*.[9]

In response to Flynn's protest, Ned ordered the ship's launches to slow down in the harbor, then he sent Flynn a handwritten invitation to dine on board *Salamonie*—the invitation was delivered by a uniformed officer of the ship. The invitation was answered with a polite refusal and a further list of grievances. Matters worsened when an inebriated Flynn encountered Ned and some of the crew while ashore. Flynn proceeded to insult Ned, the crew of *Salamonie*, the U.S. Navy, and the United States. According to Michael McAllister, who was with the group thus confronted by Flynn, "Captain Ned kept his cool, [and] told the crew to disregard him [Flynn]." Later, however, according to McAllister, "A skinny SH2 named 'Pop Faulkner,' about 130 lbs., knocked Flynn on his ass."[10] Like Horatio Nelson, Ned turned a blind eye to Faulkner's actions, as no disciplinary action was taken according to McAllister.

[3]

Whether facing tests of bravery at sea or of diplomacy involving civilians ashore, there were bigger challenges Ned faced while on *Salamonie*. His seamanship was sorely challenged during a man-overboard emergency in the Atlantic off the coast of Spain in May 1957. Heavy weather—sixty mile-per-hour winds, waves between forty and sixty feet high—was playing havoc with the four destroyers that were escorting *Salamonie*. Low on fuel, the destroyers lacked the weight that would give them the stability to weather the storm. With full fuel bunkers, the "tin cans," as destroyers were known, would have had enough mass and lowered centers of gravity to better hold their own in the heavy seas, but with fuel bunkers nearly empty, they needed refueling immediately—both to keep their boilers lit and to make them more seaworthy.

Underway refueling is a dangerous operation under ideal conditions, but in the heavy seas facing *Salamonie* and her consorts, it was a nightmare. As Old Sal approached USS *Gearing* (DD-710) from astern, SN George D. Schack was suddenly washed overboard when a giant wave engulfed *Gearing*. All ships in the task group were immediately notified "man overboard," with every ship sending extra lookouts to their topside stations to try to spot the missing sailor amid the giant waves.

Nine minutes after the signal was sent, crew members of Old Sal spotted Schack off their port bow. Ned then signaled that he was maneuvering to pick up the man, having stationed thirty extra men to keep the struggling sailor in constant view. Ned attempted to bring Old Sal into a position so the seaman would be in the lee of the ship, thus protecting Schack from the worst of the wind and waves. Unable to turn quickly enough to do so, Old Sal had to make a complete 360° turn before placing herself between the wind and the quickly tiring sailor.

Louis Colbus, who was a junior officer on board one of the escorting destroyers at the time, would later recall that Ned "took that big oiler, just moved everything the way he had to," to pick up the man.[11] It was normal in these situations for one of the destroyers to attempt the recovery since they are more agile than a huge tanker—but Ned and *Salamonie* proceeded as if plucking a sailor from a rough sea was an everyday operation for them.

Realizing that the heavy seas made lowering a lifeboat impossible, GM2 Lawrence W. Beckhaus volunteered to dive into the ocean to assist the exhausted Schack. Wearing a rescue harness attached to a line running back to Old Sal, Beckhaus reached the cold and tired Schack after ten minutes of strenuous swimming. Quick and expert work on the part of Old Sal's deck hands brought Schack and Beckhaus alongside and then on board smartly as a huge wave washed across the ship's well deck.[12]

Joseph Felt, who was the ship's first lieutenant at the time and in charge of deck operations on *Salamonie* during the rescue—and therefore of the crew members handling the line that hauled Beckhaus and Schack on board—adds that the tension of the moment was increased when one of the escorting destroyers lost steering and rammed *Salamonie*, puncturing a hole in one of Old Sal's living compartments aft.[13] Eventually, all four destroyers were refueled, further damage averted, and no one else was injured. The harrowing incident and Ned's expert seamanship, however, entered into the lore of Old Sal.

Ned's handling of *Salamonie* during the man-overboard crisis prompted his squadron commander, Capt. W. T. Nelson, USN, to comment that Ned "is an excellent ship handler."[14] This comment appeared on Ned's next fitness report. While Ned's handling of the large tanker was proof itself of his ship-handling abilities, the statement to that effect in his fitness report stands in contrast to the fact that in his fitness reports for the period of 1939 to 1945, the only category for which he consistently received low scores was ship handling. On the 4.0 scale used at the time, his lowest score was a 3.4, and that was ship handling. Overall, his average was 3.88 on the eighteen fitness reports that were written on his performance from the time he was commissioned until the Navy dropped the 4.0 scale at the end of World War II.

For his efforts, Beckhaus was awarded the Navy and Marine Corps Medal, one of the highest peacetime awards given by the Navy. Presentation of the medal was made by Rear Adm. John C. Daniel, USN, commander, Destroyer Force, Atlantic. Assembled on the deck of *Salamonie* back at Newport for the ceremony were the crew of *Salamonie*, plus Schack's parents and fiancée. Schack had already returned to duty on board *Gearing*, which was still at sea. Beckhaus' wife and four children also attended the ceremony.[15]

As if foreshadowing events soon to come to fruition, Rear Admiral Daniel told the assembled sailors, press, and family members at the ceremony that someday the Navy would have nuclear-powered surface ships, thereby making at-sea refueling unnecessary.[16]

[4]

In the period Ned served in the White House, his family had grown used to his being home most evenings. His return to sea duty on board *Salamonie* resulted in some adjustments on the part of both Ingrid and the children. During the several years following his detachment from the post of naval aide to the president, his absence from home became more common than his presence.

The Beach household was a great one for nicknames. The children called their father "Did," although no one today is sure of the exact origin of the usage. Sometimes he was called "Did-Bo" by his eldest, who was himself known as "Ned-Bo" to his father. Second child Hugh was called "Hugh-go" by his father, while the youngest, Ingrid Alice, was called "Ping." Within the family, their mother was known as "Mo." In time, all the children's friends, as well as some close friends of the family, came to call Ned "Did."

One of the important elements of the family milieu was the intellectual stimulation the parents carefully maintained. Mealtimes, especially the evening meal, were frequently the forums for long and heated debates. Topics ranged across the whole of current events, with everyone free to take a "devil's advocate" position, or their own, and defend it to the bitter end. Emphasis was also placed on listening to each other's arguments. Ned would frequently stop an ongoing debate to ensure Ping had a chance to voice her opinion. As the youngest, she was frequently drowned out by her elder brothers, but Ned took care to include her, helping her to develop her own self-identity and self-worth.[17]

An aspect of these dinnertime disputations that left a lasting impression on all three children was that, often days after a particular debate, Ned, when alone with one of his children, would recall arguments the child had made, suggesting other avenues of thought or alternative points from which to argue the same idea. On a preconscious level then, but very much in their consciousness today, each child came to realize that their ideas were being carefully listened to by the adults during those discussions.

When his sons were ages six and eight, Ned taught them Morse code. The boys tried to use the system to communicate between their beds when they were supposed to be asleep, but as Hugh recalls, they were so bad at it that the struggle to beep or tap out coherent messages soon lulled them into the slumber their parents wanted. On one occasion, when Ned was to pick up his sons at some arranged spot after a now-forgotten activity, Ned was stuck in traffic some blocks away, so he began beeping out the Morse code dots and dashes for "Hugh" and "Ned." Picking up on the signal, the boys ran to find their father, saving him a considerable wait in traffic.[18] No memory exists of the reaction of the other drivers stuck in traffic to the constant honking of one car.

Ned very much enjoyed telling his children bedtime stories, especially ones he seemed to have made up himself. He would often tell stories of two imaginary brothers and their sister named Billy, Bobby, and Hobby, who matched the ages of the three Beach children. The children of the stories were somewhat mischievous, but their adventures always ended well, with right triumphing through the good efforts of the children. Working mostly ad lib, Ned crafted stories that had general themes like "Honesty is the best policy." Not until the last months of his life did Ned reveal to his children that the idea of telling them such stories—which they had always assumed he had created from his own imagination—came from his father, who had told such stories to Ned and his brother and sister.[19] Ned modified and updated the stories, but the lessons the stories taught did not change.

In addition to the bedtime stories, the children also relished their father's reading to them. One perennial favorite was Howard Pyle's *The Story of King Arthur and His Knights*. Adapting the text from Sir Thomas Mallory's *Morte d'Arthur*, Pyle kept the florid, courtly language associated with the high Middle Ages, making the book special for the children because of its use of language as much as for its plot.[20] Ned always provided additional sound effects and unique approaches to each character's vocalization for any story he read.

An especially fond memory for the children was a Disney cartoon on 8mm film that the family owned, titled *Pluto and the Little Chickens*. It was without sound, so Ned would narrate the film, adding new and enlarged interpretations with each viewing. He did unique voices for each character and often provided narrative—in the character's voice—as to what a character might be thinking at any given point of the film. Ned's grandchildren would also enjoy his oral interpretation of their favorite books, as well as his narration of the Pluto cartoon.

Ingrid's influence in these areas was also critical in the development of the children. An avid aficionado of the arts, she passed on to her children a strong sense of visual and musical taste. In the context of the family dinner discussions, she always maintained a mind and values of her own, but encouraged each of the children to develop as independent thinkers.[21]

For those who are not trained in child psychology, it is sometimes surprising what memories stick in a child's mind. Son Hugh was always taken by the manner in which his father put on his pants. "He did it a very special way by holding the end of each pant leg folded back to the belt. Then as he inserted his leg, he would let go of the pant leg, and it would snap smartly into place."[22] While serving on board ships, Ned had learned that the deck, even of his cabin, could be dirty and oily, so he had learned how to put on his pants without dragging the pant legs across the deck.

[5]

Ned was never happier than when he was engaged in some project around the house. All the homes in which the Beaches resided were fair game for do-it-yourself projects, none ever being too small or too large. When it came to these projects, he was no Mr. Micawber, in that he had the skill and temperament to successfully complete anything he undertook. He re-plumbed the home at 29 Gravel Drive in Mystic, Connecticut, as well as created a library/office in the unfinished attic.[23] For the three-story (plus basement) home in Georgetown, he installed a buzzer system from floor-to-floor, so whoever answered the phone on one floor did not have to trundle up or down the stairs to inform another family member that the call was for him (or her).

Chief among Ned's home-improvement schemes was his great love of digging, especially to create new rooms under a house. For the Mystic home, which was just down the street, around the corner, and a short walk from the Mystic Pizza shop of movie fame, he installed a bomb shelter in the event of a nuclear attack. Having developed plans for such shelters for the White House during his time there as naval aide, he was familiar with the type of structure needed, though his home version was somewhat less sophisticated than the one he designed for the executive mansion.[24] When the local press took notice of the shelter, however, some of the Navy's brass were fearful it sent the wrong message to the general public.[25] A later owner converted Ned's excavation into "a very good wine cellar."[26]

Ned's propensity for underground excavation was seemingly unlimited. He added several basement rooms to the family's Georgetown residence, including the one that became his writing office and library. When he and Ingrid purchased an apartment building down the street and around the corner from their Georgetown residence, Ned began a year-long effort to put a basement under the apartment building. Daughter Ingie "often mused over the relationship between being an accomplished submariner and his predilection for being subterranean."[27] Always possessing a very fit and trim physique, Ned's hard labors in mining had the additional benefit of helping to maintain his prime physical condition over the years.

A major by-product of all that digging was the need to dispose of the excavated earth. Friends were readily supplied with any and all the fill dirt they needed. Ned even took to clandestinely putting three to four inches of dirt in the bottom of each neighbor's trash cans just before the weekly garbage pickup. When all else failed, he finally purchased an old pickup truck from friends Peter and Mary Beth Durant. Lining the pickup's bed with sheet metal to make unloading easier, he would sortie on nocturnal ventures, where he would truck the freshly mined loam to construction sites near and far. There, the unwanted substance of his subsurface labors was deposited to blend in with the piles of dirt already removed by the construction crews.

The secreting of excavated dirt into the neighbor's trash cans was in part possible because Ned was the self-appointed "King of the Alley." The block in Georgetown where the Beaches resided was one of the few in the area with an alleyway. This meant the residents did not have to cart their trash out to the curb in front of their homes for pickup. However, the refuse removal company could not get its truck down the alley if the legal parking space at the end of the alley was occupied by anything larger than a compact car. When this happened the regular collection was skipped.

In speaking with the man who supervised the rubbish collection in their neighborhood, Ned discovered he was a former Navy chief boatswain's mate, so the two immediately got along very well and were soon working to ensure a smoother operation. In one instance, Ned sent a two-page, single-spaced, typed letter to all the residents on the block, outlining the ongoing problems with trash collection. The letter spoke to the issue of the limited alley access if the first parking slot was occupied by a full-size car and included other suggestions for making the regular collection of trash hassle-free.[28]

A secondary issue the letter addressed was the problem of wild animals and the plastic bags used by some residents. Ned noted that the "wildlife (I mean small animals) living in the alley bank or possibly in the wilderness area at the bottom of the [Katharine] Graham property" were ripping open the plastic bags at night.[29] Reporting that he had often seen raccoons and an opossum with babies in the area, Ned wanted his neighbors to know that the "attractive odors" of their garbage were leading to scattered debris along the alley, something Ned himself frequently cleaned up, or paid someone to clean up. The inequality of the situation was something about which he thought everyone on the block ought to be aware.

[6]

Given Ned's professions as a naval officer and as a writer of naval history, an important hobby that occupied his time was collecting museum-quality ship models. One of his most prized acquisitions was a beautiful, solid walnut replica of USS *Lea* (DD-118). Beginning his naval career as a junior officer on board *Lea*, Ned developed an emotional attachment to the ship from which he was eventually transferred to serve in submarines. The 3/32nd-inch scale custom model was built by Dave Davenport, who also produced a custom model of USS *Trigger* (SS-237) for Ned.[30]

Ned's collection of seventeen large-scale custom-built models included: a magnificent wood and brass rendition of HMS *Victory*—Nelson's flagship at the Battle of Trafalgar in October 1805; an equally marvelous model of USS *Constitution*; and two versions of USS *Constellation*—each showing the configuration of the ship at different periods in her history. There is also a very large-scale model of *Triton* (SSR[N]-586). Some of the models of ships from the "age of fighting sail" are over six feet in length, from the tip of the jib boom to the tip of the spanker boom. All the running rigging is present in intricate detail. Model builder Lou Montanaro of Rockville, Maryland, built several of the items in Ned's collection.

[7]

Eventually, Ned's time as skipper of Old Sal came to an end. On departing *Salamonie* in January 1958, he began one of the most intellectually challenging chapters of his career in the Navy. It would also prove to be the apex of a career that already had many high points.

Part VII: 1958–1961—*Triton*

[1]

It was a windy day on the Thames River in May 1960 as the Navy's largest submarine, USS *Triton,* made her way upstream to the submarine base at Groton having just completed a record-setting submerged circumnavigation of the globe. The steady breeze kept the Stars and Stripes stretched stiff as the national emblem flew from one of *Triton*'s periscopes, but the schooled observer might have noticed that the huge, and somewhat faded, flag bore only forty-eight stars. The submarine's crew had not erred in using a flag that did not recognize the recent admissions of Alaska and Hawaii to the Union; rather, the forty-eight star flag was provided by Ned, *Triton*'s skipper. It was the same flag that had flown from USS *Memphis* on the day she was swamped by a tidal wave and destroyed. On that day in May, Ned was paying tribute to his father, Edward L. Beach Sr., who had been commanding *Memphis* on a fateful day in 1916.[1]

[2]

"The big project, of course, is to get such a power plant [nuclear] into a submarine. This is possible, and, boy, what a sub that would be!" So wrote Ned to his wife Ingrid in 1947 as he attended his first nuclear power school at Oak Ridge, Tennessee.[2] There is no doubt that, as Ned penned those lines, he was thinking about what it would be like to command such a submarine, but in 1947 he was just getting his feet wet amid the internal and external political struggles of Op-36.

[3]

Some observers have speculated that behind Ned's selection as PCO of *Triton* was the hidden hand of President Eisenhower. When Ike asked Ned to remain as his naval aide after the president's heart attack in 1955, Ike was aware of the potential harm that could be done to Ned's career if he remained too long in the White House. When Ned was promoted to the rank of captain in October 1956, he became senior to the men who were then being given command of the Navy's newly emerging nuclear submarine fleet.

Eisenhower's influence in deciding who would command *Triton* may have been a factor, but the decision was subject to the tremendous influence of Rear Adm. Hyman G. Rickover. With an iron hand Rickover controlled the Navy's nuclear program down to the slightest detail—especially its training. The selection of commanding officers was not a prerogative with which Rickover would have easily parted during the early years of the program, not even at the bidding of his commander in chief. Rickover had defied Ike before, even in public, as in 1955 when Rickover responded to a reporter's question regarding orders from the president: "I can be directed to do things and do them in a half-hearted way, you know."[3]

Hyman G. Rickover was, and still is, a legend in the U.S. Navy. Lewis L. Strauss, who was chairman of the Atomic Energy Commission and who worked with Rickover in the early days of the development of nuclear power, describes Rickover as "an officer who combined some of the qualities of Henry Ford, Admiral Farragut, and (if one listened to his detractors) Simon Legree."[4] When it came to the operation of nuclear reactors, Rickover was a fanatic for precision, detail, and professionalism. As a result, he exercised rigid and unilateral control over who was admitted to the training program. One of the most infamous practices that Rickover maintained was the interview process officers had to endure to be admitted to the program. One junior officer who was subjected to the Rickover interview found the experience "harrowing"—his name was Jimmy Carter.[5]

Will Adams, who was destined to be the executive officer on *Triton*, reports that Rickover threw Adams out of his office three times during his own interview. Lieutenant Commander Adams was then the commanding officer of USS *Pickerel* (SS-524), stationed at Pearl Harbor, when he was summoned to Washington for an interview with Rickover. Adams had applied for the nuclear power program, and the only way in was through Rickover's office. The interview was held on a Saturday, with Adams due back at Pearl Harbor on Sunday since *Pickerel* was scheduled to depart on Monday for exercises. After Rickover had thrown Adams out of his office a second time and called him back a second time, Adams asked Rickover's aide to inform him when the time came for Adams to leave to catch his flight back to Hawaii. Rickover became further enraged and told Adams if there were things more important to him than the nuclear power program he should just leave immediately. Adams departed believing he had forever lost the chance of being selected for nuclear subs. Much to his surprise, he was later given orders posting him to the nuclear program as prospective executive officer of USS *Triton*.[6]

Lest the reader believe Rickover was some sort of madman, Ned's views of the man known as the "Father of the Nuclear Navy" might be helpful: "I think he's [Rickover] one of the only [*sic*] people I've ever seen who had complete personal control of his adrenaline valves. In other words, he can get mad intentionally and deliberately."[7] The ability Ned suspected Rickover of having was often exhibited in the applicant interviews. Determining how an officer reacted to stress was an important marker on Rickover's yardstick of the qualities necessary for a good nuclear plant operator. Cool-headedness under extreme tension was a crucial personality trait in Rickover's view.

In an oral history interview for Columbia University, Ned assessed Rickover as "a man of vision, but he couldn't have told you what the vision was, he just had visions of the limitless horizon sitting out there, you know, and everybody else was putting fences around this horizon and not looking beyond the fence, and that's where they were wrong and he was right, because a man of vision has got to recognize that what he's looking at is an infinite distance, and he's only able to see the beginning of it."[8]

Many of the ill feelings against Rickover originated in the ways he treated people. Ingrid Beach felt that most people misunderstood Rickover. "I always took him with a grain of salt, and never took him too seriously. I think part of the time he was just being sarcastic and liked to project this 'meanie' sense of humor."[9] Junior officers seeking admission to the exclusive club of the nuclear-powered Navy, however, could ill afford Ingrid's more tolerant views after having been subjected to a Rickover barb. Will Adams notes that Rickover's prickly personality earned him the nickname "K.O.G. (Kindly Old Gentleman)" as a common substitute for the more profane names many officers would like to have publicly expressed about the man.

So why did Rickover want Ned to command *Triton*, even if doing so was only in acquiescence to a directive from the White House? The negative column for Ned to command included both his seniority, plus his not having been part of the long and rigorous training program already in place for officers in the nuclear power program. While Ned had early contact with the Navy's nuclear power program, including a key role in getting CNO Fleet Admiral Nimitz to sign off on the initial concept, he would have to be completely trained—in a very short time—in order to take command of *Triton* as scheduled.

Rickover's policy was that officers commanding nuclear submarines had to first be qualified as nuclear power plant operators. This requirement was a source of much irritation for the Navy's diesel-powered submarine officer corps, as it limited who could command any of the nuclear-powered submarines then being built, or being planned, and it gave Rickover unprecedented control of the command selection process. Between the submarine officers he chose to bypass and the numerous other naval officers his roughshod tactics had stung, there was always strong opposition to Rickover.

Rickover had a distinct dislike for the Navy's system of rotating officers between billets. Specialists who spent their entire careers doing those things for which they were trained remained his idea of the way to run the Navy—no jack-of-all trades for Rickover.[10] While Ned was a submariner, he had yet to prove himself in Rickover's nuclear-power training meat grinder. What Ned had that Rickover seemed to value in an officer more than anything else was the courage of his convictions. As historian Michael Isenberg described him, "Rickover expected every man to stand his ground and battle for his ideas."[11] Ned was never a man to lamely accept the professional opinions of higher ranking officers—just ask anyone who was subjected to his criticism of the flaws in *Trigger II*. It is possible that the reputation Ned earned for his actions concerning *Trigger II* is what made him attractive to Rickover. In addition, Ned had a demonstrated ability for problem solving, especially during stressful situations, and he displayed remarkable staying power once involved in a project.

In a fitness report of Ned while he was in the nuclear-power training program, Rickover noted that the seven-day weeks with sixteen-hour days that Ned had endured were to Ned's credit. Then Rickover goes on to note, "He was selected for this assignment from among the most outstanding submarine officers of his experience level."[12] Still, Rickover gives no direct hint as to why Ned was selected for command of *Triton*.

Since the Navy's nuclear program was producing a steady supply of officers who could run both the nuclear reactors on board submarines and were qualified for command, the question remains as to why Rickover was willing to take someone from outside the existing cadre of trained officers and arrange a special program to get that someone trained up to Rickover's high standards. There had to be at least half a dozen officers who were junior to Ned, but who possessed the necessary skill set to take command of *Triton*. So, why Ned?

Naval historian Paul Stillwell offers one possible rationale—publicity.[13] There would have been little doubt in the minds of most submariners in the mid-1950s as to who was the most well-known submariner in America—Ned Beach. The initial linking of Ned's name with the command spot of *Nautilus* before that historic ship even had her keel laid was based on Ned's image, both within and outside the Navy. His exposure to the public as Eisenhower's naval aide, the long list of articles he had authored, coupled with his best-selling novel and his successful book of World War II submarine stories all added up to a visibility for Ned that no other submarine officer could match. In short, where Ned went, headlines followed.

For Rickover, a master at manipulating both the political system and the Navy's bureaucracy to achieve his goals, the Navy's nuclear program was in need of a sustained push in the late 1950s. Submarines in general had suffered in the postwar years when it came to budgets. Carrier aviation dominated the Navy, as well as the public's view of the Navy, and funding was a function of that image. The public attention that accompanied the commissioning of *Nautilus* in 1954 was sustained to a certain degree, and the voyages under the polar icecap by nuclear boats even led to subsequent bumps in public awareness, but what Rickover sought was a definite intensification of the limelight.

The need to create a platform from which to launch nuclear-armed missiles that did not have the vulnerability of land-based missiles had led to the initial funding of the Polaris submarine program by Congress. That program did promise a bright future for nuclear-powered submarines, even as some in the Navy began to stiffen in their opposition to an all-nuclear submarine force. Even with *Nautilus* and her three sister "nukes" already in commission, there were those in the submarine service who staunchly opposed a complete conversion of the nation's submarine force to all nuclear power, and they had allies on Capitol Hill.

Rickover might also have been looking for someone who could generate some positive publicity for Rickover himself. Ned had always been very much aware of the need to keep Rickover involved on the public side of the nuclear submarine program. When Ned arranged for First Lady Mamie Eisenhower to launch *Nautilus*, he made certain Rickover had a front-row seat, with due recognition for his role in the development of the nation's first nuclear submarine. Prior and subsequent public ceremonies marking the accomplishments of the nuclear-power program usually found Rickover in the back rows or not invited at all. For example, when the voyage of *Nautilus* under the polar icecap was feted at the White House, Rickover was not even invited, an apparent intentional slight arranged by Adm. James Russell, who was acting chief of naval operations at the time (filling in for an absent Adm. Arleigh Burke). Russell dismissed criticism of Rickover's absence by noting that Rickover had opposed the polar voyage and there was no point in his being there. In fact, according to historian Francis Duncan, Russell as a young officer had endured one of Rickover's scathing reprimands, and had vowed revenge some day.[14] White House press secretary James Hagerty was left with the unenviable task of justifying Rickover's absence to an inquisitive press.

In addition to his demand of hegemony over who would be qualified for command of nuclear boats, Rickover also demanded input in both the design and operation of nuclear-powered submarines. The push for *Triton* to have two nuclear reactors was in large part due to Rickover's belief that the planned submarines that were to be armed with the Polaris missile ought to have two reactors to improve reliability and speed, especially since they were to operate under the polar icecap. As far as most of the rest of the Navy was concerned, Rickover should have been confined solely to the development of reactors, leaving ship design and operational matters to others. CNO Arleigh Burke made sure of that by specifically barring Rickover from other facets in the development of the Polaris program.[15] Rickover found in Ned a commanding officer who could generate headlines for the Navy's nuclear program, as well as someone who would ensure that Rickover got the credit he deserved for those successes. Additionally, he found an officer who had the courage of his convictions.

"Triton was the trumpeter of the Sea. His trumpet was a great shell," according to Edith Hamilton's classic work on Greek mythology.[16] If Rickover's motive for selecting Ned as the PCO of *Triton* was to find someone who could give his nuclear program a publicity boost, then the choosing of Ned to be a new "trumpeter of the Sea" was apropos to say the least. Like a consummate chess player, Rickover moved pieces on the game board by uniting the most well-known submariner of the day with the Navy's biggest and newest nuclear submarine.

[4]

As early as January 1957, months before Ned had to contend with an angry Errol Flynn on the island of Majorca, the decision was made to appoint Ned as PCO of USS *Triton* (SSR[N]-586), scheduled to be the Navy's fifth nuclear-powered submarine and then under construction at General Dynamics' Electric Boat Division in Groton.[17] Notification of his selection was sent to Ned in August 1957 by the Bureau of Naval Personnel. Attached to the official Navy letter was a copy of a memorandum from Rear Admiral Rickover to Vice Adm. James L. Holloway Jr., chief of naval personnel, which outlined a timetable of training to prepare Ned to command *Triton*.[18]

The *Triton* to which Ned was assigned was the fifth ship of the U.S. Navy to bear that name. Postwar Navy policy was to name new submarines after those lost during the war. The one exception was *Nautilus,* which was named as much for Jules Verne's well-known submarine of fiction as it was for the three previous Navy ships to bear that name.

Triton's immediate predecessor, with the hull number of SS-201, had a spectacular career during World War II battling the forces of the Imperial Japanese Navy, and earning five battle stars. *Triton* was lost on 15 March 1943 to depth charges dropped by Japanese destroyers. Ironically, it may have been USS *Trigger* (SS-237), with Ned on board, that was the last U.S. Navy ship to have any contact with *Triton,* as *Trigger,* from a distance of some ten miles, heard the underwater explosions that evidenced the fatal attack on *Triton.*[19]

The differences between submarines *Triton III* and *Triton V* (there was a *Triton IV*—Coast Guard Patrol Boat No. 16) are astonishing. While the older *Triton* was 307 feet long and displaced 2,370 tons submerged, the nuclear-powered *Triton* was 447 feet long and displaced 7,900 tons submerged. The World War II submarine could make 20 knots surfaced and 8.76 knots submerged (but for only a very short time), while her namesake could make 27 knots surfaced while making at least 18 knots submerged, both for indefinite periods of time. The later *Triton* was designed for exactly one hundred more crew members than the fifty-nine for which her eponym had been designed.[20]

The new *Triton*'s size was in part a reflection of the fact that she was the first—and only—U.S. submarine to have two nuclear reactors. In fact, *Triton* was the largest submarine the United States had built up to that time. The genesis of *Triton*'s design and size lies in two unrelated areas. In the first, Rickover was always looking at the construction of nuclear-powered submarines in the 1950s as platforms on which to test his evolving technologies. The previous four nuclear submarines the Navy had launched all had single-reactor power plants. Since nuclear power was a science still in its infancy, questions nagged the engineers and scientists as to reliability, especially with the planned routine patrols under the polar icecap, where a reactor malfunction could strand a submarine in an unreachable location. The idea of a submarine with what amounted to a backup reactor was appealing. *Triton*'s claim to greater reliability was also linked to the fact that she had two propellers and two propeller shafts, allowing her to continue to move under her own power even if damage was sustained to half of her propulsion train.

An additional rationale for a dual-reactor arrangement was a desire to experiment with the underwater speeds that might be obtained from twin reactors. Unfortunately for *Triton*, she was not designed with what became the most optimum hull for underwater speed. Later hull designs for nuclear-powered submarines would achieve higher submerged speeds than *Triton*, albeit with single reactors.

Another factor in the design of *Triton*, though not necessarily in second place, at least in the thinking of the rest of the Navy outside Rickover's domain, was the need to develop a submarine that could serve as a radar picket platform in advance of carrier battle groups. Experiences during World War II in the Pacific pointed to the need to have radar probing far ahead of carrier battle groups to provide sufficient warning of approaching enemy planes. The technological state of radar during the war advanced rapidly, but it still had a range limit that allowed little time for an aircraft carrier to launch planes with which to defend herself. Longer warning periods were achieved during the war using destroyers, but the fragile tin cans were highly vulnerable to attack by the enemy planes they were trying to spot.

As planning progressed for the invasion of the Japanese Home Islands, technical planners developed the idea to use submarines as radar pickets and as forward air controllers. A submarine would have the advantage of being able to submerge in the face of oncoming enemy planes, and once the threat had passed it could return to its mission of being the forward eyes of the fleet and to direct the air battle in its assigned area. The problem with using submarines in this role stemmed from the already cramped spaces in a submarine and the need to install additional radar and communications gear, all requiring more electricity, more crew members, and more air conditioning to keep all the electronics cool and in an atmosphere of relatively low humidity.

Several submarines underwent conversion to the radar picket configuration—they were designated as SSRs, the "R" for radar—before the war ended. After the war, the idea was not discarded, but expanded, as the dominant arm of the Navy—carrier aviation—pressed its need for advance warning of enemy aircraft. The Navy developed various configurations, and even some submarines that had been under construction when the war ended were partially redesigned for the radar picket role, but it soon became clear that none of these diesel/electric-powered boats could keep far enough ahead of a fast-moving carrier if the submarines were forced to submerge.[21]

The sustained speeds, both surfaced and submerged, that could be achieved with a nuclear-powered submarine seemed to provide a solution to the radar picket quandary. With that role in mind, the new *Triton* was designed and constructed. She was to be large enough to accommodate the necessary communications and radar gear to serve as the "eyes of the fleet" while having the speed to keep one station ahead of the fast-moving carriers.

[5]

The keel for USS *Triton* (SSR[N]-586) was laid down on 29 May 1956 at Groton by General Dynamics' Electric Boat Division. She would be launched on 19 August 1958 and placed into commission on 10 November 1959. Seven months before *Triton*'s launch, in January 1958, Ned entered into a series of highly strenuous and technically challenging training programs designed to make him qualified to command a nuclear submarine. As previously noted, Rickover's stringent rules required that any officer who aspired to command a nuclear submarine had to first qualify as a nuclear reactor operator. Ned, as he approached his fortieth birthday, was plunged into the Navy's most intellectually demanding and rigorous training program. The result of the training was to enable him to operate the reactors with which *Triton* was equipped, and to be able to handle "all conceivable functions and malfunctions" of those reactors.[22]

An integral part of the Rickover training program required both officers and enlisted men who were to operate reactors to train on the prototype of their respective reactors. Every reactor the Navy installed on board a ship had a prototype on land that was used as much for training purposes as it was to prove the feasibility of the reactor's design. *Triton* was to be equipped with two S4G nuclear power plants (S = submarine; 4 = fourth model; G = General Electric, the designer/builder). Before Ned and Will Adams were trained on the S3G (the land-based version of the reactors that would power *Triton*), they had to first undergo a sort of "basic" training on the S1W (Submarine Model 1 Westinghouse) at the National Reactor Testing Station in Idaho. The S1W was the land-based prototype for the S2W that was operational on board *Nautilus*. Specific training followed at West Milton, New York, on the S3G.[23]

Will Mont Adams Jr., Naval Academy Class of 1945 (but graduated in 1944 for World War II service), who at the time was assigned as prospective executive officer of *Triton*, went through the training with Ned. Adams recalled that, because he and Ned both had command experience, their training program was not the typical one followed by less senior officers. He believes that their program of study was more intense, if for no other reason than they were taken through the program outside the normal training cycles—they were their own "class" of two students. Adams also notes that Rickover seemed to have implemented a spy system to keep the pair under constant surveillance.

While in Arco, Idaho, at the National Reactor Test Station, Ned and Adams were subjected to the typical seven to eight hours' worth of lectures per day followed by several hours' worth of "homework." After about five weeks of the seven-day weeks of pure instruction, they began to also stand "watches" on the operating reactor, all under the scrutiny of their instructors. Rickover did not believe in "simulations," lest the students get the idea that making mistakes had no consequences.[24]

As the two neared the end of the first phase of their training cycle and were scheduled to return to Washington, D.C., to Naval Reactor Headquarters, Rickover suddenly extended their time at Arco by several weeks. Adams then became concerned that his hair had grown too long and he badly needed a haircut. Unwilling to ask anyone at the training facility to cut his hair, he received permission from the officer in charge of the facility to borrow a car to drive into town for a haircut. Before Adams got back, Ned received a phone call from Rickover, who wanted to know why Adams had left the training facility and who had given him permission to go.[25] It was clear to Ned and Adams that only Rickover had the authority to grant them leave from the training program, even for a haircut.

Months later, while the two were undergoing additional training at the General Electric facility in Schenectady, New York, they were invited to have lunch in a dining room reserved for the plant's staff and visitors. Before the meal was over, Ned received a phone call from Rickover (who was in Washington, D.C.) informing Ned he had no right to eat in that dining room, that he was a trainee and he must eat only where other trainees were allowed.[26] Because Ned was a well-known author, he was frequently running into people who wanted to single him out for a conversation, or to autograph one of his books. Rickover seems to have anticipated the potential for special treatment being accorded Ned, so every move out of the ordinary by Ned and Adams was somehow reported immediately to Rickover.

[6]

By the end of July 1958, Ned had completed the prescribed training programs, was deemed qualified to operate both the S1W and S4G reactors, and arrived at Groton to take charge of *Triton*. The submarine was launched on 19 August 1958 and the process of crew training and oversight of the final stages of construction became Ned's immediate tasks. The training and prep work for the new command were so demanding of Ned's time and energy that his personal files are devoid of any writing, fiction or nonfiction. This is one of the rare periods in his life when he did not have some personal writing project to which he devoted his spare time. *Triton* was commissioned on 10 November 1959, over a year having elapsed between her launching and her acceptance by the Navy as a completed ship. At the commissioning ceremony, Ned addressed his crew and the gathered dignitaries:

> Men of *Triton*, our honored guests, ladies and gentlemen. Placing a ship of the United States Navy into commission is a most serious duty. In the first place, it culminates a long period of preparedness and labor. In the second, it is an undertaking before many witnesses, both seen and unseen. In the third place, we and our ship now take our position in our country's battle forces, assuming the responsibility for readiness, efficiency, [and] effectiveness in our assigned missions. We have been brought to this point by the Navy and the Navy's supporters, who have, in effect, been our supporters, too. All this now changes and we become responsible for our destiny in ways hitherto but lightly thought of.
>
> And remember likewise our predecessors in whose path we follow. The men and ships of the Navy who have gone before and who, by their daring, competence, and strength in years past, have given us the traditions we follow. Remember the men who preserved our country from defeat at sea; the men who gave their all in our Navy's wars from ages past—who lie indeed with the first *Triton*. Remember, in fact, the men who lie with all those submarines which did not come back—do we not owe them something as the name *Triton* returns to the fleet's rosters? We cannot deny our heritage. We can only wonder when the accounts are finally cast for the mighty ship on whose deck we stand, how she will compare with the standard against which she will have been measured.[27]

With these words, followed by the reading of the Navy's orders to place her in commission, *Triton* became an active ship of the U.S. Navy, but she was still a long way from being ready to assume any frontline position in the Cold War for which she had been built. Even as her crew labored to meld themselves and her inanimate steel into an axe of war with the ultimate goal of defending the peace, plans were being discussed in other places that would give *Triton* an opportunity to prove herself in ways no one on her crew—not even her skipper—could have imagined.

[7]

When the Soviet Union announced the successful launch of its first satellite *Sputnik* on 4 October 1957, many in the U.S. government were caught by surprise, even if American scientists working on similar projects were not.

A stunned American public, egged on by politicians with their own agenda of pet projects, began to look for ways to increase American technological advancements to outpace the Russians. Regardless of the minimal immediate impact *Sputnik* had on the military side of the Cold War, the technology race of the Cold War began with a starter's pistol that sounded much like the "beep, beep" of *Sputnik*'s radio beacon.

Within the Eisenhower administration, the launch of the Soviet satellite also initiated a hunt for potential "firsts" that the United States might achieve through technology. Within a month of *Sputnik*'s appearance in the earth's atmosphere, the National Security Council considered the possibility of *Nautilus*' making a submerged circumnavigation of the world via the Arctic Basin.[28] The idea was shelved for a time, but it reemerged within a few months of *Triton*'s commissioning.

Capt. E. P. Aurand, USN, naval aide to President Eisenhower and Ned's successor in that post, proposed in a classified memorandum to Adm. Arleigh Burke, chief of naval operations, a series of "projects" the U.S. Navy ought to consider completing before the Russians did. The memorandum from the White House to the CNO is indicative of the Eisenhower administration's quest for some "one-upmanship" on the Soviets. Aurand prefaced his proposals with the following: "There is no doubt that sooner or later the USSR will put some nuclear submarine to sea. It would be a shame if we permit them to announce this to the world by virtue of some dramatic feat which we could have done ourselves. This would be Sputnik all over again, but without any excuses."[29]

The second item on Aurand's list of "projects" was "Around the world submerged (particularly the Magellan route)." He went on to state at the end of his list that, "'Project Magellan' is, in my estimation, head and shoulders above any of the remainder as a feat of submarine navigation and a demonstration of the global range of nuclear submarines."[30]

The chief of naval operations' classified response to Aurand's suggestions came within twelve short days, making particular note that the "Magellan route" could be accomplished by *Triton* in "56 days at 20 knots or 75 days at 15 knots" at a cost of $3.34 million in terms of nuclear fuel consumed at the higher of the two proposed speeds.[31]

President Eisenhower had already scheduled a summit meeting for the summer of 1960 in Paris with Soviet Premier Nikita Khrushchev, as well as with the British and French heads of state. That meeting was to be followed by a tour of the Soviet Union with Eisenhower as Khrushchev's special guest. With CNO Burke's assessment of the Magellan route and his recommendation of *Triton* as the submarine to make the voyage, Aurand forwarded to James Hagerty, Eisenhower's press secretary, a classified memorandum on 26 January 1960 that outlined the Magellan route for further discussion with the president. Included in Aurand's list of "pertinent" facts about the project was that the twin reactors of *Triton* made the submarine the "logical choice" for the trip, and that "the cruise could be scheduled for completion about 15 May."[32] Once the idea was presented to Eisenhower, a decision was quickly made, and a very surprised Ned found himself being summoned to Washington for a meeting with top Navy brass on 4 February 1960.

Directed to arrive at the Pentagon in a business suit instead of his uniform (so as not to draw attention), Ned was ushered into a meeting with Vice Adm. Wallace M. Beakley, deputy chief of naval operations, Fleet Operations and Readiness, and Rear Adm. L. R. Daspit, commander, Submarines, Atlantic Fleet, as well as several other admirals, captains, and commanders. Ned had hardly a chance to sit down when he was asked point blank whether or not *Triton* could go around the world submerged instead of on her scheduled shakedown cruise. Ned later wrote in his account of the voyage that prosaic words that might have been quoted by future generations of seamen failed him at that point, "[A]nd, after a sudden, nervous cough, I said 'Yes, sir!' That was all I could say."[33]

[8]

In 1492, Christopher Columbus believed he had reached islands off the coast of India, but follow-on voyages by others soon proved that the lands Columbus had found were not anywhere close to India. Once Vasco Balboa reached the western shore of the Isthmus of Panama, it became clear that another body of water lay between the newly discovered lands and the far eastern nations to which Spain and other European nations wanted easier access.

In 1519, a Portuguese sea captain named Ferdinand Magellan was commissioned by Spain to cross Balboa's newly discovered and named Pacific Ocean to measure its true width. Departing with five ships, the voyage would become one of the most celebrated journeys of exploration in human history. After three years, a single ship, leaking badly, with a greatly depleted crew, arrived back in Spain, having provided the first measure of the width of the Pacific and the true magnitude of the world's size. Unfortunately, the man whose name is associated with this monumental voyage did not survive to see his vision fulfilled.

As the U.S. Navy planned to demonstrate the capabilities of its nuclear submarines with a submerged circumnavigation of the earth in 1960, the route followed by Magellan's ships in 1519 seemed to offer a fitting historical link in what was hoped to be another epic chapter in human exploration.

As a consequence of the discussions about the historical links to Magellan, *Triton* was ordered to follow in the wake of Magellan's voyage.

[9]

The decision to use *Triton* as a demonstration of American technical capabilities may not have been a difficult one to make for the president or a group of men sitting around a table in the Pentagon, but the translation of that decision into reality—one that had to be cloaked in secrecy until it was accomplished—now fell on Ned's shoulders. Admiral Beakley's instructions were to keep the entire trip classified until it was completed, and that the voyage had to be completed by 10 May 1960, which gave Ned only twelve days from the time the verbal order was received until his ship and crew were to depart. Curiously, no one said—and Ned did not ask why—the deadline of 10 May was so important. The discussion at the White House had indicated 15 May, but did the Navy's leadership want a five-day cushion on the president's target date?

The classified voyage was given the code name "Sandblast," and *Triton*'s skipper was to be code named "Sand." Several of the high-ranking officers in on the project found the code name amusing for a person whose real surname was "Beach." For his part, Ned was not particularly amused. Between the time *Sputnik* was launched and the *Triton* voyage was approved, the United States had suffered a number of humiliations on the technology front. In a quest to regain some of the momentum in the technological space race, the United States attempted several very public launchings of satellites, only to have them collapse in balls of flame before newsreel cameras. To avoid any such future embarrassments, Eisenhower's staff wanted to keep *Triton*'s trek secret lest it, too, should fail.

The problems of past failures and the public relations nightmares that ensued were part of the matrix of details with which Ned had to contend during the brief twelve days he had to ready *Triton*. The logistics of getting *Triton* ready for a voyage of such length without arousing the suspicions of the men on the ship, as well as anyone at the submarine base in Groton, however, was one of the most difficult tasks he faced.

Not being able to tell the crew was especially worrisome. Normally, when a ship puts to sea for a long voyage, the crew knows in advance at least when they will return so they can make arrangements for their dependents' financial and other needs. In addition, both the crew members and their families can prepare emotionally for a long separation. In this case, however, all that the families would know was that the submarine was to go on a shakedown cruise scheduled to last a month or so. In cases where a ship's mission was changed and the return home was delayed, both the crew and their families had the security of knowing what was happening, and a flow of diverted mail could help alleviate some of the anxiety such situations produce. The nature of *Triton*'s mission meant there would be no mail, while the location and activities of the ship would remain unknown to the families. Conversely, the men on board *Triton* would be faced with not knowing how their families were getting along in their absence.

In an effort to lessen the strains that a long, unplanned voyage would create, Ned did warn his crew that due to some "bureaucratic" foul-up, there was the possibility of *Triton*'s being sent on for further tests in the Caribbean once she had completed her shakedown in the North Atlantic. Each crew member was required to complete a checklist of items that needed to be taken care of before *Triton* departed—car insurance, rent, utility, and other payments. Ned would later write, "Though income tax deadline was still two months off, the men had been advised to file their returns before leaving."[34]

Ingrid became one of the important links between the crew and their families during the voyage. Ned informed his wife of the general nature of the mission, but she was enjoined from revealing anything to anyone, even the family members of the ship's crew. Periodically, Rickover, or some other Navy official, would call Ingrid and simply inform her, "Everything is fine."[35] Ingrid would then pass that word along to the families of crew members, though she was not allowed to tell anyone how she came by the information or who provided it. In a further effort to relieve some of the anxiety of the wives of crew members, Ingrid and several of the officers' wives hosted a "coffee," which was attended by eighty of the 106 wives of crew members.[36] Such an occasion provided an outlet for emotions while helping to engender mutual support.

Then there was the problem of navigating a journey of a projected thirty-four thousand miles. Just acquiring all the necessary charts (Navy lingo for maps) to cover the entire journey was a task—one that fell on the shoulders of XO Will Adams, OPSO Bob Bulmer, and CQM William J. Marshall, all of whom had to be told about the nature of the mission beforehand.

The actual route that Magellan's ships took in 1519 had to be researched, then the navigation had to be worked out taking into consideration the depth of the ocean all along the route. The projected course *Triton* would follow had to be filed with the Navy prior to departure so the Navy would have an idea where *Triton* was at any given point of the voyage. The various commands of the Navy had to be informed of *Triton*'s presence while in their areas so that some mischance detection of an unidentified submarine did not result in alarms being sounded.

In planning his voyage, Magellan assumed there would be a way around the southern end of what today is known as South America, just as there was a point at which the African continent ended and a ship could begin a northward journey again. The passage at the southern end of South America that Magellan eventually found, the one that bears his name, took a month for his three ships to navigate due to its forty-foot tides, rocky barren shores, and swift currents.[37]

During the Pentagon meeting when Ned was ordered to attempt the submerged circumnavigation following Magellan's route, it was decided that passing through the Straits of Magellan was not feasible. The Straits were legally the waters of Chile and Argentina, and it would have been necessary to obtain permission to travel through those territorial waters. Even if such permission could be secured on short notice and without compromising the secrecy of the mission, the size of *Triton* meant she would need a considerable amount of room in which to maneuver, something the narrow and sometimes shallow channels of the Straits could not provide, especially if *Triton* were to encounter a large surface ship. As a result, *Triton* crossed from the Atlantic to the Pacific by rounding Cape Horn at the southern end of the South American continent.

Triton had been designed to carry seventy-five days' worth of food for her crew of 159, but that was not sufficient for the projected eighty-five days of this trip. Additionally, Ned felt it necessary to provide food for a total of 120 days in case some unforeseen circumstances forced *Triton* to remain at sea longer.[38] In calculating food needs, consideration also had to be given to providing for the eight "technical" specialists that were being sent along on the voyage.

The Navy had decided to use *Triton* as a laboratory to measure the psychological effects of long periods in a submerged submarine. To that end, a psychologist, Dr. Benjamin R. Weybrew, from the Naval Medical Research Laboratory, came on board. The Navy may have wanted data on the long-term effects of life on board a submarine, but the crew had other ideas about the nature of Dr. Weybrew's work, as shall be seen later.

Two civilian engineers, one from General Dynamics, the builder of the boat, and one from Sperry, the company that had designed the inertial navigation system, were also assigned to the crew. These two men were to provide technical backup in case problems arose, as well as to monitor various aspects of the sub and its systems. In the case of the SINS (Ship's Inertial Navigation System), the original design of *Triton* did not call for such a system, so it was much to the surprise of Will Adams when technicians suddenly arrived to install a SINS for the supposed "shakedown cruise." Designed for the fleet ballistic missile submarines then being planned by the Navy, the SINS carried on board *Triton* proved to be an utter failure according to Adams.[39] The SINS did become a reliable and essential part of the ballistic missile submarines in the years that followed, but its trial on board *Triton* was not an auspicious beginning.

Three civilians from the Navy's Hydrographic Office were detailed to join the voyage. One of the most important scientific projects that *Triton*'s journey fulfilled was the accumulation of gravitational and oceanographic data gleaned from a single platform with continuous use of the same instruments on a circumnavigation. The Navy desired a baseline set of data that such a circumnavigation could provide, and the scientists at the Hydrographic Office realized the best data would be achieved by a sub-merged ship, something that heretofore had been impossible to facilitate.

To measure ocean currents, *Triton* was to periodically eject sealed glass bottles containing instructions for anyone finding such a bottle to forward the contents to the nearest U.S. embassy or consulate. Each "note in a bottle" contained coded information as to the time, longitude, and latitude that it had been deposited in the sea. Knowing when and where a bottle was retrieved would assist the Navy in furthering its knowledge of ocean currents.

To provide a photographic record of the journey, Earnest R. Meadows, a Navy photographer, and Cdr. J. Baylor Roberts, USNR, were selected by the office of the chief of naval information to make the trip. Roberts was a highly respected photographer for the National Geographic Society. Their still and motion picture photography provided a visual record of the journey. The film footage was eventually edited into a forty-five minute documentary, but the voiceover of the narrative script and sound were never added. Ned came to own a 16-mm print of the documentary, which he would narrate live when making presentations in the years that followed. In 2006, Will Adams recorded a narrative sound track for the National Geographic documentary, which had been converted to VHS and DVD. Copies of the program have been deposited with the Naval Historical Foundation in Washington, D.C., and the Submarine Force Museum in Groton, Connecticut. Whether the program will ever be made available to the public is still undecided.

General Dynamics also released a documentary on the voyage using some of Roberts' film footage. Titled *Beyond Magellan*, the video version of that thirty-minute documentary can still be found for sale from various vendors specializing in military programming.

All the scientific measurements, plus those that engineers sought, required not only additional personnel, but also the installation or stowage of their equipment—not to mention all the cameras and film for Roberts.

Triton may have been the largest submarine the Navy had ever built, but it was still crowded because of the two reactors. Adding more equipment, more personnel, and enough food to feed everyone for four months required all the creative storage skills for which submariners are rightly famous.

[10]

Triton eased away from her dock and into the channel of the Thames River on Tuesday, 16 February 1960, a little after 1400. Except for a few of the officers and a very limited number of enlisted men, no one on board knew the true nature of her pending voyage. As far as the Navy personnel at the Groton submarine base were concerned, *Triton* was heading out on her shakedown cruise in the North Atlantic. The vast majority of the men on board believed they were eventually headed to Hawaii. That bit of misinformation was due to an inadvertent comment by XO Will Adams. The crew members were to each take along a sports shirt for use in the traditional high jinks when *Triton* crossed the equator, but Adams informed the crew they would need an "Aloha shirt."[40] Having lived in Hawaii for so long, Adams had become accustomed to calling sports shirts by their popular Hawaiian name.

It was not until noon of the day after *Triton* departed that Ned announced to the crew the exact orders under which they were sailing. Unlike the dramatic scenes depicted in films, Ned did not provide an impassioned reading of COMSUBLANT's (Commander, Submarine Force, U.S. Atlantic Fleet) Operation Order 5-60, nor did the crew spontaneously burst into applause or patriotic song when the announcement was finished. Ned would later attribute the silence that followed his announcement to "the unofficial code of the sailor that requires that he remain outwardly unaffected by words of praise or blame, condemnation or exhortation. Yet I knew, deep inside, the thrill of the adventure must be stirring in their chests as it was in mine, along with a fervent determination to see it through."[41] Will Adams suspects that the silence was a stunned reaction to the hoped-for Hawaiian visit that had been thwarted.

[11]

In planning the submerged circumnavigation, Ned and his officers were aware of the need to be precise in the manner in which they could prove that they had accomplished their quest. Magellan had left from Spain, while *Triton* was departing from the eastern coast of the United States. Was the circumnavigation to be measured from Groton back to Groton? If so, then part of the journey would be over the same ocean area twice. After discussions of the problem, Ned and his officers planned to measure their record-setting journey from the middle of the Atlantic, rather than from Groton. The result was that a little-known and seldom-seen set of small rocky islands was selected as the actual beginning and ending point of the submerged circumnavigation.

St. Peter and St. Paul's Rocks, an archipelago in the North Atlantic, became the marker by which *Triton* measured her voyage. Having submerged off the eastern coast of the United States on 16 February, *Triton* reached St. Peter and St. Paul's Rocks on the twenty-fourth. After observing and photographing the barren stone islands, *Triton* began the first leg of the journey as she headed for the southern tip of South America. A routine set in on board ship as the miles and hours passed.

Navigation was an important factor in the journey, which necessitated that *Triton* approach periscope depth once a day to make a celestial observation in order to determine the submarine's exact location. Fortunately, *Triton* was equipped with a new type of periscope that allowed celestial observations through its specially constructed lens. World War II-era submarines had to run many hours on the surface both to charge batteries and to make any speed on long passages, a practice that allowed for regular navigational fixes using the traditional sextant. Nuclear-powered submarines did not need to surface, so engineers had developed a method for observing the sun, moon, and stars through a periscope that was designed to function in place of the sextant.

As a precaution in determining *Triton*'s location, XO Will Adams and CQM William Marshall worked as the primary navigation team while Lt. Cdr. Robert W. Bulmer and QM1C Curtis Nedam worked as the secondary, or backup, team. Each team took independent observations and calculated the ship's location before comparing them. If the two did not agree, another set of observations was made and the ship's location recalculated. Once agreement had been reached, the results were presented to Ned.

The daily routine of moving up to periscope depth was time-consuming. Since higher speeds with a much quieter transit could be achieved at greater depths, the process of coming up to a depth where the periscopes could be used was laborious and potentially dangerous. As she came up, *Triton* had to slow down since high speeds could damage a raised periscope. In addition, on the way up, she had to stop periodically and listen with her passive sonar for surface ships. Coming up too quickly and not knowing what was on the surface was an invitation for disaster. All of this took time and impacted the tight schedule that needed to be kept to meet the deadline imposed by the White House.

While at periscope depth, the snorkel pipe was extended, allowing fresh air to be sucked into the ship and the stale air expelled. This practice also conserved oxygen, which normally was to be released into the ship's atmosphere whenever the ambient oxygen level fell below the percentage determined to be optimal for human activity (16.2 percent). The crew seemed to welcome the fresh air, but Ned was always concerned with the tight schedule that had to be maintained.

Triton had been selected for the mission of submerged circumnavigation because of her twin reactors and the reliability they presupposed. Nonetheless, Ned recognized that even if at least one of the reactors could be kept working properly, the mission could still be endangered by some other system failure. Granted, *Triton* had been to sea for several short trips to test systems, but none had even remotely approached the length of a normal shakedown, let alone a circumnavigation. *Triton* was, after all, on a shakedown cruise, the very nature of which was to determine whether all her systems were functioning properly. It was not uncommon for a ship on its shakedown to come back with long lists of repairs, and even with major problems, as Ned had experienced with *Trigger II*. In addition to possible unforeseen technical or mechanical problems, *Triton*, like any other ship, was potentially limited by her all-too-human crew.

No sooner had *Triton* gotten into the first leg of the voyage when the ship's medical officer, Cdr. James E. Stark, MC, USN, approached Ned with word that one of the crew had been taken seriously ill. CRdM J. R. Poole was suffering from kidney stones. Stark told Ned that initially the ailment could be dealt with on board ship, but if Poole's situation worsened, he would need to be transferred to a hospital. When Poole's symptoms lessened, the crisis seemed to have passed, but soon the pains returned in even greater measure.

Once it became clear that the sailor needed to be moved to a medical facility, Ned began to consider how that could be done without violating the parameters of a submerged circumnavigation. *Triton* was just north of the Falkland Islands in the South Atlantic when Ned and Stark concluded that Poole needed more help than he could get on board *Triton*. Having been briefed on the location of most Navy ships along *Triton*'s projected route, Ned knew that the cruiser USS *Macon* (CA-132) was somewhere in the vicinity of Montevideo, Uruguay.

As the radio messages were exchanged to set up a rendezvous with *Macon*, Ned pondered the problem of getting Poole off *Triton* and onto the cruiser without having to surface. After discussions with some of the officers, a consensus was reached that it would be possible to "broach" *Triton*, exposing only enough of her to allow the opening of a hatch through which Poole could be moved, thereby preserving the distance already covered in the quest for the submerged circumnavigation record.

The timing of the transfer was determined by how quickly the two ships could reach each other, so it happened that Poole was transferred to *Macon* in the middle of the night. With both ships dead in the water, Ned raised both of *Triton*'s periscopes. One had been rigged by several of the quartermasters with a light inside a tin can that was held against the eyepiece of the periscope. A switch allowed the light to be flashed off and on, sending the same sort of blinker signal that could be sent on the surface. While the jury-rigged signal light operated on one periscope, Ned manned the other, reading the return signals from *Macon*.[42] Both ships having exchanged recognition signals, Ned ordered *Triton* brought up to forty-eight feet with only her sail—the vertical projection from her hull sometimes called the conning tower—broaching the surface. Crew members from *Triton* would bring Poole up through a hatch and help place him in a launch that *Macon* was to send across the six hundred yards separating the two ships.

When Ned was satisfied that the sail was above water, and that the hatch that led to that part of the submarine was also above water, he ordered the hatch opened. Concerned that the calculations might have been inaccurate about how much air would be needed in *Triton*'s tanks in order to hold the sail above water, or that the water density might change during the operation, thereby making the ship ride lower in the water, Ned had stationed QM1C Curtis Nedam at the hatch with instructions to keep the hatch only slightly ajar, lest *Triton* begin to ship water. There was also concern that choppy seas or rough waves might develop, either of which could cause *Triton* to take on water.

Having made his way to the bridge, Ned found himself standing on the deck of an 8,000-ton ship that was 99 percent submerged. Alone and in the darkness, Ned called for the line-handling party to come into the lower portion of the conning tower as a preparation to take *Macon*'s launch alongside. Two crew members had come topside with paint buckets and brushes to paint over the large "586" on her sail—for the security of the mission, Ned and his officers had decided that it would be unwise to allow someone on *Macon* with binoculars to determine the identity of *Triton*.

The waves proved to be higher than Ned had first anticipated—the line-handling crew were covered in seawater up to their necks as they held on to the side of the conning tower. A one-second burst of air was ordered into *Triton*'s forward tanks, raising the sub enough so that the entire conning tower was clear of all but the highest waves. The lower conning tower hatch was opened and a second hatch in the side of the conning tower was also opened. The line-handling party received lines heaved from *Macon*'s launch, and Poole—very relaxed on painkillers—stepped from *Triton* to the waiting boat, getting only the soles of his shoes wet.

With the ailing sailor safely on board *Macon*, *Triton* slipped completely back below the waves and resumed her voyage, having lost about seven days on her schedule. A rumor persists among the crew that Poole ended up in an Argentinean hospital where doctors "cured" his condition by forcing him to drink vast quantities of beer until the kidney stones had passed out of his urinary tract. The beer was supposed to have eased the pain of the stones' passage. This rumor has often been repeated but remains unconfirmed because its basic idea is so appealing to the crew that they never want to have it proved false.

[12]

When Magellan departed Sanlúcar, Spain, on his voyage of discovery, one of his worries was the morale of his crew, for mutiny was always a possibility. Magellan also had five ships under his nominal command, but he could not always control the actions of the other ships. The pilot and captain of the *San Antonio* refused to enter what became known as the Straits of Magellan, fearing for the safety of the ship. So Magellan and his remaining four ships pressed on into the straits. *San Antonio* headed back to Spain; even before Magellan entered the Pacific, he had lost one-fifth of his command.

Ned supposed that he did not have the navigational worries that faced Magellan because of the charts the Navy provided. The decision already having been made to avoid the Straits of Magellan, *Triton* traveled around Cape Horn, avoiding the dangerous waters that had proved so terrifying to Magellan's men. When *Triton* got to the Pacific and began a northward leg toward Easter Island, Will Adams made a startling discovery.

The Navy maps covering the Pacific from Cape Horn to Easter Island did not contain indications of the depth of the ocean along the projected route. It appeared few ships equipped with a fathometer had ever made the passage while recording depth readings as they went. The problem now faced by *Triton*'s navigators was exacerbated by Will Adams' discovery that the ship's fathometer had stopped working, making it difficult for the navigators to know the exact depth of the water through which the submerged ship was traveling.

In submarines from an earlier era that operated submerged only for short periods at depths never below several hundred feet, the loss of a fathometer was not a traumatic event. On board a nuclear-powered submarine that was charging along at 20+ knots and at depths of over five hundred feet, there was grave concern over the inability to quickly and accurately determine the depth of the water under the submarine. Prior to the loss of the fathometer, while in the mid-Atlantic, *Triton* detected an underwater mountain that was not on the charts. Only the watchful eyes of the on-duty personnel noted the quickly rising bottom, and *Triton* had to decrease her depth to avoid hitting the side of the uncharted undersea mountain. Even if their training had not taught the crew to be vigilant, the harrowing experience of the underwater mountain had indeed instilled in them a greater degree of caution.

Various jury-rigs were attempted to replace the fathometer, including lowering a home-made device through the garbage disposal unit. That effort was fruitless and resulted in damage to the garbage disposal unit, much to the dismay of the torpedo room personnel, who had to suffer the indignity of their torpedo tubes being used to expel garbage for the rest of the voyage.

Now *Triton*, sans a fathometer, faced having to keep her steady pace in order to regain and then keep to her schedule, but through waters of unknown depths. The submarine's sonar in its active mode could be used to estimate depth through triangulation, and it had been regularly employed for that purpose since the fathometer had malfunctioned, but the degree of accuracy and reliability of that system when it was being used for a secondary purpose was worrisome. The use of the sonar to constantly monitor depth required personnel on duty in the control center to utilize unpracticed procedures when guiding *Triton* through the depths of the ocean. A secondary worry about use of the sonar in active mode was that it would reveal *Triton*'s presence to any other ship or submarine in the area using passive sonar, violating *Triton*'s mission directive to remain undetected during her circumnavigation.

[13]

As part of an ongoing study of the psychological effects of long-term submerged travel, the Navy had sent along psychologist Dr. Weybrew, as previously noted. Crew members were asked to volunteer to participate in his study. Those who did were given questionnaires to be completed each day. The surveys asked the sailors to describe their feelings regarding their general well-being, toward others, missing their loved ones, and so on. One sailor, tired of having to take the time to complete the questionnaire each day, was seen filling out all of his at one time and then handing in one each day.

Participants in the study were also asked to meet with Dr. Weybrew for one-on-one sessions every couple of weeks. After *Triton* had been submerged for more than a month, a sailor was participating in one of his regular meetings with Dr. Weybrew when another sailor walked in, sat down next to the sailor being interviewed, kissed the interviewee on the cheek and then left. Dr. Weybrew asked, "Who was that?" "Don't know," was the reply. "He must be a new crew member."[43]

EN2 Philip P. Mortimer Jr., who worked in the engineering section, informed Dr. Weybrew that he would not give up his sack time or his chow time for the one-on-one interviews, so if the psychologist wanted an interview, he'd have to come to the engineering spaces to talk while the sailor was on duty. Dr. Weybrew complied with the request, but during every interview, Mortimer would suddenly stop, stare down at the doctor's feet and inform the psychologist that he was standing in the sailor's strawberry patch. This pattern was repeated many times. At the end of the cruise, when a Navy psychiatrist came on board to review Dr. Weybrew's work, Weybrew insisted that the psychiatrist meet this strange sailor with the imaginary strawberry patch. After a number of minutes while Mortimer and the psychiatrist calmly chatted, Weybrew could no longer stand the strain, so he asked, "When are you going to tell him to get out of your strawberry patch?" With a straight face, Mortimer looked at Weybrew and said, "What strawberry patch?"[44] It would appear that Engineman 2nd Mortimer may have been familiar with the James Thurber story "The Unicorn in the Garden." (This story appeared in the *New Yorker* on 21 October 1939 and was published the following year in Thurber's *Fables of Our Time and Famous Poems Illustrated*.)

Ingrid does not believe her husband was aware of the crew's "toying" with Dr. Weybrew. "I never heard Ned mention any of these amusing pranks so I don't know if he was aware of the ribbings." She also believes that, in spite of his well-known sense of humor, Ned "would not have approved of such disrespect."[45]

In the fall of 1960, when *Triton* was participating in NATO exercises in the North Atlantic, several of the wives of men on board mentioned to Ingrid that letters they had been receiving indicated the crew was weary of the long periods submerged. Ingrid noted that the Navy might have been better off doing the psychological study on a normal deployment, not on the submerged circumnavigation when crew morale was high due to their determination to complete its special mission.[46] Perhaps the reported high jinks of the crew during the submerged circumnavigation underscore Ingrid's assessment.

[14]

Part of the responsibility Magellan accepted in his journey was the conversion of indigenous peoples to Christianity. When the intrepid seafarer arrived in the Philippine archipelago, he found numerous tribes willing to convert. However, when one reluctant chief refused, Magellan—against the advice of his officers—decided to force the man to convert. With that purpose in mind, Magellan and about fifty men landed on the island of Mactan, only to be attacked by fifteen hundred natives who did not appreciate the point of a sword being used as a method of proselytizing.[47] In the ensuing battle, Magellan was killed. Later, the Spanish occupiers erected a large monument to Magellan in the surf near the spot where the famed explorer died.

Following his route was not the only homage to Magellan planned for *Triton*'s epic voyage. A carefully designed part of the trip was an offshore visit to Mactan's Magellan Bay. Dubbed a "periscope liberty," each crew member was allowed into the conning tower to take a brief look at Magellan's monument through one of the two periscopes. Having already traveled over 19,000 miles before arriving at Magellan Bay, the crew considered the viewing a welcome diversion. This "periscope liberty" was not the first on the voyage, as each crew member had been allowed to view Cape Horn. Tradition holds that any sailor who views Cape Horn can then safely spit to windward—a perk for which *Triton*'s long-submerged sailors had little use—but traditions at sea must be honored, even if more in the breach than in the keeping.

When *Triton* entered Mindanao Sea from the east, using Surigao Strait, she traversed the same passage Magellan had used as he wound his way through the Philippine archipelago in 1521. This was also the same Surigao Strait through which Vice Admiral Shoji Nishimura, Imperial Japanese Navy, led his force of two battleships, a heavy cruiser, and four destroyers on the night of 24–25 October 1944. Part of the complicated Japanese plan to attack American ships unloading troops and supplies at Leyte Gulf, Nishimura's task force was met by an American force of six old battleships, some resurrected from the wreckage of Pearl Harbor. In what will probably remain history's last sea battle fought by ships armed with large guns, American Rear Adm. Jesse B. Oldendorf's force devastated the approaching enemy, thereby turning back one of the pincer movements aimed at the vulnerable transports at Leyte Gulf.[48]

The narrow confines of Surigao Strait were an aid in Oldendorf's battle plan, but maneuvering a submerged submarine as large as *Triton* through those tight waters was no easy task. The situation was complicated by the presence of surface traffic, especially non-motorized sailing craft that *Triton* could not detect except through visual sightings using her periscopes. Having the periscope spotted might cause some alarm to be raised, thereby jeopardizing the secretiveness of *Triton*'s mission.

It was while in the waters of the Philippines that Ned peered through the periscope as it broke surface and found himself looking at a Filipino in a dugout canoe. Not only was the young man looking back at Ned, whom he could not really see, but he was paddling his canoe on a course parallel to *Triton*'s, easily keeping pace with the submarine's slow speed. Ned quickly ordered the periscope lowered and informed the control room crew of what he had seen. Commander Roberts asked permission to snap a picture of the Filipino. Ned agreed, the resulting picture later being published in *National Geographic* magazine as part of *Triton*'s post-voyage story.

Having been the only unauthorized civilian to see *Triton* during her classified voyage, the nineteen-year-old was eventually tracked down by investigators sent by *National Geographic*. According to the *Charleston* (West Virginia) *Gazette,* the young man was Rufino Baring, who admitted he had spent many sleepless nights after sighting what he thought was "part of a very big monster."[49] In an effort to ward off future sea monsters, Baring repainted his canoe and painted the names of two saints on it for protection—St. Peter and St. Paul, a curious coincidence with the starting and ending points of *Triton*'s submerged circumnavigation.

Once Baring was located, he exchanged correspondence with Ned. In 1976, Ned sent him several 8 x 10 color prints of Roberts' periscope photo, plus an inscribed copy of *Around the World Submerged*, in spite of Ned's doubts that Baring was indeed the young man photographed in the canoe.[50] For a time Baring wrote letters to Ned telling of his family's financial hardships and their extreme hunger, and asking for money. Baring noted that Ned had made money by using Baring's picture, and Baring was entitled to something, too. Over a period of four years, the Beaches sent what amounted to several hundred dollars to Baring and his family, but each gift was answered by yet another letter asking for more. Finally, Ned sent Baring a letter which stated that if Baring was going to continue to beg for money, the correspondence should halt. That was the last of the letters exchanged between the two.[51]

[15]

Having spent several years of his early youth in what was aptly named Poor Valley in southwestern Virginia, Allen Steele lived most of the rest of his youth in Gaithersburg, Maryland. He would later describe himself as the "world's worst student, and if not, I was runner-up—I'd skip school a couple days a week to go to work to earn money."[52] In the process of cutting a class one day, he ducked into the school library to hide from a teacher, thinking the library was the last place the teacher would look for him. Needing something to camouflage his true intent, he grabbed a book off a table of newly arrived books. That was a life-changing moment. The book was *Run Silent, Run Deep*. In a short time, Steele was engrossed in Ned's novel, and when he finished it, Steele told himself, "This is what I want to do in life."[53] Not too many years later, Torpedoman 3rd Class Steele found himself assigned to *Triton* and serving under the command of the man who had inspired his career in the U.S. Navy.

Triton was only twenty-four hours from returning to St. Peter and St. Paul's Rocks, bringing the official submerged circumnavigation to an end, and Ned was beginning to breathe a little easier, while the crew was anticipating being reunited with family and friends. A little after 2000, Steele was on watch in the after torpedo room when he heard what he thought was a muffled explosion followed by the sounds of a heavy spraying. As the room began to fill with a mist of atomized hydraulic fluid, he notified the control room over the ship's 7MC announcing system that there was a major hydraulic leak on the stern plane mechanism.

Like many mechanical systems on a submarine, the stern and bow planes were operated through the use of hydraulics. In this case, the system maintained a constant pressure of three thousand pounds per square inch. A valve had failed near the stern planes, depriving the control room of the ability to maneuver them. The loss of hydraulic pressure was noticed in the control room even before Steele's immediate report, and the system was switched to its emergency backup.

With hydraulic fluid misting throughout the compartment, Steele worked his way down to the system's lines and managed to close a valve that controlled the non-pressurized part of the line. He then began to struggle to close the valve that had three thousand pounds of pressurized fluid spraying out. The oil mist had immediately coated all the surfaces, making it very difficult to grip the valve and equally difficult to gain any footing from which to exert the force necessary to rotate it.

Steele's desperate struggle to close the valve was aided by EN3 Harlan F. Martin, who had rushed to Steele's assistance. The total elapsed time from the failure in the hydraulic system's line to the closing of the last valve was less than thirty seconds. In that time, the torpedo room was fogged with a choking, highly explosive hydraulic mist. Off-duty sailors sleeping in the compartment had to be roused out of their bunks to evacuate the space.

Of the 120 gallons of hydraulic fluid in the ship's entire system, almost one-fourth was lost in those brief seconds after the rupture. Any further loss of fluid would have seriously compromised both the steering and diving plane systems before emergency controls could have been triggered.[54] For his quick action, Steele was awarded the Navy Commendation Medal, which was presented to him by Secretary of the Navy William B. Franke at a ceremony following the voyage.[55] Ned's novel inspired Steele to a career in submarines, but it was Steele's quick action that saved *Triton* from a potential disaster even as the sub neared the end of its historic journey.

The mishap in the stern torpedo room was the last hurdle *Triton* and her crew had to face on their record-setting journey. On 25 April, *Triton* reached the mid-Atlantic point from which her circumnavigation of the globe was being measured—St. Peter and St. Paul's Rocks. To ensure that there was no doubt about the true completion of the feat, she circled the rocks completely before heading north. Ned would later recall that, as the last few hours ticked away before *Triton* reached St. Peter and St. Paul's Rocks, several crewmen congregated in the forward torpedo room trying to jockey for position to be the most forward man on the sub, thereby being able to claim the bragging rights of being the "first man to circumnavigate the globe submerged."

Word of the successful mission was relayed up through the Navy's chain of command and then on to President Eisenhower. Col. Walter R. Tkach, USAF, Eisenhower's Air Force aide, later reported to Ned that on Sunday, 8 May, he was with President and Mrs. Eisenhower at their Gettysburg residence, and that, "The President was so excited about this [*Triton*'s accomplishment] that he stated in his own inimitable way that if we could keep it secret he would tell us what was going to happen in a few days."[56] "A few days" was 10 May, the deadline Ned had been given to complete his mission, and the date *Triton*'s feat would be made public just prior to Eisenhower's departure for the summit in Paris. Ike's desire of "one-upmanship" was to be fulfilled.

[16]

Three years after setting sail, the sole remaining ship of Magellan's tiny fleet arrived back in Spain. Of the 240 men who had departed with him, only eighteen survived. Hostile natives, scurvy, storms, starvation, mutiny, and accidents had taken a horrendous toll, including the famous leader whose name would be forever linked to the expedition.[57]

One final honor was to be paid to Magellan by *Triton*. Before leaving Groton, the ship's company had provided funds for the casting of a bronze plaque that would be delivered to the Spanish government upon completion of the submerged circumnavigation. Bearing the Latin inscription *Ave Nobilis Dux Iterum Factum Est* ("Hail, Noble Captain—It is Done Again"), the plaque also bore the dates 1519 and 1960 along with olive branches and the U.S. Navy's Submarine Force twin dolphin insignia. The shiny brass plaque, twenty-three inches in diameter (its size determined by the requirement that it be able to fit through one of *Triton*'s hatches) was to be shuttled from *Triton* to Spain when *Triton* reached a mid-ocean point closest to Cadiz (Magellan's home port). Using the same technique of "broaching" the ship as had been used to transfer off Chief Radarman Poole, *Triton* passed the plaque to USS *John W. Weeks* (DD-701) on 2 May in mid-ocean while off the Spanish port. The American destroyer then conveyed it to the American ambassador to Spain, who in turn presented it on behalf of the submarine's crew. The plaque was placed in the city hall of Cadiz.

A curious footnote to the story of the bronze plaque is that the Latin inscription was obtained from a Latin teacher known to Ned. In what was probably an error in transcription as the words were written down during a phone call, the word *factum* was misspelled *sactum*, a word that does not exist in Latin.[58] The error was not discovered until *Triton* was on her submerged journey, so a new plaque had to be cast with the corrected word. That plaque was flown out to *John W. Weeks* and substituted for the one transferred from *Triton*. The plaque that went to Cadiz does commemorate the voyages of both Magellan and *Triton*, but it did not accompany *Triton*.

[17]

The triumphal return of *Triton* from her record-setting trek was still in the offing when events on another side of the world were conspiring to deprive her and her crew of the kudos they had earned and the technological masterstroke Eisenhower had sought. On 30 April, an American U-2 spy plane was shot down by the Soviets over their own territory. The highly secret photographic missions had been going on for several years, but the high-altitude planes had gradually become more and more vulnerable to advances in Soviet missile technology. When a U-2 plane piloted by Francis Gary Powers went down, the promises made to Eisenhower by Allen Dulles, director of central intelligence—that either the pilots of such missions would never survive a shootdown or, if they did, they would kill themselves before being captured—did not materialize.[59]

On 5 May, Soviet Premier Nikita Khrushchev announced that Soviet forces had shot down an American spy plane. Eisenhower had already been informed that a U-2 plane was missing and presumed down with the pilot dead, but the Soviet leader slyly did not reveal on 5 May that the pilot had been captured. The Eisenhower administration, in releasing a statement claiming the plane was an off-course weather plane, had walked into the Soviet trap. On Sunday, 8 May—the same day Eisenhower's exhilaration over the success of the *Triton* mission had caused him to prematurely reveal its existence to his wife and his Air Force aide—Khrushchev announced that the Soviets had the pilot alive, and that the pilot admitted to being on a spy mission. The Soviets then produced photos from the U-2's camera to further back up their claims of intentional violations of their air space.

The U-2 incident seemed to loom ever larger, like an oncoming thunderstorm, resulting in the *Triton* voyage receiving little of the attention it deserved. From *Sputnik* on, the American public had hungered for some feat that would signal a resurgence of national technical prowess. *Triton*'s exploit was that feat, but no one will ever know the true expression of American feelings that might have been released over *Triton*'s accomplishments—the story had too much competition for headlines.

In May 1960, Ned poses at the White House with the log of the Triton*'s record-setting voyage and a map of the route in the background.*

Triton was still on her way back to Groton when she surfaced off Rehoboth Beach, Delaware, so that a helicopter could take Ned to the White House for the formal announcement of the remarkable accomplishment. Waiting at the White House were Ingrid, Vice Admiral Rickover, and President Eisenhower. Missing in the White House spotlight were the top admirals in the submarine force hierarchy. For reasons unknown to Ned, they had not been invited. Perhaps it was Rickover's payback for prior slights but, regardless of the reasons, Ned had nothing to do with the invitation list. Nonetheless, some of those neglected took umbrage at what may have been a simple oversight. Unfortunately, some of that dismay was later directed at Ned.

All of that backstage drama was not on Ned's mind when, with cameras rolling, Ike presented him with the Legion of Merit. The official citation noted that Captain Beach "led his crew with courage, foresight, and determination in an unprecedented circumnavigation of the globe, proving man's ability under trying conditions to accomplish prolonged submerged missions as well as testing new and complex equipment in the world's largest submarine."[60]

The previous Sunday's newspapers had carried headlines and op-ed articles questioning Ike's leadership and the seeming lack of command authority he exercised over the CIA, all due to the U-2 crisis.[61] The ensuing days were harrowing for the president as he publicly took the blame for the entire U-2 debacle. Ike was in low spirits by the time Ned reached the White House. Aides to the President were therefore puzzled when he released a heartfelt laugh as Ned presented him with some object. When later asked the reason for the President's sudden outburst of mirth, Ned had to admit that when he presented his commander-in-chief with a letter and envelope specially created by *Triton*'s crew as mementos of the voyage, the president was reacting to the paper in which the souvenirs were wrapped.

As a commemorative of the record-setting voyage, *Triton*'s crew had created special envelopes that were postmarked on board the ship. In addition, they had created a certificate announcing the accomplishment. Both of these items were to be sent to various dignitaries in the government, plus the family and friends of the crew. Due to a shortage of ink on board, the crew had to create their own ink for the mass printing of the certificates and envelopes. After some experimentation, they developed a mixture of hydraulic oil, ground charcoal, and insulating paint. The president was to receive the first one, but the ink had trouble drying, so Ned had wrapped it in a highly absorbent paper to prevent smudging. The root of the president's good humor was being handed his memento wrapped in toilet paper, as Ned had neglected to remove the wrapper prior to the presentation.[62] A brief return of the president's good humor only momentarily dispersed the clouds of the U-2 incident, something about which Ned had not heard. When White House Press Secretary James Hagerty asked Ned if he had heard about the U-2, Ned responded innocently, "No. What is it—a new German submarine?"[63] The ensuing laughter was also short-lived.

The commander of Submarine Squadron Ten, to which *Triton* was assigned, Capt. T. H. Henry, USN, wrote in Ned's fitness report, "This successful exploit bears witness to the professional competence, imagination, drive, and intelligence of this outstanding officer."[64] In a later fitness report dated in March of 1961, Captain Henry is the first officer to evaluate Ned while noting that Ned had "flag rank" potential.[65]

[18]

Phileas Fogg, the fictional globetrotter, may have taken eighty days to go around the world in the Jules Verne classic, but *Triton* took only sixty days, twenty-one hours to travel the 26,723 nautical miles (30,752 statute miles) from St. Peter and St. Paul's Rocks and back again. From the time she dove beneath the waves on 16 February until she surfaced on 10 May, *Triton* had spent eighty-three days, nine hours, and fifty-four minutes submerged, traveling 35,979.1 nautical miles (41,411.9 statute miles). The total voyage, from the time she left the dock at Groton until she docked again on 11 May, encompassed eighty-four days, nineteen hours, and eight minutes—a total of 36,335.1 nautical miles having been covered (41,821.7 statute miles).[66] The Knolls Atomic Power Laboratory, which developed the power plants on *Triton*, calculated that the ship's average underwater speed on the circumnavigation was eighteen knots.[67]

The Navy reported that eight crewmen became fathers during the voyage, while forty-two members of the crew received notice that they had advanced in rank or rate.[68] One of those who received advancement in rating was SO1 Lawrence W. Beckhaus, who became qualified to wear the twin dolphins pin of a submariner. Beckhaus was the valiant sailor who volunteered to jump overboard to rescue a fellow sailor off the coast of Spain when Ned commanded *Salamonie*. Having requested assignment to *Triton* when Ned was given command of the submarine, Beckhaus was pleased when Ned had asked the Navy's Bureau of Personnel to arrange for the transfer.

[19]

The coverage by newspapers quickly passed, but other publications took up *Triton*'s story. The November 1960 issue of *National Geographic* featured an article on the voyage written by Ned and lavishly illustrated with J. Baylor Roberts' photographs. The *Saturday Evening Post* (22 October 1960) ran a six-page story with numerous photos, and the August 1960 issue of *Argosy* magazine declared Ned the "Magellan of the Deep" as it presented him its "Giant of Adventure" award for 1960.

Though a relatively new medium, television did not ignore the event. Ned appeared on CBS' *Face the Nation* on 15 May, a program broadcast on both television and radio. Several crew members made appearances on *What's My Line?*, a game-show hosted by Gary Moore. Later in May, Ned was a guest of Senator Prescott Bush (R-CT) on a program that was aired on TV and radio stations across Connecticut.[69] Bush, the father of future President George H. W. Bush, was a major supporter of the Navy's Polaris submarine program, a fact not too difficult to understand since the submarines were to be built in his home state.

Just as in today's world of late-night TV hosts/comedians, Ned and *Triton* became the sources of material for several popular comedians. For example, Mort Sahl in a recording of one of his live performances titled "Mort Sahl at the Hungry i" joked that the reason President Eisenhower gave Captain Beach a medal was because Ned was "one of the few officers whose whereabouts he knows."[70] The punch line came after a reference to Gary Powers and the U-2 incident, and the early claim by the White House that the president did not know about the flight.

The close resemblance between *Triton*'s astonishing voyage and a comedy routine by Bob Newhart led some to believe Newhart based his material on the actual events. However, Newhart's first album, "The Button-Down Mind of Bob Newhart," which contained a track titled, "The Cruise of the USS *Codfish*," was released on 10 February 1960, before *Triton* had completed the submerged circumnavigation. Perhaps Newhart had some knowledge of the classified mission, but that is extremely doubtful. The Newhart routine is based on the premise that the fictitious *Codfish* is completing a two-year submerged voyage, and the skipper of the sub is addressing the crew on various matters—including asking for the return of the executive officer who has been kidnapped by some of the crew and hidden somewhere on the submarine. Ned capitalized on it and played the track over *Triton*'s PA (public address) system during later NATO (North Atlantic Treaty Organization) exercises. Ned admitted that many who heard the Newhart routine thought Newhart and Ned sounded remarkably alike.[71] In 2006, Newhart told listeners of *Talk of the Nation*, hosted by Neal Conan on National Public Radio, that the publicity from the *Triton* voyage had been a "spur" to the popularity of his "Codfish" routine.

For many years after the return of *Triton*, Ned was in demand as a speaker. Asked to discuss the submerged circumnavigation and show the National Geographic film taken by Roberts, Ned spoke to such diverse groups as the National Geographic Society itself (27 May 1960), the American Philosophical Society (22 April 1961), the Society for Non-Destructive Testing (8 May 1965), and an Eagle Scout Recognition Dinner in Chicago (4 November 1965).

An informative sideline to the Eagle Scout Recognition Dinner in Chicago was that Ned shared his speaking time with a sailor he brought with him—Allen Steele. The torpedoman who had heroically dealt with the leak in *Triton*'s hydraulic system on the last day of the submerged circumnavigation, Steele had pursued a college degree and then entered the

Navy's Officer Candidate School (OCS). In the midst of his OCS courses, he was surprised to be asked to accompany Ned to Chicago and then told that he was to be part of the program, speaking on his experiences in the Navy. Citing Steele as an example, Ned explained to the Eagle Scouts how an enterprising person could enter the Navy at even the lowest level and achieve a commission through hard work and dedication. With encouragement from Ned, Steele did earn his commission and returned to service on board submarines, eventually retiring from the Navy with the rank of commander.[72] In Ned's mind, Allen was an incarnation of the luck-and-pluck characters that peopled the novels of Ned's father.

Being skipper of *Triton* produced an additional honor when American International College in Springfield, Massachusetts, presented Ned with an honorary Doctor of Science degree in June 1961.[73]

[20]

From the time Ned left the White House in March 1957 until his return from the submerged circumnavigation voyage in May 1960, he did very little writing of his own. The demanding training schedule in nuclear reactors, as well as the burden of being PCO for a nuclear submarine, allowed little time to write. However, that changed once *Triton* returned from her daring trek. Many view Ned's log of *Triton* as a literary tour de force itself; today, the log is on display in Beach Hall at the Naval Academy. Using the log as a basis, Ned wrote *Around the World Submerged: The Voyage of the Triton*, which was published by Henry Holt in 1962.

His publisher had been after him for another book, and he made promises of a book-length study of the epic Civil War struggle between USS *Monitor* and CSS *Virginia* (*Merrimack*). That book would never be completed and there is little in Ned's files today to show that he began any really serious work on it. He did have ideas for another novel—featuring the hero of *Run Silent, Run Deep*, but the work on that project would be delayed until Ned was retired from active duty.

[21]

The NATO exercises during which Ned played the Bob Newhart album for his crew took place in the fall of 1960. *Triton* was one of numerous American ships that participated in the massive exercise, which involved ships from all the member nations. Part of *Triton*'s role included being the subject of anti-submarine hunts by various units of the strike fleet. As the exercises ended, the ships involved gathered around oilers for refueling and *Triton* surfaced and moved among them, chiding them about their need to refuel.[74]

[22]

Ned relinquished command of *Triton* in July 1961 when he was named commander, Submarine Squadron Eight. In the three years that had elapsed from his having taken over as prospective commanding officer, *Triton* had amassed an impressive record. The U.S. Navy has not replicated *Triton*'s submerged circumnavigation feat, and no other nation has claimed to have done so, either.

Ironically, the purpose for which *Triton* had been designed was out-dated even as she completed her world voyage. The Navy's aircraft carriers were soon to be equipped with the E-1B "Tracer," an airborne radar and control system that was the predecessor of today's E-2C Hawkeye. The need for the SSRs—submarines equipped as advanced radar warning and control platforms—was eliminated by new technologies. In March 1961, *Triton* was re-designated an SSN (submarine–nuclear), her radar picket role removed.[75]

Consideration was given to converting *Triton* to a seagoing command center for the president in the event of a national emergency, but the costs for retrofitting proved to be prohibitive. While she was the largest subma-rine in the Navy until the *Ohio*-class submarines were built in the 1980s, she had only six torpedo tubes—four forward and two aft—and a designed capacity to carry only fifteen torpedoes.[76] Consequently, she would have been of little use as an attack submarine. Lack of space also made her unsuitable for renovation as a missile-launching platform.

On 3 May 1969, *Triton* was decommissioned, the first American nuclear submarine to be taken out of service. She was stricken from the Navy's list on 30 April 1986, relegating her to the ignominious status of waiting to be dismantled and sold for scrap. Towed to Bremerton, Washington, her reactors removed, and tied up in the Puget Sound Naval Shipyard, she became part of the Navy's Nuclear Powered Ship and Submarine Recycling Program. At a cost estimated to be between $25 million and $50 million, her recycling began on 1 October 2007 and was still in progress in May 2008. Her steel and other scrap metals will be sold for recycling while her reactor compartments are to be packaged and shipped to Hanford, Washington, where they are to be buried.[77]

Efforts to preserve *Triton* as a museum proved futile. All that remains of her for public view is her stern planes diving stick (similar to a steer-ing wheel), which is on display in Beach Hall on the campus of the U.S. Naval Academy. In June of 2004, the Navy's Great Lakes Training Center named one of its new barracks *Triton* in honor of both the 586 and the 201 submarines.

[23]

The last entry Ned made into *Triton*'s log on 9 May 1960 told the story of *Memphis*, his father, and of the flag that had last flown on that ill-fated ship. Ned went on to tell how he had borrowed the "rather old and slightly weather beaten set of colors" from two former crew members of *Memphis*— Stanley P. Moran and Sam Worth—who had come into possession of it. He concludes his explanation in the log of why the cherished ensign would be flying from the highest periscope of *Triton* when she entered the Thames River on 11 May with the following: "The Navy is composed of ships, and men, and long-held traditions—all melded together in dedicated service to their country. It is more fitting that the last sight graced by this old flag should be one of gladness, rather than disaster and death."[78]

Part VIII: 1961–1966

[1]

Upon being detached from *Triton* in July 1961, Ned assumed command of Submarine Squadron Eight (SubRon 8 in Navy terminology) headquartered at Groton. Taking command of a squadron was a significant item on the list of accomplishments that an officer needed to fulfill in order to be promoted beyond the rank of captain. Ned relinquished command of SubRon 8 in August 1962 when he was assigned to attend the National War College.

Located in Washington, D.C., the National War College offers postgraduate training for officers of all branches of the armed forces. Emphasis is on strategic thinking and the policy-making process within the U.S. government. An officer's chances for promotion beyond certain levels can be enhanced by successful completion of a course at either the National War College or one of the postgraduate programs offered through each branch of the military. Soon after completion of his course work at the National War College in July 1963, Ned was awarded a Master of Arts degree in International Affairs from George Washington University. The pursuit of a master's degree in a field related to high-level work within the military command structure is a common practice that is usually coupled with attendance at the National War College or the Naval War College. Incidental to, but totally unrelated to, his Master of Arts degree, Ned was also awarded in the same year his second honorary doctorate—a Doctor of Laws (LLD) by the University of Bridgeport (Connecticut).

Upon completion of the National War College program in August 1963, Ned was named director, Joint Congressional and Special Material Division (Op-90A), Office of General Planning and Programming, Office of the Chief of Naval Operations (CNO). That mouthful of a job title meant Ned was responsible for preparing the secretary of the Navy and the CNO for budget and oversight hearings before Congress. Adm. David L. McDonald, USN, assumed the post of CNO the same month Ned moved into his new job. McDonald served as CNO from August 1963 to August 1967. The Vietnam War was just beginning to heat up as both Ned and McDonald settled into their new positions.

Congressional hearings have long been one of the major venues through which congressmen and senators closely monitor senior military leaders, as well as the civilian leadership of the services. Having a staff that can thoroughly prepare anyone called to testify is a key to making the hearing process as surprise- and trouble-free as possible.

Almost as soon as he reported to his new duty assignment, Ned was heavily involved in preparations for the 1965 Defense Posture Hearings. His work in preparation for the hearings resulted in an appreciative response from Secretary of the Navy Paul H. Nitze. In commending Ned, the memorandum from SecNav states in part: "The briefings referred to, relating to matters of highest national policy and importance, were prepared under your immediate direction and under extreme urgency. I am informed that they were in every respect among the best heard by this body [Preparedness Investigating Subcommittee of the Senate Armed Services Committee] in a considerable period of time." Nitze goes on to conclude, "Please accept also my personal appreciation for the outstanding job you did in support of myself and the CNO during the recently concluded Posture Hearings in Congress."[1]

Secretary Nitze was not the only person who expressed appreciation for Ned's work, as CNO McDonald commended Ned for his efforts in "the editing and sanitization of the transcripts of the testimony, including the provision of insertions for the record, reviewing under conditions of urgency the entire Navy record of testimony to the end that a coherent consistent whole was presented." McDonald's remarks end with, "Your knowledge, prolonged effort under great pressure, and considered advice were outstanding. Well done."[2]

The 1965 Posture Hearings were among the many for which Ned had to prepare materials to assist his superiors for their testimony. The budget process is an ongoing one, as an organization as large as the U.S. Navy undergoes continual monitoring from the congressional and executive branches. For his part Ned was soon recognized, both by his superiors as well as by the legislative bodies before which testimony was given, as a consummate master of the labyrinth that constituted the Navy's budget. While engaged in congressional relations on behalf of the Navy and its budgets, Ned developed a reputation as an honest, fair, and cooperative officer—especially among the staff members who worked for the various congressional committees—that would serve him well later.

At age forty-five, Ned took up the task of mastering the complexities of defense budgets and the craft of prepping for congressional hearings. Just as he had quickly absorbed the details of nuclear reactor operations through intense course work that was usually intended for younger men, his intellectual powers quickly grasped budgets, hearings, and the politics of congressional relations.

[2]

By the time Ned had begun the training program in preparation for taking command of *Triton*, his family had settled into a pattern of living either in the Washington, D.C., area or near the submarine base in Groton, Connecticut. His two sons, Edward (called Ned or Ned Jr. by the family, but referred to here by his given name to avoid confusion with his father) and Hugh, and daughter Ingie were educated at private schools—primarily at Pine Point School in Connecticut and then at Sidwell Friends School in D.C. Both sons, as well as their sister, graduated from Sidwell Friends School and would go on to successful professional careers. (See Appendix III for brief biographical sketches of Edward, Hugh, and Ingie.)

Ingrid was a full-time mother, also serving as surrogate father when Ned was at sea or away during training programs. Once the family moved back to the Washington area after Ned began course work at the National War College, Ingrid started working as a guide for Swedish tourists to Washington, a job that eventually led to her teaching at the Foreign Language Institute of the U.S. Department of State. Having grown up in a bilingual home—her mother was born and raised in Sweden—and having traveled to Sweden frequently with her mother for years, Ingrid was as proficient in Swedish as any native-born person. Ingrid taught at the Foreign Language Institute for fifteen years; her pupils were mainly diplomats bound for assignment to the U.S. embassy in Stockholm.

By 1966, Ned's job at the Pentagon had brought him into direct contact with the political realities of the war in Vietnam as the "hawks and doves" began political contention over the war. At home, Ned was facing his own struggle over the war as his elder son Edward neared his eighteenth birthday and the requirement to register for the Selective Service System. Shaped by his lifelong belief in the sanctity of life and his intellectual affinity for philosophy, Edward had developed into—and still remains today—a steadfast pacifist. As a result, he felt compelled to register as a conscientious objector.

The draft board of the Selective Service System for Chevy Chase, Maryland, where the Beaches resided at the time, had a reputation in the

1960s as one of the toughest from which to obtain conscientious objector status. So it was with trepidation that Edward thought about his appearance before that board in 1966. The issue had been discussed within the family for some time, placing in sharp focus the split that can occur between a person's public and private lives. At the time, Ned's work in the Pentagon was to help secure continuing congressional financial support for the Navy and its role in the Vietnam War, making his son's pacifist views a potential professional embarrassment. "Yet he [Ned] understood my principled stand," notes Edward.[3]

> I labored long and hard to assemble a convincing case to persuade the Draft Board of the strength of my convictions and integrity. I asserted that, if I were denied recognition as a CO [conscientious objector], I would face imprisonment rather than participate in the taking of human life. I prepared a personal statement articulating my ethical values and I gathered sixteen letters of support, including several from members of the military, testifying to my honorable character. Still, chances appeared slim that my application would receive a favorable ruling.[4]

On the morning of the dreaded draft board hearing, Ned asked his son if he wanted his dad to accompany him to the hearing. It was with a sense of relief and surprise that Edward accepted his father's offer.[5] According to Edward, "The meeting was difficult and tense."[6] After his son had presented his case, Ned asked to address the draft board. Edward recalls that his father spoke with "dignity and eloquence in my support, telling the Board members that since he was a professional military man he found it hard to accept his son's pacifism, but that he could testify to his absolute integrity."[7] In the end, Edward was granted conscientious objector status. "I was the only youth so exempted in that Draft Board area that year."[8] Edward has always felt that it was his father's presence that made the difference.

Further insight into Ned's family relationships can be seen in his willingness to drive Ingrid to antiwar rallies and then go back to pick her up afterwards. While Ned held strong views on the Cold War and the necessity of the United States to not back away from its policy of containment, he never forced those views on his family.

Son Hugh, who was sixteen months Edward's junior, was never called by the Selective Service System due to his birth date being outside those called when the system began using the birthday lottery to determine the order of call.

[3]

All the while that Ned was immersed in the budget and posture hearings the Navy's system of promotions was doing its work. In order to examine the issues surrounding Ned's last years of active duty, a brief review of the Navy's promotion process is in order for the uninitiated. Promotion of officers up to the level of rear admiral are handled by regularly convened boards composed of officers of higher rank. From among the pool of eligible officers at a given time, the promotion board selects those it feels are the most qualified. The proceedings of promotion boards are closed and the participants are sworn never to reveal what transpires during the board's deliberations.

The Navy's system of evaluation of its officers is based on the theory of determining if the individual is "best fitted" for higher rank. Success at one level does not ensure advancement. An officer who is an outstanding skipper of a ship may not have the additional skills necessary to exercise command at higher levels. As a result, captains passed over for promotion to rear admiral three times are unlikely ever to be promoted. In such circumstances, a captain could continue to serve until forced to retire after thirty years of commissioned service. Many captains faced with this situation, however, retire rather than face years of service when promotion is virtually impossible. With what is sometimes referred to as the "up or out" system, the Navy seeks to ensure that a large number of officers unqualified for promotion do not clog the upper ranks of its officer corps.

Unlike most civilian promotion systems, there is no feedback for naval officers not selected. The officer passed over is not informed of the reasons someone else was selected. There is no rubric that can tell an officer what needs to be done to improve for the "next time." One reason promotion boards do not provide feedback is that there are no hard-and-fast criteria. This is in part due to the fact that, from one promotion board to the next, there are never a constant number of promotions to be granted. For example, a promotion board meeting to select rear admirals may be tasked to select five captains because that's how many openings there are at the time. The next promotion board to be convened may be tasked to select seven. A captain who was ranked sixth by the first board would be passed over, while in the second instance, someone ranked sixth would be selected, a fact that may seem unfair to the sixth-ranked officer from the previous selection pool, but the Navy maintains that its system has proven its value over time.

A factor that had some implications for Ned's promotion was that, during the post-World War II years, the Navy came to be dominated by the carrier and destroyer communities, thereby limiting the number of submariners who were being promoted to flag rank. It was not until the Polaris submarine program got into full swing in the early 1970s that the number of submarine-qualified captains being promoted to rear admiral began to noticeably increase.[9]

In Ned's case, his class (1939—the year he received his commission) came up for "early selection" for rear admiral in 1964–1965. Early selection is a designation that allows a promotion board to dip into a pool of younger officers to select someone of exceptional quality for promotion ahead of his normal eligibility. When Ned was promoted to captain, he was a benefactor of the "early selection" option.

From 1966 to 1967, Ned's class was in "the zone," meaning the pool of captains eligible for promotion to rear admiral consisted of everyone who: (1) was in "year group 1939"; (2) had attained the rank of captain; and (3) had the requisite number of years at that rank. The year for "late selection" for Ned's class was 1968, meaning anyone eligible in 1966–1967 who had not been selected could be reconsidered. Late selections are usually limited, with promotion boards sometimes being allowed to make only one selection from the pool of eligible captains.

The names of the officers who serve on selection boards are routinely held in confidence, yet within the small circle of officers at the ranks of rear admiral, vice admiral, and admiral, the identity of who has been tapped to serve on a particular board is often not hard to discern. Knowledge of who might be serving on a particular promotion board should not provide an opportunity to influence that board's decisions, but human nature being what it is, from time to time efforts have been attempted. Nonetheless, attempting to influence a member of a selection board is "highly unethical," according to Rear Adm. Maurice "Mike" Rindskopf.[10]

Ned indicates in his memoirs that five selection boards for rear admiral met while he was eligible for either "early" or "in the zone" promotion.[11] That does not mean he was passed over five times. Some selection boards are convened for the specific purpose of selecting a limited number of individuals for very clearly defined positions, the result being that not everyone who is in the class and eligible for promotion was actually under consideration by a particular board. After the second official notice of having been passed over, Ned decided to apply for retirement from active duty, not wishing to risk an attempt for a late promotion.

There still remains the question of why Ned was denied something that so many thought would be his for the taking. According to William Tuohy, biographer of Richard O'Kane, one of the Navy's outstanding submariners of World War II, Ned was one submariner "who many combat veterans thought was destined for four stars [full Admiral]."[12] Apart from the opinions of fellow officers like O'Kane, Ned's fitness reports from the time he took command of *Triton* began suggesting that he should be selected and promoted to flag rank. Capt. Francis D. Walker, USN, who commanded SubRon 10 to which *Triton* was assigned, noted in 1961, "He has the breadth of experience afloat and ashore and the high quality intellect necessary for flag rank."[13]

Rear Adm. Robert R. Moore, USN, commander, Iceland Defense Force, under whom Ned's squadron served during exercises in the spring and summer of 1962, noted, "He is strongly recommended for promotion."[14] Ned's overall superior, Vice Adm. Elton W. Grenfell, USN, commander, Submarines, Atlantic Fleet, endorsed Moore's fitness report of Ned without additional comment on 14 July 1962.

During Ned's tour on the staff of the assistant chief of naval operations—General Planning and Programming—the issue of selection for flag rank is repeatedly noted in his fitness reports. Rear Adm. H. A. Renken, USN, who was Ned's immediate boss in General Planning and Programming, noted the following: "He is recommended for selection to flag rank" (2 April 1964); "He is recommended for selection to flag rank (9 April 1965); "He is highly recommended for selection to flag rank now" (11 June 1965).[15]

Renken's replacement at General Planning and Programming, Rear Adm. Paul Masterton, USN, wrote in a fitness report he prepared on Ned: "It is no mystery to me that this officer was an early selectee to Captain, but it is a mystery that he has not been selected to flag rank. He is younger than his contemporaries, is fully and completely qualified and should be selected not only for his past contributions, but also more particularly for his future potential. I most strongly recommend his selection and promotion." Elsewhere in the same fitness report, Masterton added, "For the good of the Navy, this capable, dedicated officer should be selected and promoted."[16]

Since the proceedings of the selection boards are sealed and no one who served on any selection board when Ned was up for rear admiral has broken his oath of silence, the balance of this discussion must be based on opinions—albeit some well-informed ones.

[4]

To those who asked why he never made rear admiral—there were many, many people, both within and outside the Navy, who did ask that question—Ned replied with the story of his encounter with a person to whom he always referred to as "Joe Blunt." As he relates the story in his memoir, Ned tells of Joe Blunt, a character in his novels *Run Silent, Run Deep* and

Dust on the Sea. Ned used the name because his father had a character of that name in several of his novels—a character who had a positive influence on the events of the story—and it is clear in *Run Silent, Run Deep* that Joe Blunt is such a benign character.

In Ned's novel, Joe Blunt is on the staff of the commander of all submarines in the Pacific, and had been a mentor to the novel's protagonist, "Rich" Richardson. As many novelists do, Ned had based the character of Joe Blunt on an actual person and, just as in the novel, that real officer had been Ned's mentor during his early days serving on board submarines.

After *Run Silent, Run Deep* was published, the real officer upon whom the fictional Joe Blunt was based called Ned at his White House office and asked if the character of Joe Blunt was based on him. Not yet wise to the pressures that can be exerted on novelists by people who see themselves in fictional characters, Ned answered in the affirmative. It was Ned's conviction, as he would later note, that from that time forward the real "Joe Blunt" assumed that Ned "owed him" for having used him as a basis for a character.[17]

Later, "Joe Blunt" approached Ned, who was still serving as naval aide to the president, requesting that Ned write an article for the U.S. Naval Institute's *Proceedings* magazine indicating that the excellent war records of submariners (implicitly like "Joe Blunt") ought to be the basis for the kind of officers promoted to rear admiral. In Ned's view, the implication of such an article would be that President Eisenhower had somehow authorized or endorsed the concept, and indirectly the specific promotion of "Joe Blunt." Ned replied that while he wholeheartedly supported the concept of promoting submarine officers with outstanding war records, he could in no way use his position in the White House to try to influence a promotion board, especially if it implied that the president was behind the endorsement.[18]

Incensed with what he felt was a rebuke, "Joe Blunt" seemed to drop the issue. However, upon being promoted to rear admiral in spite of not getting an implied White House endorsement, he let Ned know that Ned had let him down and that he resented it. Within the relatively small community of high-ranking submarine officers in the 1960s, the real "Joe Blunt" would remain within Ned's chain of command for many years—especially while Ned was in command of *Triton* and later of SubRon 8.

According to Ned's version of events, "Joe Blunt" then proceeded to push men junior to Ned for early promotion. In so doing, "Joe Blunt" did not openly lobby against Ned, but by pushing officers who would be in competition with Ned for one of the coveted rear admiral slots open to submariners, he may have effectively, but indirectly, blocked Ned's promotion.

Outside his family, Ned never mentioned the real name of "Joe Blunt." Even at home the man was usually only referred to as "Joe Blunt." The reason Ned never would reveal the real "Joe Blunt" was that, in the absence of either a direct statement from "Joe Blunt," in front of witnesses, that he had indeed influenced selection boards, or a statement from a member of one of the selection boards that "Joe Blunt" had influenced their decisions, Ned was left with only his own speculations. Nevertheless, his own love of the Navy and his deep-seated conviction that the Navy was an honorable organization could not allow Ned to accept the fact that less honorable officers would do something unethical to a fellow officer or that the Navy would allow such a thing to happen.[19]

According to Ingrid, Ned did feel he had earned the promotion, and his bitterness over not achieving it was never completely eased. Only the dedication of Beach Hall at the Naval Academy years later seemed to lessen his anguish. Ingrid tried to point out to her husband that most admirals are forgotten by history, but that his writings had created a name that would be remembered by many future generations.[20] "Joe Blunt" will probably remain among the hundreds of officers who served their nation and their Navy in high-ranking positions of authority, but whose careers would never merit consideration by biographers.

As to the identity of "Joe Blunt," the list of suspects is easily compiled. There were only a few officers on the staff of COMSUBPAC (Commander, Submarine Force, Pacific Fleet) during the war who eventually made flag rank and who were still on active duty when Ned came up for promotion. In this case, however, this author has decided to respect Ned's own practice and not speculate on who "Joe Blunt" might have been. As noted before, in the absence of hard evidence, a discussion of possible culprits would only serve to potentially sully the reputations of men who were not involved without any surety of naming the right one, if indeed there was such meddling in the promotion process. In Ned's mind, that did occur. Whether "Joe Blunt" had any direct influence on events is probably unknowable. It is possible that the only revenge "Joe Blunt" was able to take was to convince Ned that somehow he had a hand in blocking the promotion, when in fact he had been unable to influence events. There are those who do offer other rationales for why Ned was denied flag rank, and those possibilities cannot be totally discounted.

Five, in fact, can be readily discerned. Not necessarily in order of probability, the reasons include: too much time in Washington during tours of duty not at sea; lack of a desire to work the "good old boy" system; Ned's harsh criticism of his superiors over the *Trigger II* problems; inherent prejudice in the Navy against officers who theorize and write; and the very nature of the "silent service." Each of these shall be examined in turn.

In looking at Ned's career, some have speculated that he spent too much time in Washington. Rear Adm. Corwin Mendenhall, USN, a classmate and rival of Ned's at the Academy, expressed the opinion that Ned "while not on sea duty spent a great deal of his career in Washington."[21] Ned did remain in the post of naval aide to the president longer than any peacetime naval officer. Additionally, almost all of Ned's other tours of shore duty were within the higher circles of the Navy or the chairman of the Joint Chiefs of Staff's office, when he wasn't in some training program or enrolled at the National War College.

In Ned's defense, it is important to note that he reluctantly accepted the second tour as naval aide to Eisenhower, and did so only at the president's request following Ike's heart attack. (Ned noted in his memoir, *Salt and Steel: Reflections of a Submariner*, that he is the only presidential naval aide who did not make rear admiral.)[22] Additionally, while Ned's assignment as aide to the chief of naval personnel (December 1945 to March 1947) was done by the Bureau of Personnel through its own processes, his later selection as an aide to General Bradley (September 1949 to March 1951) was on the recommendation of his former boss at Naval Personnel— Admiral Denfeld. These were not positions Ned sought, as he was commanding *Trigger II* when he got the call for the White House job, and commanding *Amberjack* when he got the call for the job as Bradley's aide. His detractors would note that in these instances Ned could have declined the appointments, and that his willingness to accept them showed a strong desire to be near the seats of power, something that can cause flags of caution to be raised by some on selection boards. Few know that, just prior to being tabbed for the job with General Bradley, Ned had passed on a job offer from then-Capt. Arleigh Burke in the Op-23 office in the Pentagon.[23] If Ned had an unbridled desire to remain near the seats of power, he would have quickly shed his command at sea for another chance for a desk in the Pentagon. Ingrid is quick to point out that her husband was never happier than when he was at sea in command of a ship. Only reluctantly would he give up command on one of his "beloved ships" and he "never sought" assignments in Washington.[24]

An additional argument contrary to Mendenhall's suggestion of too much time in Washington is that tours in Washington are almost an unwritten requirement for achieving flag rank. The Navy needs to know how an officer will react in its halls of highest power. There is also a need for an up-and-coming officer to get noticed by high-ranking officers in order to have some recognition when promotions are discussed. As should be clear, tours of duty in Washington can be a two-edged sword even if a major downside is having others not tabbed for such duties question the motives of those who are.

Coupled with the "too much time in Washington" factor was what some saw as Ned's role in passing directives from the White House to top Navy brass on behalf of the president. Capt. Slade Cutter, another of the legends of the submarine war against Japan, observed, "I think what hurt Ned was that he ruffled some feathers when he was President Eisenhower's aide. He was right. He did what was right, but he was a Commander and the people he was ruffling were flag officers. Then they sit on the selection board, so what happens? They have a chance to get back, you know. That's human nature."[25] In the type of instances Cutter describes, Ned was performing in the same manner in which he approached every task he undertook: Be the very best by doing your very best. If the president wanted the Navy's top officers to understand some position the president had taken on a budget issue, and Ned was delegated to carry that message to the Navy Department, then Ned did his very best to ensure that the message got through. Unfortunately, the tight purse strings Eisenhower tried to enforce during his years in office were a "major migraine" for the Navy, according to naval historian Michael Isenberg.[26] The impact of the manner in which such messages were delivered, coupled with the unwanted nature of the messages, could have doubled the tendency to "shoot the messenger."

Perhaps the single greatest argument against claims that Ned was overly enamored with Washington was the fact that he was far from the socializer Washington politics demanded. "He was not the type of person who sought to ingratiate himself with his superiors in social settings," notes Ingrid.[27] That fact, however, could also have been a factor—albeit a minor one—in his not being selected for flag rank. While his fellow workers, whether in the White House or the Pentagon, were out playing golf or tennis after work and creating the network of connections the "old boy" system demanded, Ned was devoting most of his spare time to writing. For the most part, Ned was not too happy with the typical cocktail circuit of Washington that took time away from his writing. Moreover, he was also often frustrated in such social settings. Ned admitted that he got indignant in such situations when someone would ask him about his White House work, or about submarines and, when his answers became too lengthy, they would get distracted and move on to talk to another person. The frustration came in part because Ned felt people did not want to listen to the answer once they asked the question. Ingrid tried to tell him that in the context of cocktail party small talk, people do not want detailed answers to inquiries.[28] In his youth, Ned admitted he had difficulty in engaging his peers, especially in what he called "general bantering conversation."[29]

Other observers of Ned's situation at the time of his retirement from active duty have suggested it was the stink Ned raised over the problems with *Trigger II* that came back to bite him when he came up for promotion. Sending official communications that declared *Trigger II* unfit for deployment when the squadron commander had listed the submarine as deployable caused a great deal of trouble. As noted before, Ned stated, "But I should have had the sense to realize that this thing I was saying was a pretty strong thing, and I'd better check with the admiral first, and that's where I wasn't so smart."[30] In a letter to Ingrid written during the time when a promotion board was meeting and he was eligible for early promotion, Ned noted that, "Were it not for Admiral . . . being on the board I'd be a lot more cheerful." (In the letter Ned used only the first letter of the admiral's name, but it has been omitted here.) In this case the admiral referred to had been the squadron commander for *Trigger II* when Ned was raising so much hell. Ned went on to write, "But since he's the submarine member [of the selection board], and presumably knows the qualifications of the submarine officers, they'll expect an accurate and knowledgeable judgment from him."[31] Ned was not surprised when he was not selected for early promotion given the person the Pentagon rumor mill said was on the promotion board. Even so, Ned felt in later years that he had done the right thing when it came to complaining about the problems with *Trigger II*.[32]

Naval historian Michael Isenberg aptly lays out the argument that there was a degree of inherent hostility within the Navy toward those who wrote, especially for the general public: "The successful naval officer should know a bit of everything, be broad in his duties (this was part of the in-house prejudice against Rickover), and above all, live the life of the sea. Most senior officers felt certain contempt toward those who wandered off into other, proscribed areas—such as writing or theorizing. Alfred Thayer Mahan suffered from this prejudice all his professional life, and Ned Beach, a successful author even before he skippered *Triton* around the world, never made Flag Plot."[33]

Coupled with the perception that writing was somehow outside the realm of what effective naval officers ought to be doing was the belief that the time it took to write was perhaps a distraction from the regular duties of an officer. Ned faced some of this criticism, and it forced him to eliminate scheduled interviews and appearances connected with the publication of *Run Silent, Run Deep*. There were questions raised at the time about officers earning money for writing that was done while on active duty. (Many who held this opinion viewed active duty as more than a nine-to-five job.) There is a further possibility that a successful writer can be subject to the jealousy of those not so gifted.

Another element that could have played into the denial of a promotion was the mystique of submarines. Especially during World War II, when the submarine arm of the Navy had earned the moniker "the silent service," the ethos of the submariner was to find satisfaction for jobs well done from within the submarine community itself since outside publicity was generally denied for security reasons. While the vast majority of enlisted men and junior officers of the submarine service celebrated the writings of Ned about the war, there may have been a certain feeling of betrayal on the part of some who saw Ned's work as a demystification of what had been accomplished during the war. In breaking the wall of silence, which no longer bore an official prohibition for security reasons, Ned may have been proclaiming the heroism of his fellow submariners, but he brought a certain degree of fame to himself as author, too.

The general perception within the submarine force that Ned was the most visible submariner in the Navy by the late 1950s, thus overshadowing officers who had legitimate claims to even more distinguished war records, could also have been a source of some jealousy and dislike. It is ironic that the very reason Rickover may have worked with Ned to acquire the command of *Triton*—Ned's stature with the public—could have been a factor against Ned when it came to promotion.

Even a cursory review of American naval history will reveal that few naval officers have ever achieved long-term public fame. There are indeed few American naval heroes that the general public can readily name. John Paul Jones, George Dewey, Stephen Decatur, "Bull" Halsey, Arleigh Burke, and perhaps Chester Nimitz might be called to mind, but, in general, naval officers, either by design or accident, have avoided the type of public acclaim accorded other military leaders. There has never been a naval officer who earned fame in battle and then went on to the presidency, while American history is replete with generals who have turned military success, or a perception of success, into political capital. The reasons for this are varied and complicated, but there nonetheless seems to reside within the generally accepted paradigm for career naval officers a strong belief that seeking public attention is to be avoided. In the end, if Ned became a victim of that unwritten code after he did more than anyone else to highlight the heroism of the submariners who so devastated the enemy during World War II, it would be a sad payback.

[5]

Having been passed over a second time, Ned decided to apply for retirement from active duty. Had he known of the comments written in his fitness reports by officers like Masterton, Ned might have considered waiting for the late selection board to meet. While it is impossible to say how much weight prior promotion boards had given to Ned's fitness reports, or whether comments by officers like Masterton might sway a late selection board, it seems clear from the fitness reports at least that there were some high-ranking officers pushing his cause. His wife and family urged him to hang on for the possibility of that late selection, but his pride could not suffer the humiliation that would have followed a third rejection. Better to walk away of his own volition than to be seen as having been forced out.

In December 1966, after twenty-seven years and six months of active duty in the only job he had ever wanted, Ned retired from the Navy. During his career, Ned had been awarded the Navy Cross; the Silver Star Medal with Gold Star (in lieu of a second Silver Star); the Legion of Merit (presented by the president of the United States); the Bronze Star Medal with Gold Star and Combat "V"; the Commendation Ribbon with Star and Combat "V"; the Ribbons for three Presidential Unit Citations and one Navy Unit Citation; the American Defense Service Medal; Atlantic Fleet Clasp; the Asiatic-Pacific Campaign Medal with three engagement stars; the American Campaign Medal; the World War II Victory Medal; and the National Defense Service Medal. He left with an enviable record, but it was a bittersweet passage.

When he left the Academy, he had dreamed of commanding a battleship like his father, and there was deeply imbedded in him a desire to achieve the flag rank his father had been denied. The battleship command never came, as battleships had been retired from the fleet by the 1960s. *Triton* was, however, a crowning achievement for commands at sea, and with *Triton* he had also accomplished something no one else had—the submerged circumnavigation of the world.

Rear Adm. Fred G. Bennett, USN, Ned's last boss at General Planning and Programming, wrote on Ned's final fitness report, "Captain Ned was an inspiration to all with whom he associated and it is with the deepest regret that this truly outstanding officer is retired from active duty."[34]

The failure to earn the right to fly his own flag as an admiral cast a shadow over the end of an otherwise stellar career. Even with that burden, Ned did not look to retirement from active duty as the end of his useful life. He was forty-eight years old and determined to make further contributions to his nation and humanity. Others would be left to puzzle the reasons the Navy had passed him over, and those reasons would from time to time haunt his thoughts. However, as he looked to the future Ned's own nature as a hard worker and optimist could not be repressed.

Part IX: 1966–2002

When Ned ended his active duty career, he was looking forward to having more time to write. While his literary output had been somewhat diminished after *Run Silent, Run Deep* was published, he had not stopped writing completely. Reviews and a few nonfiction articles still occasionally flowed from his typewriter, and with the completion of *Triton*'s voyage, he produced a book on the trip along with several magazine articles. One reason for the decline in pages of text had been the intense program of study at nuclear reactor school, which was followed by the prep for the submerged circumnavigation. Another factor, however, that intruded on his productivity was the criticism that had been leveled at him when *Run Silent, Run Deep* appeared. There were those both within and outside the Navy who publicly and privately raised the issue of a full-time officer writing for commercial pay.

Feeling the urge to get back to writing, Ned accepted a position teaching at the Naval War College, becoming the Stephen B. Luce Chair of Naval Science at the Navy's postgraduate school. (Stephen B. Luce [1827–1917] founded the Naval War College in 1884 to provide officers with advanced training in strategic thinking, policy analysis, tactics, and logistics.) It was Ned's hope that, in accepting the post, he would carry a light enough teaching load that he could devote time to his writing. That hope proved to be a false one. In addition to teaching, his job description included editing the *Naval War College Review* and shepherding the writings of others through the publication process. Finally realizing that his writing time would forever be compromised by the demands of teaching and editing, Ned left the Naval War College in 1969, after only two years on the faculty.

Just as Ned retired from active duty, his third nonfiction work was published, *The Wreck of the* Memphis. This work was written while Ned was prepping the CNO and the secretary of the Navy for congressional budget and oversight hearings. USS *Memphis* (ACR-10) was a heavy cruiser that

Ned's father was commanding on 29 August 1916 when it was destroyed by a tidal wave while at anchor in the harbor of Santo Domingo, Dominican Republic. Forty-three of the crew were killed and another two hundred were injured. *Memphis* was a total loss. A Navy court-martial—believing as most of the scientific community did at the time that tidal waves were a by-product of weather conditions and, therefore, predictable—convicted Ned's father of not having sufficient steam ready in the ship's engines to get under way on "short notice."

Ned always felt his father had been dealt a grave injustice by the Navy, particularly because the number of boilers the elder Beach kept lit at all times was the result of orders from his squadron commander. Those orders were not in writing and the admiral in question did not volunteer to testify, while Ned's father refused to have him subpoenaed because the elder Beach believed that, as a matter of honor, the admiral should appear of his own volition.

The court-martial sentenced Ned's father to having his name moved back twenty places on the Navy's seniority list, a relatively light sentence, but the fact that he was found guilty at all meant he would probably never be promoted. In reviewing the findings of the court, then-secretary of the Navy Josephus Daniels reduced the sentence to moving back five places on the seniority list, but let the conviction stand. Later, Daniels vacated the conviction. Ned's book *The Wreck of the* Memphis is a re-arguing of his father's case.

Also in 1966, Ned joined with John V. Noel Jr. to produce the second edition of *The Naval Terms Dictionary*. That standard reference work would continue under their dual editorship for the third (1971), fourth (1978), and fifth (1988) editions.

Ned's return to writing fiction coincided with his leaving the Naval War College and assuming duties as secretary and staff director of the SRPC (Senate Republican Policy Committee) in 1969. By this time, Ned and his family had settled into a spacious home in Georgetown and he found more and more time to write. In 1972, Henry Holt and Company published *Dust on the Sea*, a sequel to *Run Silent, Run Deep*. Following the same characters as *Run Silent, Run Deep*, this novel traces the exploits of Rich Richardson's submarine war against the Japanese while turning the benign Joe Blunt from the earlier novel into a raving coward and incompetent squadron commander. Whether Ned intended to exact a little revenge on the man upon whom the character was based is uncertain, especially considering that, at the end of the novel, it is revealed that Joe Blunt's actions are the result of a brain tumor that also leads to his death.

Run Silent, Run Deep and *Dust on the Sea* can be seen as two parts of a single book in that they share two halves of the same theme—the morality and motivations "of men forced by tremendous, terrible circumstance to bear the enormous responsibilities inherent in war." *Dust on the Sea* attempts to answer the question that *Run Silent, Run Deep* asks the reader to ponder: What is the warrior's moral obligation in war?[1] Ned noted with the publication of *Dust on the Sea* that the adrenaline that motivates men in combat cannot be easily turned off once the war is over. For his part, Ned said the outlet for his adrenaline was found when "I began to write about it."[2]

[2]

One of the lesser known aspects of Ned's life was the eight years he spent as secretary and staff director for the SRPC. Senator Everett McKinley Dirksen (R-IL), the minority leader in the Senate, died on 7 September 1969 due to heart failure following surgery to remove a cancerous lung.[3] His unexpected passing led to a reshuffling of leadership roles among Republicans in the Senate, boosting Senator Gordon Allott (R-CO) to the number three position in Republican leadership—a position that included chairmanship of the SRPC. Allott wanted a Republican academic for the position of secretary and staff director to ensure that Republican senators could be provided with in-depth research on current issues being debated. The primary function of the SRPC was to do the research for senators on bills and resolutions that came before the Senate.

One of the results of Allott's redefining the role of the SRPC was that there was at least one other candidate for the position besides Ned—a young university professor by the name of George F. Will.[4] When Ned was selected for the staff director's job in September 1969, Will was then offered a position as one of the professional staff members at SRPC. Will accepted the offer, holding the position about six months before being moved into the speechwriting post on Senator Allott's personal staff.[5] Dr. Will would later note that, at the time, Ned was "just the right man to lead the Republican Policy Committee."[6]

The makeup of the Republicans in the U.S. Senate in 1969 was remarkably diverse by today's standards. The spread of political ideologies from liberal to conservative was very broad, with senators like Edward W. Brooke of Massachusetts and Jacob K. Javits of New York typical of the liberal wing of the party, while senators like Barry Goldwater of Arizona and John Tower of Texas were on the opposite end of the ideological spectrum—and all still remained under the umbrella of the Republican Party. As a result, the position of secretary and staff director of the SRPC required an ability to please a very diverse set of views. The reputation Ned had earned while serving as the Navy's point man for preparing the CNO and secretary of the Navy for congressional testimony was a significant factor in his selection for the SRPC post.

According to Donald deKieffer, who was a member of the SRPC professional staff during much of Ned's tenure as staff director, Ned was the ideal person for the position. Mollifying the egos of such a broad spectrum of senators was no easy task. While SRPC chair Allott was a "mountain state conservative," he saw the role of the SRPC as one of pushing only those political issues on which consensus could be reached among Senate Republicans.[7] The SRPC was also charged with tracking all legislation in the Senate. This included keeping voting records on each item, from committees to the floor of the Senate, as well as providing background studies. Coordination of legislation with the Republicans in the House of Representatives also fell within the duties assigned to the SRPC.

A part of Ned's job was to keep his boss—Senator Allott—happy, who in turn had to keep the rest of the Republican senators happy. Walking that tightrope also required not letting the Nixon White House co-opt the SRPC for its own uses. Having worked in the White House, Ned was not awed by a phone call from someone in the West Wing, which helped the SRPC staff remain outside policy disputes between the Nixon administration and Republicans in the Senate.

The position of staff director also provided Ned with a good number of perks. Invitations to all sorts of diplomatic, governmental, and political functions readily flowed to his desk. Ned's personal preferences to write or be with his family in the evenings led him to more than willingly defer such perks to his staff. He would even solicit an invitation to some event if a staffer wanted to attend. "Anyone want to attend the reception at the British embassy in honor of the Queen's birthday? Here's an invitation," he was known to have said.[8]

Wanting to impress his fiancée, deKieffer asked Ned for tickets to an inaugural ball in 1969. Ned soon produced a packet of tickets and invitations to all the events of the first Nixon inauguration. Being a part-time student at Georgetown University Law School at the time, as well as working on the SRPC staff, deKieffer's financial means did not permit him to attend all the events, but he did manage to duly impress the future Mrs. deKieffer.[9]

Working relationships with the staffers of parallel Democratic committees were seldom called for, but on occasion they were needed. The one topic on which some staffers on both sides of the aisle collaborated as a running joke was the sponsorship of proposed legislation to halt or limit the pirating of music by Asian record companies. Repeated efforts were made to get Louisiana's Senator Russell B. Long, Hawaii's Senator Hiram L. Fong, and Virginia's Senator William Spong to co-sponsor such legislation just so it could be labeled the "Long-Fong-Spong Hong Kong Song Bill." Sensibly, all three senators kept declining requests to have their names attached to such a bill.

Assignments made by Ned sometimes carried heavy responsibilities. In 1969, El Salvador and Honduras initiated military actions against each other on the pretext of mistreatment of each other's citizens at World Cup Soccer preliminary matches. In reality, what became known as the "Soccer War" was about economic problems, overcrowding, illegal immigration, and political unrest. The Nixon administration issued a stern warning to all employees of the federal government to remain absolutely neutral, and for all foreign nations, especially the Soviets, to also remain outside the conflict.

With both nations seeking to have their cases heard by someone in the U.S. government, the word came down that a staffer from the SRPC would have to be the official "ears" of the Nixon administration. Realizing that, by handing the assignment to the SRPC, the White House was signaling to the two governments just how disdainful it was of the events, Ned in turn assigned the task to his most junior staffer—deKieffer. This was the political equivalent of a very junior Ensign Beach having been sent to inform the commanding officer of a British cruiser that had entered the port at Key West during World War II that he was violating neutrality laws.

After being picked up by limo by first one embassy and then the other, deKieffer was treated to a lavish dinner laid on at each embassy while he was also fed the hosting country's views of the conflict. Under strict orders to express no opinions whatsoever and to divulge nothing he heard in the briefings, deKieffer found himself sitting like the sphinx while he was wined and dined. Ned's judgment on which staffer could handle the situation proved correct as the unspoken message of deKieffer's stoic silence effectively conveyed the policy of the United States.

Growing pressure from the Organization of American States and the deep freeze under which the United States had placed the conflict combined to bring about a halt in the shooting after four days. It would take another ten years for the two nations to formally settle their differences, but the conflict was kept from spreading into something that might have pulled in the superpowers.

Ned's service as staff director of the SRPC came to an end in the same manner in which it started. A reshuffling of the Republican leadership in the Senate brought John Tower (R-TX) into the number three slot of

Republican leadership. Tower, along with the other new leadership of the Republicans in the Senate, was determined to force ideological purity on fellow Republicans, so he sought a staff for the SRPC that would help bend less conservative Republican senators to his views.

At age fifty-nine, Ned was not too concerned about his own dismissal, but his sense of honor was highly offended when he discovered that the rest of the staff, save one female secretary (a "good friend" of Tower), was also being dismissed, but no one with the incoming regime had bothered to inform the old staff. It fell to Ned to tell his staff that they, too, were going—and on very short notice—just before Christmas in 1976. His last weeks at the SRPC were spent frantically helping his staff find jobs in other offices on Capitol Hill.

[3]

While he was spending his days on Capitol Hill, in the evenings Ned was busy at home writing—always writing. The third novel in what could be called the Rich Richardson series, *Cold is the Sea*, was published by Henry Holt in 1978. This novel finds the protagonist now a nuclear-powered submarine squadron commander who is facing espionage and an aggressive Soviet plot to occupy parts of the Arctic icecap. Much of the novel is the stuff of the techno-thriller later popularized by Tom Clancy and others.

Interestingly, this was not Ned's first venture into that ilk of fiction. An August 1950 issue of *Esquire* magazine carried a short story titled "Mission in 1956," by one Beachley Edwards, a nom de plume for Ned. Set on board a nuclear-powered submarine, and written years before the United States began to build such ships, it tells the tale of how a futuristic American submarine had to find and sink a Soviet nuclear-powered submarine before it could approach the coast of the United States and launch missiles armed with atomic warheads. "Only this green shakedown crew stood between the U.S. and its terrible enemy," reads one of the sub-headings for the story.[10]

In a minor act of prescience, the fictional nuclear-powered submarine in the story is named *Nautilus*, Ned having chosen the name for his story several years before the Navy began construction of its first nuclear-powered submarine, which happened to carry the same name.[11] A second element of the story that would later suggest Ned had some mystic power to see the future is that the crew of the fictional submarine is on a shakedown cruise when it is informed of its mission, something the crew of *Triton* would experience almost ten years later. While Ned's speculation on some of the technical aspects of future nuclear-powered submarines did not match their eventual reality, he did rightly predict the development of missiles capable of being launched from submerged submarines, and the difficulty the United States would face in guarding against such surprise attacks.

[4]

For the four years of the Carter administration, Ned spent much of his time writing, but when Ronald Reagan entered the White House in January 1981, the political winds of change that brought Reagan into office also brought Jeremiah A. Denton into the U.S. Senate. A retired naval officer, Naval Academy Class of 1947, Denton had been a prisoner of war in North Vietnam for over seven years. He was promoted to rear admiral after his release from captivity and he retired to his hometown of Mobile, Alabama. Then he decided to enter politics, becoming the first Republican ever elected by popular vote to the U.S. Senate from Alabama.

A novice in the world of Washington politics, Denton sought an experienced hand to run his D.C. office, turning to Ned to serve as his "administrative assistant"—the highest-ranking official in a senatorial office (next to the Senator, of course). At age sixty-two, a still fit and trim Ned, but now sporting white hair, once more entered the fray of Washington politics. What Ned brought to the job was an insider's knowledge of the workings of the Senate.

Ned had to manage a staff of twenty-five as they struggled to answer three to four thousand letters a week, 250 to four hundred phone calls per day, and sometimes as many as seventy-five visitors to the office per day. The Reagan Revolution was on, and the conservatives had another new champion in Denton, who was besieged with requests and demands on his time from a much wider audience than his Alabama constituency. In demand as a speaker all around the country, Denton soon came under fire in his home state because he seldom had time to visit there. Denton's prestige generated national press coverage, resulting in Alabamians knowing that he was playing tennis in Arizona but that letters and calls from home were going unanswered.[12]

Ned served as Denton's administrative assistant from December 1980 to April 1981, and it was a tough time for both. Several of the people who had worked to get Denton elected felt they were cheated when it came to passing out the jobs in Washington. As a result, an internecine war broke out between the staffs in the Alabama and D.C. offices. Caught in the middle, Ned seemed powerless to stop it. Letters, calls, and messages transferred from the Alabama offices to the D.C. office were "lost." Voters were angered by lost letters, scheduling foul-ups, and a seeming overall lack of attention from Denton, with the blame always being passed on to the D.C. office and Ned.

In the midst of all the turmoil, stress, and whirlwind activities of a new senator's office, Ned may have paused now and then to ponder what his life might have been like had his application for the post of U.S. Ambassador to Sweden been treated favorably by the Reagan administration. Senator Howard Baker (R-TN) had written a letter of endorsement, which he forwarded to the Reagan-Bush transition team in December 1980 along with Ned's application.[13] Curiously, Ingrid never knew of the application and the Baker endorsement until research for this book uncovered it. Perhaps never a realistic dream on Ned's part, the ambassadorial post in the land of Ingrid's ancestors could have been an interesting and challenging job, but it never came to pass.

The turmoil in the senator's office was only briefly reprieved when Ned was notified that he was to receive the prestigious Alfred Thayer Mahan Award for Literary Achievement from the Navy League of the United States. He would win the award again in 2000, being the first writer to be twice honored. In 1987, Ned would be further honored with the Roosevelt Naval History Prize. All three awards serve as testimony to his skills as a writer, but the turmoil he faced each day in Denton's office was not mitigated.

When Denton announced Ned's departure from his staff, he sent a letter to Ned in which he noted, "We all agree that we could solve most of our problems if I were able to find an Administrative Assistant fully grounded in the ways of Capitol Hill, highly proficient as a manager and head of a Senatorial staff, who not only speaks fluent Alabama, but is widely known and respected throughout the State. Believe me, I would love to have such a person."[14] Ned fulfilled the first parts of Denton's ideal candidate, but he was compromised by his lack of respect from Denton's Alabama constituency.

In accepting the post to help out an old Navy friend, Ned had stepped into the middle of Alabama politics, about which he knew nothing. He also had to create a staff where none had existed before. Unlike his experience with the SRPC, Ned did not inherit a veteran staff when it came to Denton's office. The staff he did put together had to be made to run efficiently in spite of internal tensions he could not control. With a great deal of grace and dignity, he stepped aside, leaving those in Alabama who saw him as the symbol of their discontent to cheer his departure. Denton, however, never blamed Ned, stating, "By the time he departed my office, I felt comfortable and confident. . . . He did a great job and I had full confidence in him."[15]

[5]

As Ned left the last formal job he would ever hold, his thoughts had already turned back to a much heavier schedule of writing. There were still stories to be told and history to be dissected. A timely offer from the Naval Institute—an organization his father had once served as secretary—to prepare the text of a coffee-table book on the Navy (*Keepers of the Sea*) came along at this time and Ned seized the opportunity as a way to step down with some dignity from his position in Denton's office.[16]

Others of Ned's age might have sought the tranquil life of retirement, but the habits of a lifetime developed through the discipline of a writer who worked at his art with the same passion he had brought to all ventures would not allow him to retire to a life of quiet, and he was soon to take up a crusade that would become the focus of the last two decades of his life.

[6]

As a writer, Ned's practice of the physical act of writing evolved as technology changed during his lifetime. Much of his early work, including his novel *Run Silent, Run Deep*, was laid down in longhand before it was typed. The World War II submarine stories he turned into articles for *Blue Book* and other publications were also rendered in their initial form in longhand. In an interview with *All Hands* in 1999, Beach explained how he wrote *Run Silent, Run Deep* using a clipboard and seated on the couch in his living room in the evenings, aiming to write two pages of text per night.[17]

An examination of the manuscripts for his early works reveals that once a typewritten page was produced little was changed in the text, with the exception of corrections of spelling, grammar, and typographical errors. Subsequent works, where the early drafts were produced on a typewriter, show extensive revision of the text from one draft to the next. By the early 1960s, as the cash advances from publishers grew, he was able to utilize tape-recorded dictation of some works, with a typist employed to produce the early drafts.[18] When Ned acquired a word processor, hard copies of drafts began to disappear from his files, making it difficult to analyze the evolution of his thinking.

Ingrid states that her husband was frequently frustrated with word processors because the screen did not readily display what he had already written farther up the page. This caused Ned to repeat himself at times, a fact he found annoying. For virtually all his work, Ingrid was his first editor, as well as the first set of eyes to read any and all subsequent drafts. This working arrangement provided a reliable sounding board. Ideas and structure for entire projects, plus for individual chapters, were discussed between the two at length, resulting in her editorial suggestions going to issues of both grammar and style and, more important, to the broader issues of theme and the stream of the narrative.

When it came to revisions, Ned constantly reworked his texts. In a letter to a sixteen-year-old boy who had sought Ned's assistance by sending him the draft of a submarine novel, Ned responded, "Even with plenty of practice, it *never* comes out right the first time [emphasis in the original]."[19] He went on to offer advice to the would-be author: "Writing *is* indeed eighty percent work, but the other twenty percent is knowing something about your subject."[20]

While his early writing career saw Ned sitting in his living room in the evenings, clipboard on his lap, in later years the family moved to homes with space for an office/library that afforded a quieter environment. Once the family moved into the much roomier house in Georgetown that was to be their home the last forty years of his life, an even more reclusive writing enclave was possible. Both the first and second floors of the three-story home have rooms used as libraries, but Ned did his writing in a basement-level room that seems to have been created to match the tight quarters of a submarine. Walls lined with shelves crammed full of books on naval topics, models and paintings of ships filling the higher wall spaces, and a homemade desktop supported by file cabinets all add to the feeling of being wrapped in a cocoon of naval history. The only outside light into the space is provided through two ship's brass portholes that have been installed where a couple of basement windows originally stood. The portholes were a gift from longtime friend Gary Steinhaus.

Ingrid was always amazed at her husband's powers of concentration. He could work for hours on end on any project requiring his attention. Whether writing, editing, or installing new flooring, Ned was capable of a continuous concentrated effort that far exceeded the stamina of anyone else around him.[21] Even with his ability to focus on his work, the normal routine of a household, especially with children, could still intrude on writing time. As a result, Ned did seek times and places where he was guaranteed periods free of intrusions.

For three of his books—*The Wreck of the* Memphis, *Cold is the Sea*, and *The United States Navy: 200 Years*—Ned was awarded admittance to Yaddo, an exclusive retreat for artists, writers, and musicians in Saratoga Springs, New York. In 1965, again in 1977, and finally in 1993, Ned was provided room, board, and work space on Yaddo's extensive campus for work periods that lasted several weeks for each visit. With visitors and family barred from the campus, the atmosphere allowed him to concentrate solely on the book at hand, as well as enjoy the opportunity to share ideas with fellow writers and artists.

On a few other occasions, friends offered Ned invitations to visit their homes, with the proviso that he would be allowed uninterrupted writing time. Mary and Vance Gordon twice hosted Ned in their Colorado home under such conditions while he was working on *The United States Navy: 200 Years.*[22] The Beaches and Gordons had become good friends in 1944 when both young couples were temporarily located near the Portsmouth Navy Yard. Vance and Ned were assigned to submarines under construction, and their time together grew into a lifelong friendship.

[7]

For some time, Ned had toyed with the idea of writing a general history of the U.S. Navy. As early as 1974, he approached the Naval Institute Press with the idea.[23] Eventually, Henry Holt accepted his conception for the book and Ned began researching in earnest. Published in 1986, *The United States Navy: 200 Years* is 544 pages of text, including a bibliography and appendix, as well as photos and reproduced images of famous people, events, and ships from the Navy's past.

In approaching the work, the reader is first advised that, "This book is not a history but a progress."[24] Operating on the thesis that World War II, especially the year 1942, was the Armageddon at sea, "the great test for which our navy had been created," Ned's book sets off to delineate how the history of the U.S. Navy, along with its traditions, customs, and esprit de corps, led to triumph in 1945.[25] Curiously, the book deals little with World War II itself, but concentrates on the events and people who shaped the U.S. Navy into a force that was able to meet the demands of a global war for national survival.

In his telling of the story, Ned sees an unbroken heritage from the days of Lambert Wickes and John Paul Jones in the Revolutionary War, to Stephen Decatur during the War of 1812, thence on to David Glasgow Farragut during the Civil War, and then the careers of the men who shaped the Naval Academy—like George Bancroft and Franklin Buchanan. Although *The United States Navy: 200 Years* is meticulously researched, its focus is more on the contributions of the men who established the traditions and training programs of the Navy than it is on operational details.

The modern, traditional, general histories of the U.S. Navy—works like Kenneth J. Hagan's *This People's Navy: The Making of American Sea Power*, or Stephen Howarth's *To Shining Sea: A History of the United States Navy 1775–1991*—focus on details of various operations over time and on the development of the theoretical foundations of American naval strategy. While he never spoke of it in any formal setting, Ned was aware he had no academic credentials as a professional historian. He was, however, a career officer who possessed a strong sense of history.

The greatest value of Ned's book is its insights into his ideas of leadership gained from his long career of active duty—in times of war and peace. The "traditions" of the Navy, as Ned saw them, that enabled the United States to emerge victorious from the two-ocean conflict that was World War II were the ones handed down from John Paul Jones directly to George Street III. The courage and leadership skills required for an officer like Isaac Hull to lay his ship—USS *Constitution*—alongside the British frigate HMS *Guerriere* in 1812 and battle it out, were the same as those required of the submariner skippers during the war with Japan—when men like Roy S. Benson, Dusty Dornin, Slade Cutter, and Mike Rindskopf fearlessly pushed their fragile submarines into the enemy's home waters to deal death blows to imperial ambitions.

In Ned's view, it was the core of leaders, both commissioned and noncommissioned, who were there to check the advance of the rampaging enemy in 1942, and who then provided the foundation on which to train the personnel of the hugely expanded Navy that eventually won the war. Not just commanders of individual ships—in Ned's view—but task force and unit commanders like Arleigh Burke and Marc Mitscher of World War II shared a heritage with naval officers like George Dewey.

[8]

At the request of Senator Strom Thurmond (R-SC), a meeting was convened on 27 April 1995 in Washington, D.C., to discuss the status of the long-deceased Rear Adm. Husband E. Kimmel, USN. Thurmond was chair of the Senate Armed Services Committee at the time, and the meeting was held in his committee's meeting room. Among those attending the meeting were Deputy Secretary of Defense John Deutch, and Secretary of the Navy John Dalton, as well as Ned. The meeting was the product of a long-running effort to bring political pressure to bear on the Navy Department and the Department of Defense regarding a posthumous restoration of rank to Husband Kimmel. (For a full account of the events leading up to and following this meeting, see Fred Broach and Daniel Martinze, *Kimmel, Short, and Pearl Harbor: The Final Report Revealed*).

Rear Admiral Kimmel had been ordered to command of the U.S. Pacific Fleet in 1941, a position that required an officer with the rank of full admiral. As was customary in such circumstances, he was granted a temporary promotion. After the Japanese attack on Pearl Harbor, Kimmel was relieved of command, reverted to his permanent rank, and eventually forced to retire from active duty. Subsequent action by Congress in 1947 allowed all flag and general officers who had received similar temporary promotions to higher rank during the war to retire from active duty at the higher rank as an acknowledgement of their achievements while on active duty during the war. Such promotions are sometimes referred to as "tombstone promotions" since they only impact how the individual is addressed. Kimmel and his U.S. Army counterpart, Brig. Gen. Walter C. Short, were punitively excluded from that privilege. Feeling Kimmel had been unfairly blamed for the disaster that befell the Navy at Pearl Harbor, the Kimmel family, aided by several historians and friends, have been seeking for many years to have the rank of admiral restored posthumously as a symbolic gesture to correct what they see as an injustice.

For ten years prior to the meeting in the Senate Armed Forces Committee room, Ned had been actively working to gain what he had come to view as a restoration of honor on the part of the Navy. Historian Paul Stillwell, in summing up Ned's emotional involvement in the Kimmel case, noted, "Ned Beach lives by a high sense of honor. He feels that an injustice was committed against Kimmel and that the Navy has dishonored itself by how it allowed Kimmel to be treated."[26]

In a series of videotaped interviews conducted with Ned by his son Edward, the same theme was expounded. Pointing out that at the Naval Academy, midshipmen training drums into their heads that they should never lie, cheat, or steal, Ned then spoke of the "betrayal" to the midshipman's code of honor that occurs when the government itself lies or cheats.[27] "The idea of personal honor is very important and should not be put aside," Ned said in discussing the Kimmel case.[28]

For the most part, Ned's advocacy for the Kimmel case came from his perception that officers in the Navy in positions higher than Kimmel's bore much of the blame for the disaster at Pearl Harbor, and that honor demanded they also should have shouldered a proportionate part of the blame. Understanding that wartime circumstances mitigated against punishing officers whose skills were needed in the war effort, Ned nevertheless contended that once the war was over, remedial action ought to have been initiated.

Controversy over the Pearl Harbor attack, especially theories of conspiracies, began to burst into flame even before the smoldering ruins of the Pacific fleet had turned back to cold steel. Ned sometimes gave lip service to such theories, but he never accepted them to a full extent. He preferred to argue that information gleaned from the Magic code-breaking program had been withheld from Kimmel. The state of ignorance in which Kimmel was forced to operate, in Ned's view, was the product of bureaucratic turf wars and interservice rivalry, not a covert conspiracy to allow the attack to go on undeterred. That being the case, Ned asserted, the "blame" for the disaster at Pearl Harbor should be shifted to all the officers whose conduct led to the loss of lives, ships, planes, and equipment.

In support of his assertions that the U.S. government should and could act to redress the wrong done to Kimmel, Ned pointed to several precedents where previous "wrongs" in history had been righted. In 1952, Congress directed the president to correct the record of William Cox, an officer on board USS *Chesapeake*, when it was preemptively attacked by HMS *Leopard* in 1807. Cox was court-martialed for his actions during the incident and found guilty in an atmosphere where the general public demanded a scapegoat.[29] President Eisenhower corrected the historical record as he came into office by officially issuing Cox a commission as a third lieutenant in the U.S. Navy.

Ned saw two examples from World War II where mistakes were later redressed. The payment of reparations to the Japanese-Americans for their internment during the war was one. The other was the case of Cdr. Joseph John Rochefort, USN, who was head of the Naval Intelligence Unit at Pearl Harbor. Against the wishes of his superiors in Washington, Rochefort shared his intelligence assessments with Adm. Chester Nimitz in May 1942, providing Nimitz with the information that led to the spectacular American victory in the Battle of Midway. Ned wrote: "To Commander Joe Rochefort must forever go the acclaim for having made more difference, at a more important time, than any other naval officer in history."[30] Because his actions were contrary to his chain of command—Rochefort was not directly under Nimitz' command—and in spite of the victory, Rochefort's efforts were ignored by his superiors, and he was transferred to meaningless desk jobs for the duration of the war. That wrong was redressed when President Ronald Reagan awarded Rochefort the Distinguished Service Medal posthumously in 1986.

Believing that the time was approaching when the political winds would allow for the Kimmel case to be rectified, Ned and others pushed their arguments on all who might bring about some reconsideration of the case. This effort was intensified in 1990 as the fiftieth anniversary of the Pearl Harbor attack loomed on the horizon, supporters of the Kimmel case seeing the anniversary as a prime opportunity to correct a past injustice. When then-Secretary of Defense Dick Cheney announced in 1991 that he would not recommend a change in Kimmel's status, pressure was brought to bear directly on President George H. W. Bush. In early December 1991, just days before the fiftieth anniversary, President Bush announced that he would not support a posthumous promotion for Kimmel.

In September 1991, at the Tenth Naval History Symposium at the Naval Academy, Ned served as commentator for a panel of presenters of scholarly papers on Pearl Harbor and its aftermath. In his remarks, Ned called upon the gathered naval and military historians to sign a petition that requested a re-examination of the Kimmel case. The plea resulted in very few signatures affixed to the petition as historians are divided over the general concept of using the political process to correct what some see as errors committed in the past.

Subsequent efforts to win congressional endorsement for the Kimmel case met with mixed results, as the Department of the Navy and the Department of Defense were unwilling to change their assessments of the case. At the same time Ned was serving on the Naval History Advisory Committee for the secretary of the Navy, he tried to induce that committee to push then-secretary of the Navy John H. Dalton on the Kimmel issue.[31] When that avenue dead-ended, the Kimmel family and its political allies began a letter-writing campaign in still another direct appeal to the president. On 1 December 1994, President Bill Clinton notified the Kimmel family that he would not act on the issue.[32]

In a further effort to garner public and political support for the Kimmel case, Ned wrote *Scapegoats: A Defense of Kimmel and Short at Pearl Harbor*, which was published by the Naval Institute Press in 1995. At a meeting of scholars who supported the reopening of the Kimmel case, the *Washington Post* reported that Ned announced the forthcoming publication of the book with the caveat that it would be "an 'emotional rather than a factual' rearguing of the Kimmel case."[33] That sentiment was echoed in the opening chapter of the book, where Ned wrote:

> This is, therefore, not the usual book about history. It lacks the fundamental virtue of chronology, since it is entirely focused on a single point in time. The author has not discovered new material. All of the material is already there, available to overflowing, researched and compiled by hundreds of others. While we may still seek a "smoking gun," to apply a modern term that did not exist then, there are few primary sources cited in this book. Where there is need to make reference, the reader will note that in almost every case the reference is to some other research, someone else's work, a committee report, some book or paper written by someone else. What *is* new is an effort to redirect the deluge of information and show how simple justice to the memories of our long-gone and truly heroic victims of Pearl Harbor—all 2,403 of them, in all services—requires that the stain of official blame be cleansed. The honor of the United States has needed this for years."[34]

In examining the effort—the physical, the mental, and the emotional—that Ned put into the Kimmel case, one quickly begins to see some parallels between the Kimmel case and that of Ned's father. In a 1995 interview Ned admitted that when he began working on the Kimmel case he was not conscious of those connections, but that later, as he thought about the parallels in the situation, he began to see more and more of them. Kimmel and the elder Beach both were accused of wrongs that were partially the results of actions by officers in positions over them. While the senior Beach was convicted in a court-martial (the conviction eventually being vacated), Kimmel was convicted in the court of public opinion, especially with the publication of the Roberts Commission Report in the months just after the attack. There seems little doubt that the Roberts Commission Report was intended to manipulate public opinion at a time when the Roosevelt administration was trying to unite the nation in preparation for wars against both Japan and Germany.[35] Both Kimmel and the elder Beach were defended by civilian lawyers who understood neither the military system of command nor the parameters of the military justice system, facts that seem to have hurt their cases.

An important distinction needs to be made regarding the case of Beach Sr., and the loss of *Memphis*. While his conviction was eventually vacated, there was a pall over the rest of his career, and the correction of his service record came too late. Given his professional standing and the path of his career up to the loss of *Memphis,* it is not difficult to surmise that he would have attained flag rank, probably before the end of World War I. In his father's case, Ned did not see that there was an injustice to be corrected, although he did once seek to have his father's case reexamined for a post-humous promotion.

Just how much of Ned's passion in the Kimmel case was redirected emotion over his father's treatment is impossible to know. It is safe to say that, given the immense impact his father had on his life, both profession-ally and personally, Ned's heavy emotional investment in the Kimmel case was on some preconscious level an effort to rectify the honor of the Navy all the way back to the loss of *Memphis*.

[9]

The traditional song "Navy Blue and Gold" describes the location of the Naval Academy as "[w]here Severn joins the tide."[36] That phrase has rever-berated in the hearts of hundreds of thousands who view the Academy as one of the enduring symbols of the U.S. Navy. Many of the women and men who have served in the Navy, whether with or without a commission, as well as those now serving, hold the view that the Academy is one of the

Navy's significant repositories for the traditions that hold so much meaning for them.

In addition to the beautifully designed campus at Annapolis, there are the stately buildings bearing the names of some of the Navy's, as well as the Marine Corps', greatest heroes and leaders. Many of the honored dead who have not had their names preserved in the legacy of a building lie at rest in the Academy's cemetery, forever in touch with the soil upon which the Academy stands.

At the dedication of Beach Hall—(left to right): Ned, Ingrid, Ingie, Edward ("Ned Jr."), and Hugh.

In a rare occurrence, a living person witnessed his name bestowed on a building on the Academy grounds when, in 1999, Beach Hall was dedicated. Eighty-one years and one day from Ned's birth, on 21 April 1999, the usually temperate spring on the Chesapeake gave way to cold and rain, forcing the dedication ceremony to be held inside nearby Alumni Hall. Dedicated to father and son—Edward Latimer Beach Sr. and Jr.—the newly renovated building was to serve as the headquarters of the U.S. Naval Institute. Only Adm. Hyman Rickover had previously been so honored by seeing a building on the Academy grounds named for him while he was still alive.

A wing of the Naval Hospital that had served the Academy for so long, the building that was to become Beach Hall had stood idle for some time. The growing activities and prestige of the Naval Institute had forced it out of its limited space in Preble Hall, where it had been housed since Ned graduated from the Academy in 1939. The cost of the renovations was borne jointly by the Naval Institute and the Academy. A major fund-raising campaign was run by the Institute to finance their share of the work. As was typical of building projects requiring large sums of donated money, the right to name the building would go to the person who could provide a very significant contribution.

The angel who stepped forward with that generous donation was John J. "Jack" Schiff.[37] Typical of so many who hold the Navy in their hearts, Schiff had never attended the Academy, but had served as an officer in the Navy during World War II. Like so many of his generation, Schiff viewed the Academy as one of the symbols of all the Navy stood for, and how his time in the Navy had prepared him for a later life of success. The Cincinnati resident went on to a highly successful career in the insurance business after leaving the Navy, and he wanted to give something back as an acknowledgement of his gratitude. Atypically, Schiff did not want his own name on the building for which he was making such a significant contribution. Instead, he wanted the building named for the Beaches—especially for Ned, with whom he was well acquainted and of whom he had become an ardent admirer.

The insignia for the Naval Institute bears a sword crossed with a pen, symbolic of the Institute's role as a forum for discussions of the role of the all the Sea Services—Navy, Marine Corps, and Coast Guard—in the defense of the United States. The naming of Beach Hall in honor of two men who had dedicated their lives to long careers in the Navy and to writing about the Navy was an exceptional way of showing the dual missions of the Naval Institute.

At the dedication ceremonies, Ned became quite emotional. He concluded his brief remarks with, "Thanks so much for this tribute to my father and me; I don't know what I can say but thank you." At that point, his voice broke.[38]

[10]

In the same year Beach Hall was dedicated, Ned's last book, *Salt and Steel: Reflections of a Submariner* was published. He viewed the book as a continuation of his *The United States Navy: 200 Years*. In large part, Ned wanted his memoir to show how the Navy's ideals of leadership and honor were lived out in his lifetime.

The final project on which Ned worked was prepping his father's autobiography for publication. Even though the book was not released until 2003, it had been written almost seventy years before. The published version of *From Annapolis to Scapa Flow: The Autobiography of Edward L.* *Beach Sr.*, contains material inserted by Ned to explain parts of his father's text or to add information for clarification.

As a writer, Ned published three novels and six works of nonfiction. In addition, he coauthored two works—*Naval Terms Dictionary* and *Keepers* *of the Sea*. The list of his articles and stories published in periodicals is lengthy. (See Appendix II for a complete listing of Ned's published works.) These are in addition to the numerous reviews he penned, along with prefaces and forewords for countless books by others. His writing career stands as a remarkable achievement by any standard.

Epilogue

"Father," said Ralph Osborn, looking up from the book he had been reading, "I want to go to the Naval Academy."
—Edward L. Beach Sr., *Ralph Osborn, Midshipman at Annapolis*

In their "Golden Years"—Ingrid and Ned on the island of Ljusterö, off Stockholm, Sweden, where they spent many summers after Ned's retirement moved into a slower pace.

The familiar words registered in Ned's mind even as he fought to remain awake. The words were being read to him this time as he lay quietly on a bed newly installed in his first-floor library. Cancer of the liver had been the diagnosis but five months earlier and the progression of the disease had been rapid. A profound sense of tiredness is the principal symptom of liver cancer; Ned became more and more listless. As his energies dimmed and his ability to read declined, he sought comfort in the books of his father. Ingrid, son Edward, and family friend Dena Verrill read aloud the stories of Ned's youth. In the pages of his father's novels—telling the adventures of Ned's boyhood idols Robert Drake, Roger Paulding, Ralph Osborn, and Dan Quin—Ned was able to relive his boyhood dreams and to reconnect with his father. If a novelist today were to describe this scene with old books providing an anodyne for illness, many would call it contrived, but for Ned the novels of his father were just that—they carried his mind away from his present woes and into the world his father had so richly created. In contrast to the drive and energy of his life, Ned very quietly slipped the moorings of his mortal life on Sunday, 1 December 2002. As Ingrid and son Edward cradled his head, and devoted friend Del Tanamont stood nearby, Ned finally responded to the order, "Sailor, rest your oars."

Tributes poured in from across the world, with newspapers from New York to London to Australia running obituaries. Famed novelist Tom Clancy wrote a tribute that appeared in the *Wall Street Journal* on 4 December 2002, and submariners' organizations also honored Ned. Ingrid and her family received incredible numbers of condolence cards and letters, many from previously unknown individuals attesting to Ned's having influenced them to enlist in the Navy—especially in the submarine force—and expressing gratitude for that inspiration.

With time needed for a family spread across the globe from Sweden to California to New Zealand to gather, Ned's memorial service was not held until 14 January 2003. On that day, family and friends gathered in the Naval Academy chapel as the aisles were lined by submarine veterans, each holding a flag of the submarine force. Across the nation, thousands more attended in spirit. The memorial service was led by Adm. Frank L. "Skip" Bowman, USN, head of the Navy's nuclear power program. Other eulogists included Capt. James C. Hay, USN (Ret.), Paul Stillwell and Thomas Cutler from the Naval Institute, and the three Beach children—Ingrid Alice, Hugh, and Edward. Ned's ashes were interred just below the crest of the hill on which Beach Hall stands—his final resting place among those honored in the Academy's cemetery.

How does one measure the depth and breadth of the wake his passage through life produced? There is the trivial—he was once a clue in a *New York Times* crossword puzzle.[1] At the other end of the continuum of his accomplishments, there is the building that bears his name and that of his father. In between, there are such monuments as the Naval History Prize, named in his honor and awarded annually by the Naval Historical Foundation to the Naval Academy midshipman who submits the best essay or research paper dealing with some aspect of naval history. But all of those are only the outward manifestations of the legacy Ned left.

His career of service to his nation would be one of the things Ned would list as a significant model he created for future generations. Without a doubt, his published writings would also be at the top of a list of accomplishments worthy of living past his own lifetime, especially given the fact that so many are still in print today. But the enduring heritage Ned Beach left to his country and his Navy is deeper and more valuable than either of these accomplishments.

What Ned yearned for, what he sought and fought for his whole life, was a Navy worthy of the vision his father's novels constructed. To his own credit and honor, Ned never lost his faith in a Navy that was as susceptible to the foibles of humans as any other institution. But for Ned, that was never good enough. The words "Honor, Courage, and Commitment" from the Sailor's Creed were not abstract ideals to be merely mouthed, they were to be lived, achieved—practiced in everyday life.

It was emblematic of his undying faith in the Navy that he got on so well with his juniors, men in whom he always saw the potential to achieve his vision of the Navy. Equally symbolic were his run-ins with superiors when he perceived that they had failed to live up to that same vision. He would not hold any sailor to a rubric of never making a mistake, but he would, and did, hold everyone to account for mistakes that were made and not admitted to and corrected. His passion over the Kimmel case was not one based on criticism for the errors of those in high command before the attack, but for those same individuals who, after the war was over, would not or could not own up to their mistakes by correcting the public record.

Can any institution ever lift itself above the frailty of its all-too-human members? Ned would answer with a resounding, "Yes!" The whole can be more than the sum of its parts if enough of its members strive to achieve the ideals to which the institution is dedicated. For Ned, "the Navy was the greatest organization."[2] In spite of the flaws he saw, he never abandoned faith in the Navy and the people who wear its uniform.

The Naval Academy's alma mater, in its original words, states: "For sailor men in battle fair / Since fighting days of old, / Have proved a sailor's right to wear / The Navy Blue and Gold."[3] Ned wore the uniform of the U.S. Navy with pride and in honor; he encouraged others to wear the same uniform with the same degree of pride and with the obligation to uphold its honor; and he taught our nation about the respect that is due the uniform when it is worn with the pride that comes from serving with honor.

Ave Nobilis Dux

Appendix I: A Brief Chronology of the Life of Edward L. "Ned" Beach Jr.

1918	20 Apr	Born to Edward Latimer Beach Sr. and Alice (Fouché) Beach in New York City
1934		Graduates from Palo Alto High School
1935		Enters U.S. Naval Academy
1939	1 June	Graduates from U.S. Naval Academy, second in class
		Commissioned ensign
		Assigned to USS *Chester* (CA-27)
	Sept	Reports on board USS *Lea* (DD 118)—participating in the Neutrality Patrols and the occupation of Iceland, as well as convoy duty in the North Atlantic
1941	Sept	Ordered to submarine school
	7 Dec	United States enters World War II
	Dec	Graduates from submarine school first in class
1942	1 Jan	Reports to USS *Trigger* (SS-237) at Mare Island Navy Yard, CA
	30 Jan	USS *Trigger* commissioned
1943		His father dies in Palo Alto, California, and is buried in Golden Gate National Cemetery, San Bruno, California.
1944	May	Detached from *Trigger* and ordered to new construction with leave time
	4 June	Marries Ingrid Schenck at the chapel of Stanford University in Palo Alto
	July	Reports to Prospective Commanding Officer School in New London

	Aug	Reports as PXO of USS *Tirante* (SS-420) at Portsmouth, New Hampshire
1945	April	Detached from *Tirante*
	June	Assumes command of USS *Piper* (SS-409)
	Aug	*Piper* departs Pearl Harbor on first war patrol with Ned in command
	10 Aug	Inga-Marie is born
	2 Sept	World War II ends as *Piper* enters Sea of Japan
	Dec	Ordered to Washington, D.C., for duty as personal aide to Chief of Naval Personnel Vice Adm. Louis Denfeld
1947	Mar	Assigned to Office of the Chief of Naval Operations (Op-36)—Atomic Weapons
1948	7 Feb	Edward Latimer Beach III born
	May	Assumes command of USS *Amberjack* (SS-522) based in Key West, Florida
	17 Aug	Inga-Marie dies at Key West, Florida
1949	7 June	Hugh Beach born
	31 Aug	Ordered to Washington, D.C., as naval assistant to Chairman of the Joint Chiefs of Staff Gen. Omar N. Bradley
1951	Mar	Ordered to command USS *Trigger* [II] (SS-564), then under construction
1952		*Submarine!* published
	5 Dec	Ingrid Alice Beach born
1953	Jan	Relieves Rear Adm. Dennison as naval aide to President Dwight D. Eisenhower
1954	21 Jan	USS *Nautilus* (SSN-571) christened by Mrs. Eisenhower
1955		*Run Silent, Run Deep* published
1956	1 Oct	Promoted to captain
1957	Feb	Ordered to command USS *Salamonie* (AO-26)
1958	Jan	Appointed special assistant in submarine matters to the

		Chief of Naval Reactors Branch, Division of Reactor Development, Atomic Energy Commission
		United Artists releases *Run Silent, Run Deep*, very loosely based on Ned's novel
	June	Ordered prospective commander of USS *Triton*, then under construction by General Dynamics Corporation (Electric Boat Division), Groton, CT
1959	10 Nov	Assumes command of USS *Triton* (SSR[N]-586)
1960	16 Feb–10 May	USS *Triton* completes first submerged circumnavigation of the globe
		All crew members were awarded the Presidential Unit Citation Ribbon, while Ned was also awarded the Legion of Merit Medal presented by the president of the United States.
1961	July	Commands Submarine Squadron 8
1962	Aug	Enrolled at the National War College, Washington, D.C.
		Around the World Submerged: the Voyage of the Triton published
		Awarded honorary doctorate by American International University
		Awarded *Magellanic Premium* by the American Philosophical Society
1963	July	Completes the course work at the National War College
		Assigned to the Office of the Chief of Naval Operations, Navy Department
		Earns Master of Arts degree from George Washington University
		Awarded honorary doctorate by University of Bridgeport
1966	1 Dec	Relieved of all active duty (retired)
		The Wreck of the Memphis published
		Naval Terms Dictionary, co-authored with John V. Noel Jr., is published (2nd ed.)

1967		Begins teaching at Naval War College, and serving as Stephen B. Luce Chair of Naval Science
1969	Oct	Leaves Naval War College to write full time
		Secretary and staff director for the Senate Republican Policy Committee, Washington, D.C.
1971		*Naval Terms Dictionary*—3rd edition published
1972		*Dust on the Sea* published
1977		Ends service with the Senate Republican Policy Committee
1978		*Cold is the Sea* published
		Naval Terms Dictionary—4th edition published
1979		Alice (Fouché) Beach dies in Palo Alto, California
1980		Awarded the Alfred Thayer Mahan Award for Literary Achievement by the Navy League of the United States
1981		Administrative assistant to Senator Jeremiah A. Denton
1983		*Keepers of the Sea*, co-authored with Fred J. Maroon, published
1986		*The United States Navy: 200 Years* published
1987		Awarded Roosevelt Naval History Prize
1988		*Naval Terms Dictionary*—5th edition published
1995		*Scapegoats: A Defense of Kimmel and Short at Pearl Harbor* published
1999	21 Apr	Beach Hall, on the campus of the U.S. Naval Academy, is dedicated as the headquarters of the U.S. Naval Institute named in honor of Ned and his father
		Salt and Steel: Reflections of a Submariner published
2002	1 Dec	Dies, Washington, D.C.
2003		*From Annapolis to Scapa Flow: the Autobiography of Edward L. Beach Sr.* published

Appendix II: Chronological Bibliography of the Published Writings of Edward L. Beach Jr.

Articles and Stories

"Undersea Scourge." *Shipmate*, June 1946, 20–22; 42–43.

"The *Trigger* Fights Her War." *Blue Book*, October 1946, 48–62.

"*Archerfish* Stalks the Biggest Enemy." *Blue Book*, January 1948, 88–103.

"*S-44* at Torpedo Junction." *Blue Book*, May 1948, 46–53.

"*Wahoo* Goes Brave to Battle." *Blue Book*, August 1948, 12–27.

"*Tang* Completes a Mission." *Blue Book*, November 1948, 50–64.

"Our Duty Lies Before Us." U.S. Naval Institute *Proceedings*, January 1949, 79.

"Hit 'em Again, *Harder!*" *Blue Book*, June 1949, 14–30.

"Three Strikes for *Batfish*." *Blue Book*, October 1949, 12–26.

"Battle Stations, Submerged." *Blue Book*, February 1950, 50–64.

"*Flasher* Takes the Warpath." *Blue Book*, July 1950, 36–51.

"Mission: 1956." *Esquire*, August 1950 (as "Beachley Edwards"), 26–27.

"Saga of the *Seawolf*." *Blue Book*, January 1951, 50–64.

"*Amberjack* Fights Our Own Fleet." *Blue Book*, February 1951, 12–21.

"*Trigger*-II—Sub Killer." *Argosy*, September 1951, 24–27; 72–77.

"Run Silent, Run Deep." *Collier's*, 4 March 1955, 26–27; 58–65.

"Unlucky in June: *Hiyo* Meets *Trigger*." U.S. Naval Institute *Proceedings*, April 1957, 376.

"*Triton* Follows Magellan's Wake." *National Geographic*, November 1960, 585–597; 601–615.

"Two Trips to Guam." *American Legion Magazine*, November 1961, 20–21; 50.

"The Nature of Submarining." *Proceedings of the American Philosophical Society*, 1961.

"The Influence of Nuclear Power." *Trident*, March 1962, 3–5.

"You May Fire When Ready, Gridley." U.S. Naval Institute *Proceedings*, August 1968, 118.

"Smaller, Lighter, Faster, and Deeper Diving." *Defense Electronics*, August 1979, 43–46, 111.

"Radar and Submarines in World War II." *Defense Electronics*, October 1979, 48–56.

"ELF: To Communicate With a Submerged Submarine." *Defense Electronics*, April 1980, 54–61.

"'Culpable Negligence.'" *American Heritage*, December 1980, 41–54.

"Confrontation Underseas." *American Legion Magazine*, June 1985, 20–23, 44–47.

"The Biggest Theater." *American Heritage*, December 1991, 80–90.

"Sentimental Journey to Memphis." *Naval History*, October 1993, 16–20.

"The Trouble with Admiral Sampson." *Naval History*, December 1995, 8–16 (co-authored with Martin G. Netsky).

"The U.S. Navy's Remarkable Transformation." *Sea Power*, January 2000, 5–14.

"The Submarine Mission Today." *Undersea Warfare*, Spring 2000, 1–2.

"What *is* there about the Submarine?" *Shipmate*, April 2000, 24–27.

"A Centennial Salute to the U.S. Submarine Force." *Sea Power*, July 2000, 33–40.

Books—Fiction

Run Silent, Run Deep. New York: Henry Holt & Company, 1955.

Dust on the Sea. New York: Henry Holt & Company, 1972.

Cold is the Sea. New York: Henry Holt & Company, 1978.

Books—Nonfiction

Submarine! New York: Henry Holt & Company, 1952.

Around the World Submerged: The Voyage of the Triton. New York: Henry Holt & Company, 1962. Reprint, Annapolis: Naval Institute Press, 2001.

The Wreck of the Memphis. New York: Henry Holt & Company, 1966.

Naval Terms Dictionary. Co-authored with John V. Noel Jr. 2nd edition. Annapolis: Naval Institute Press, 1966.

Naval Terms Dictionary. Co-authored with John V. Noel Jr. 3rd edition. Annapolis: Naval Institute Press, 1971.

Naval Terms Dictionary. Co-authored with John V. Noel Jr. 4th edition. Annapolis: Naval Institute Press, 1978.

Keepers of the Sea. Co-authored with Fred Maroon. Annapolis: Naval Institute Press, 1983.

The United States Navy: 200 Years. New York: Henry Holt & Company, 1985.

Naval Terms Dictionary. Co-authored with John V. Noel Jr. 5th edition. Annapolis: Naval Institute Press, 1988.

Scapegoats: A Defense of Kimmel and Short at Pearl Harbor. Annapolis: Naval Institute Press, 1995.

Salt & Steel: Reflections of a Submariner. Annapolis: Naval Institute Press, 1999.

From Annapolis to Scapa Flow: The Autobiography of Edward L. Beach Sr. (Editor.) Annapolis: Naval Institute Press, 2003.

Appendix III: Brief Biographies of Beach Family Members

Author's Note: As an avid reader of biographies, I have often been frustrated by passing mention of family members of the subject of a biography without information having been provided as to the rest of those family members' lives. As a consequence, brief biographical sketches are provided here for Ned's parents, siblings, and children, as well as his father- and mother-in-law.

Edward Latimer Beach Sr. and Alice (Fouché) Beach (Ned's Parents)

[1]

Just two years after the end of the Civil War, Edward Latimer Beach was born in Toledo, Ohio, son of Joseph Lane and Laura Colton (Osborn) Beach. The second of what would eventually be four children, he came into the world on 30 June 1867. His father had served in the Confederate Army during the Civil War, and was wounded and captured at the Battle of Antietam. In exchange for medical treatment, he agreed to swear allegiance to the Union. Later, he was paroled.

Eventually, Joseph settled in Toledo, where he sought to keep secret from his pro-Union neighbors the fact that he had fought for the Confederacy. He circulated the tale that he had been a Confederate prisoner. In Toledo, Joseph met and soon married Laura Colton Osborn of Norwalk, Ohio, who was two years his senior. They were married on 17 January 1864 in Toledo in what was probably a lavish ceremony since Laura's father, John R. Osborn, was a prominent Toledo attorney. Joseph, despite his father-in-law's professional standing, was a merchant all his life, carrying on his trade in Toledo, then Chicago, and eventually Minneapolis, Minnesota. In spite of the changes in locale for his business ventures, Joseph Beach was never successful as a merchant, ending his days being supported by and living with his second son.

Beach family records and traditions do not indicate whether or not Joseph ever revealed to his wife's family the fact that he had worn the uniform of the enemy. The fact that his wife's brother, Hartwell Osborn, served in the Union Army and later was the author of *Trials and Triumphs: The Record of the Fifty-fifth Ohio Volunteer Infantry*[1] may have been a factor in maintaining the deception. There is no documentation concerning the relationship between Joseph Beach and his brother-in-law, but avoiding frequent contacts with the Union veteran that would have resulted from living in the same city could in itself have been a reason for the move to Chicago.

Capt. Edward L. Beach Sr., USN, Ned's father.

As noted, Joseph Beach's success in business was minimal at best, his family always struggling to keep ahead of the bill collectors. As he reached his teens, an ambitious Edward Latimer Beach recognized that his parents would not be in a financial position to provide for any type of higher education, something the industrious and intelligent second son wanted. Taking matters into his own hands, Beach decided to seek an appointment to the U.S. Naval Academy as a means of providing a better future for himself. Little is known of Beach's early life in Minneapolis, his schooling, or his childhood activities. Through what he characterized as hard work and diligent study, Beach won that appointment to Annapolis by successfully competing for the endorsement of the member of Congress from his Minneapolis district. For most applicants, a mere congressional nod was not sufficient to gain admission to either the Naval Academy or the Military Academy at West Point. The appointment by a congressman, a senator, or a person in any other office who had the privilege of making such nominations all depended on rigorous competitive exams. Sufficiently intelligent and educated so as to pass the exams and earn that appointment, Beach soon found himself—in June of 1884, just short of his seventeenth birthday—entering the Naval Academy eager to begin his education. Of the ninety plebes who entered the Academy in the summer of 1884, only thirty-five would eventually graduate.

[2]

Living accommodations for the plebes were not luxurious at first. Since the plebe class was required to be on campus before the end of the previous term, the plebes were housed on board an old sailing ship—*Santee*—and forced to sleep in hammocks until the first-classmen had graduated, thereby opening space in the dormitories. *Santee* had been laid down in 1820, but due to budget constraints she was not launched until 1855 and did not see service until the Civil War. Built as a 44-gun frigate, *Santee* was used as a training ship after the Civil War, eventually being moored at Annapolis. On her decks, several generations of naval officers received their first taste of life on board ship. When Beach spent his first night at the Naval Academy on board *Santee*, she had already been serving as a training ship for twenty-nine years, and she would continue in that role until 1912.[2] Literally, the senior Beach's naval career started on the decks of a ship that had its keel laid during the "Age of Fighting Sail."

Unlike today's Academy, where a commission as an officer in either the Navy or the Marine Corps comes along with the diploma, in 1888 once a naval cadet completed the required course of study, he had to serve two years on board ship and then pass additional exams before he could be commissioned. (At the time the senior Beach attended the Naval Academy, the title of "midshipman" had not yet been adopted; in addition, the Academy did not issue college diplomas to its graduates.) After Beach and his classmates were certified as having completed the Academy's program, they were scattered to the fleet with the rank of midshipman. Beach was assigned to USS *Richmond*, a Civil War-era steam sloop-of-war.

[3]

Even with a successful two years on board ship and having passed the additional exams, gaining a commission was still almost impossible at that time. Congress limited the number of new commissions each year to the number of vacancies in the Navy created by deaths, resignations, and retirements. So it was that, in 1890, Beach and his friend Henry A. Wiley faced the possibility of not gaining commissions. The two took the issue in hand themselves and daringly approached Commo. Francis M. Ramsay, USN, chief of the Bureau of Navigation. At the time, the Bureau of Navigation was in charge of all personnel matters for the Navy. In an act that bordered on impertinence, the two midshipmen presented Ramsay with a list of officers whose names ought to have been removed from the Navy's officer list long before. While the named officers ranged from men who were so incompetent they had not been assigned duties for twenty years, to deserters and even to a murderer, the list still represented the opinions of two midshipmen. To the surprise of the brash midshipmen, the commodore accepted their list and soon everyone in the class of 1888 received commissions.[3]

[4]

In July 1890, Beach was commissioned an ensign in the U.S. Navy and was assigned to USS *Philadelphia* (C-4), one of the Navy's newest cruisers. By 1896, after he passed additional examinations, he was promoted to "assistant passed engineer" a rank equivalent to a lieutenant (junior grade) today. During those intervening years, Beach served on board the cruiser USS *New York* (ACR-2), the torpedo boat USS *Ericsson* (TB-2), and the monitor USS *Puritan*.

With tensions between the United States and Spain rising over the issue of Cuba, the Navy decided to re-commission the cruiser USS *Baltimore* (C-3) in 1897. Beach reported on board *Baltimore* just as she was being sent to join the Asiatic Fleet. Not long after *Baltimore* joined the Asiatic Fleet, the Spanish-American War broke out. *Baltimore* had been assigned to the squadron commanded by Commo. George Dewey, so she was with that group as it steamed toward the Philippines. On 1 May 1898, the *Baltimore,* in company with the rest of Dewey's squadron, entered Manila Bay and fired the opening shots of what Theodore Roosevelt would later call "that splendid little war." The stunning American victory over the Spanish at Manila Bay electrified the American public and seemed to justify the Navy's modernization program that had been started just as Beach was entering the Naval Academy.

Later, Beach would describe his part in the overwhelming naval victory as "The Battle of Irwin's Boots." He was assigned to the starboard engine room of *Baltimore* so that his view of the battle was looking upward through an engine room grating to where Ens. Noble E. Irwin stood his post directing a battery of 6-inch guns. As a result, all Beach saw of this most famous battle were the soles of Ensign Irwin's boots.[4]

While Dewey had gained a great naval victory at Manila Bay, the administration of President William McKinley was now saddled with the decision of what to do with the Philippines. There was a strong sentiment in Congress against the United States becoming a colonial power, but fears of either a German or Japanese occupation of the archipelago forced McKinley's hand, and the United States occupied the islands with the intention of eventually granting independence. In February 1899, the Philippine Insurrection broke out as the Filipinos turned against the Americans who had now replaced the Spanish as the occupiers of their islands. What followed were three years of some very vicious fighting.

There is little doubt that most of the American military forces in the Philippines viewed their Filipino enemies with a disdain born of racial prejudice. In parts of the archipelago, the suppression of the Filipino independence movement was brutal, while other areas saw little or no fighting.[5] In the midst of this war was the newly promoted Lieutenant Beach, now serving on board the gunboat USS *Helena*. Assigned the task of interdicting rebel arms and supplies moving between islands, the *Helena* regularly stopped and searched native fishing and commercial boats. While leading such a search party of one native boat, Beach discovered that his men had captured the wife of Emilio Aguinaldo, the leader of the Filipino insurrectionist movement.

The most revered figure in Philippine history, Emilio Aguinaldo had been the leader of the independence movement against the Spanish for many years before the United States and Spain declared war on each other. Living in exile when Dewey entered Manila Bay to face the Spanish fleet, Aguinaldo was hurriedly brought back to Manila by Dewey to assist in leading what was hoped to be a Filipino army allied with the Americans to defeat the Spanish army. When it became clear the Americans intended to keep the islands rather than grant immediate independence, Aguinaldo and his followers began a campaign to drive out those whom they saw as their new oppressors.

Realizing whom he had captured in the person of Aguinaldo's wife, Beach performed an act of courtesy, promptly setting Señora Aguinaldo free. As if with biblical foreshadowing, Beach's act of civility was soon repaid when he, in turn, was captured after he had become separated from a group of sailors he had led ashore in search of an insurrectionist encampment. When Aguinaldo was informed of the identity of the American naval officer who had been taken prisoner by his men, Aguinaldo ordered the young man released, but not before meeting him face-to-face, thanking him for the release of Señora Aguinaldo and treating him to a chicken dinner. As a result of that meeting, the elder Beach and Aguinaldo became friends, exchanging correspondence for many years after their initial meeting as enemies.

In the process of being moved around after his capture, Beach encountered some of the people who were supposed to be his enemies. He came to develop a sincere respect for the Filipino people and a degree of appreciation for the way in which he was treated. For the rest of his life, Beach would not hesitate to express his positive feelings about the Filipino people.

He was a frequent and welcome guest at a Filipino social club near his home in Palo Alto, California.

[5]

The war in the Philippines was beginning to wind down when Beach was assigned to teach English at the Naval Academy in the fall of 1901. During this period, the industriousness that had characterized his efforts to gain admission to the Naval Academy caused him to work beyond the hours expected of an instructor. As a result, in 1902 he completed an indexing of the U.S. Naval Institute's periodical *Proceedings*. His work covered the first twenty-seven years of the publication from its creation in 1874. He also began writing works of fiction—novels about young men in the Navy and at Annapolis. All were written for young readers and will be discussed below.

In 1904, Beach began a tour of duty as navigation officer on board USS *Nevada* (BM-8), a coastal defense monitor that had been commissioned in 1903. By 1907, however, Beach was back at the Naval Academy teaching and spending his spare time writing.

When he reported on board the newly commissioned armored cruiser USS *Montana* (ACR-13) in 1908, he continued in the role of navigation officer, his second tour as an instructor at Annapolis having lasted only one year. Life on board the fast, graceful *Montana* agreed with Beach and he was lucky enough to remain on board for two years as she patrolled the Caribbean Sea.[6] Promoted to the rank of commander on 11 March 1910, he was then assigned to the Boston Navy Yard as an engineering officer.

In the spring of 1913, Beach was posted to his first command at sea, the collier USS *Vestal*. Ships like the *Vestal* were critical in supplying coal to other ships of the fleet. While he was in command of *Vestal*, the United States occupied the Mexican port city of Vera Cruz in April 1914 as part of an effort to interdict arms being shipped to the government of Victoriano Huerta, the nominal president of Mexico. President Woodrow Wilson opposed the dictatorial Huerta, so a misunderstanding involving USS *Dolphin* at the Mexican port of Tampico was used as a pretext to seize Mexico's principal port on its east coast to prevent arms from being unloaded.

American forces seized the harbor and customs house at Vera Cruz to prevent the landing of a shipment of arms on board SS *Ypiranga*, a German-owned ship. After a force of some four thousand U.S. Navy bluejackets (sailors) and Marines made the initial foray onto the docks and streets of Vera Cruz, a contingent of U.S. Army infantry soon arrived.[7] The

Vestal was ordered to Vera Cruz to support the units of the U.S. fleet there, and Beach soon found himself not only in command of his own ship, but also in charge of a commandeered Mexican floating dry dock, warden of an island fortress turned prison called *San Juan de Ulloa*, and, for a time, "The Administrator of Customs and Captain of the Port."[8]

[6]

As the American occupation of Vera Cruz ended in November 1914, Beach was promoted to captain and ordered to command USS *Washington* (ACR-11), an armored cruiser attached to the Caribbean Squadron of the Atlantic Fleet. *Washington* was Beach's first command of a major warship. With the war in Europe just beginning and the United States strengthening its military as a precaution, he seemed to be within easy reach of achieving that highest of seagoing commands, a battleship.

Captain Beach took command of *Washington* on 12 December 1915 and, by July, he and *Washington* found themselves involved in trying to control a rebellion in the benighted Caribbean nation of Haiti. Since the U.S. had taken over the building of the Panama Canal, the nations that touched the waters of the Caribbean Sea had become of great interest to their giant neighbor to the north. Fearing further European colonization in the region that could then threaten access to the eastern end of the canal, the U.S. embarked on a policy of serving as a regional police force, whether invited or not.

In the early 1900s, Haiti suffered from overpopulation and an economy that was incapable of moving its population out of abject poverty. Once a French colony, the tiny nation that shares an island with the Dominican Republic never had been able to sustain economic growth long enough to achieve any marked increase in its standard of living. One strongman after another had seized power, using mercenary fighters. Once each new leader's foreign bank accounts were full, it seemed a new "liberator" would emerge, drive off the old one, and the cycle would began again. Sometimes these "revolutions" were bloodless, but some could result in great loss of life. Under the pretext of protecting American lives and "interests," the U.S. usually sent in the Navy and the Marine Corps to stand watch in case the fighting got out of hand. As was the case in many of the other Caribbean "hot spots" in which American military muscle was flexed, much of the policy-making was left to the admirals and generals in local command.[9]

The rebellion that brought U.S. forces to Port-au-Prince in 1915 had turned bloody when then-President Vilbrun Guillaume Sam was forcefully removed by a mob from the French embassy and beheaded. Guillaume had entered the French embassy to seek asylum, but a Haitian mob refused to honor the diplomatic sanctity accorded a foreign nation.

Beach's involvement in the affairs of Haiti extended beyond the normal duties of an officer in command of a ship sent to "protect American interests." His ability to speak French (which he learned at the Naval Academy) and the fact that he commanded the flagship of the operation meant Beach was drawn to a much greater extent into problems ashore. Soon he was assigned to serve as chief of staff for the commander of the squadron, Rear Adm. William B. Caperton (1855–1941). This was in addition to Beach's duties as commanding officer of *Washington*. Caperton did not speak French, with the result that Beach became both Caperton's closest advisor and the person delegated to negotiate directly with the Haitians.

The first action Beach took in Haiti was later described in a letter to Beach from Philippe Dartiguenave, himself destined to be a president of the Republic of Haiti:

> On July 28, 1915, the very day on which the furious mob murdered President Vilbrun Guillaume in a frenzy of rage after the massacres at the Palais National and especially those at the prison, you [Beach Sr.] landed at Port-au-Prince, unarmed, unaccompanied by a guard and before the debarkment of your troops, you crossed the city in the midst of the highly excited factions and presented yourself before the self-styled Revolutionary Committee, which had seized public power, and you informed this committee that your troops would enter the city that afternoon to protect life and property and to maintain order.[10]

With his initial success in getting the U.S. Marines ashore without incident, Beach was soon delegated more and more work by Admiral Caperton.

The Wilson administration insisted that American-style democracy should be the form of government for nations like Haiti, and naval officers in positions like Caperton's and Beach's found themselves using their military power to impose a governmental structure that seldom outlasted the steaming of American warships over the horizon. Some historians have placed blame on Beach for what happened in Haiti in the years following the 1915–1916 intervention. It is true that Beach was instrumental in negotiating a treaty between the U.S. and Haiti, and that the governmental structure in place when he left was created at the behest of the Wilson administration through the offices of Caperton and Beach.

As noted above, however, many of the policy-making decisions in these situations were left to the discretion of the local commanders, especially as the Wilson administration meddled in the affairs of more and more countries, thus losing its ability to keep close tabs on all the diplomatic balls it was trying to simultaneously juggle.[11] Even if Caperton and Beach had had close supervision from Washington, the fact that the Wilson administration wanted an American-style democracy created regardless of the needs of the indigenous people of Haiti meant the results would be unworkable.

From reading the elder Beach's own accounts of the events, it is clear that his sympathies were with the Haitian people, in spite of the known racial prejudices of Admiral Caperton.[12] In 1920, Beach authored a 221-page summation of his experiences in Haiti. Titled "Admiral Caperton in Haiti," the report is highly sympathetic to the Haitian people and outlines a suggested future policy for Haiti that would have gradually led it toward a democracy, but also would have met the short-term needs of the Haitian people.[13] The report reached the desk of the secretary of the Navy, but whether anyone in the State Department ever read it is unknown. Historian David Healy describes the report as "a surprisingly frank 'inside' view of events," and says Beach "proves to be a sensitive observer of Haitian society."[14] Other historians have not been as kind, accusing Beach of making the situation worse by imposing on the people of Haiti a form of government that could not be sustained in the face of their poverty.[15] It is clear that most historians who have so condemned Beach have not thoroughly examined his extensive report (now located in the U.S. National Archives), nor have they read his other unpublished works: "Haiti: An Essay" (1919) and "The Occupation of Haiti, 1915: The Diaries of Admiral Caperton and Captain Beach (undated)." Both of these documents were meant as extensions of the report Beach submitted to the secretary of the Navy.

As affairs in Haiti began to be completed, *Washington* was due for extensive maintenance work in a Navy yard, so she was replaced by USS *Tennessee* (ACR-10), a ship of the same class and design. As a result, Beach was transferred to command of *Tennessee* in February 1916. The Navy being satisfied with Beach's ability to handle diplomatic situations, *Tennessee* was delegated to take U.S. Secretary of the Treasury William G. McAdoo and a party of dignitaries on a two-month cruise to several South American nations. Departing on 8 March, *Tennessee* and her distinguished passengers made official calls at a number of ports, with Secretary McAdoo passing the time between port visits by playing hopscotch on deck.[16] The delegation was returned to Norfolk on 8 May just as *Tennessee* prepared for a name change.

[7]

The U.S. Navy was in the midst of expanding its fleet, so the names of states that had been originally given to the armored cruisers were to be freed for use on the new battleships under construction. The *Montana*-class armored cruisers were renamed for major cities within the states for which the cruisers were originally named. On 25 May 1916, USS *Tennessee* (ACR-10) officially became USS *Memphis* (ACR-10). With the name change, Beach and *Memphis* were ordered to rejoin the Caribbean Squadron then at Santo Domingo, Dominican Republic.

The anchorage at Santo Domingo was not protected from heavy ocean waves and bad weather, so it was customary, especially during the hurricane season, for visiting ships to keep steam in their boilers at all times so as to be able to move out of the harbor at very short notice. Large ships can survive very heavy weather more easily if they are at sea with room to maneuver, something that cannot be done inside a harbor. In an era before the satellites and instant communications of the twenty-first century, long-range forecasts of hurricanes were not possible, allowing little time for ships at sea or communities ashore to prepare. *Memphis*, however, was the flagship of Cruiser Squadron, Atlantic Fleet, and was to be anchored at Santo Domingo for an extended period. Captain Beach wanted to keep four of her sixteen boilers lit at all times, the very minimum needed to move the 13,000-ton ship. Six boilers would have been better, but he asked for four.

Rear Adm. Charles Fremont Pond (1856–1929), who had taken over as commander, Cruiser Squadron, Atlantic Fleet in July, wanted his flagship to use as little coal as possible. The re-coaling process caused massive amounts of coal dust to blanket the ship, and in a tropical climate having the ship sealed during the re-coaling process made the inside of the ship unbearable. Hence, Pond wanted only two boilers lit as a means of conserving coal.[17] As commander of *Memphis*, Beach could have insisted on having more boilers lit since he was ultimately responsible for the safety of his ship, but Beach had to get along with the admiral, who was now living on board. As a result, only two boilers were fired at a time. As a precaution, however, Beach ordered that, at all times, four additional boilers be kept in readiness for lighting on very short notice. As events would transpire, the definition of "short notice" would become crucial.

On 29 August, as *Memphis* lay peacefully in the harbor, Beach and several officers noticed a very large wave approaching the ship from seaward. Beach immediately ordered the engine room to get up steam in four additional boilers, and he ordered that a ship's boat, bringing crewmembers on shore leave back to the ship, remain at the dock. The lighting of boilers and the development of steam took time, and the giant wave, today known as a tidal wave, hit the harbor before the *Memphis* could turn to face it head on. The massive wall of water hit *Memphis* broadside, bouncing her off the bottom of the harbor and eventually throwing her like a toy upon rocks at the base of a cliff. The shore liberty party did not get the word to return to the dock and was caught in the open harbor. When the seas had returned to normal, forty-three crewmembers of *Memphis* were dead and another two hundred were injured. The ship itself was a total loss.

In a letter to his mother, dated 6 September 1916 (just eight days after the disaster), Beach wrote the following about the events: "There was no storm—at all. No wind, no roaring of any nature." In describing the actual assault on *Memphis* by the giant waves, he noted, "But now these mountains of water were picking up the ship, throwing her about, dashing her on the bottom, and hurling her toward the shore." Beach went on to conclude, "It was an agonizing experience."[18]

A court of inquiry placed the blame on Beach, so a court-martial was convened. Beach's best friend, a very well-known civilian attorney named John Blair, insisted on being part of the legal team representing Beach.[19] The rules of evidence, court procedures, and other matters in a military court differ from those in civilian courts, and were beyond the experience of Blair. Ned was always convinced that his father's eventual conviction was partially the fault of his chief lawyer's inexperience in a military court.[20]

The elder Beach was charged with numerous offenses, the main one being that he did not keep sufficient boilers lit to be able to maneuver the ship out of harm's way on "short notice." The fact that the members of the court, as well as most of the scientific community at the time, thought a tidal wave was the product of weather, and was therefore predictable, contributed to the court's verdict.[21]

Navy tradition and legal precedent firmly established that the commanding officer of a ship is ultimately responsible for everything that happens on board his ship. As Ned points out in *The Wreck of the* Memphis, the members of the court could easily envision themselves caught in the web of circumstances that led to the charges against his father. Except for a Navy judge advocate, the other members of the court were naval officers "untrained in the law, but perfectionists all in a demanding profession and essentially idealists in their outlook." Then Ned goes on to note that members of such courts "view their duties with distaste but with one emotion only: the greatest good of the naval service."[22]

The Beach legal team requested that Admiral Pond testify, but Pond asked to be excused. Beach agreed to Pond's request and then refused to allow his lawyers to subpoena the man who had insisted that only two boilers be kept lit. There being no written evidence of the exchange that led to the limitation on the number of boilers that *Memphis* had lit on the fateful day, only Pond's admission of his instructions to Beach could exonerate the captain.

Pond should have stepped forward and informed the court that he had ordered Beach to keep only two boilers lit, but he remained silent. Beach's refusal to allow Pond to be subpoenaed was based on Beach's belief that Pond was honor-bound to voluntarily appear before the Court to tell what happened. Pond never testified. In this case, the commanding officer of the ship was held solely accountable for the loss of his ship, even though the loss was directly related to having followed the wishes of his immediate superior.

The court acquitted Beach of all charges but one—not having enough steam available to get under way on short notice. The conviction rested on the definition of "short notice," which Beach and his legal team tried to define as forty-five minutes. The court defined "short notice" to mean fifteen minutes. In view of Beach's record of service and of the efforts made by Beach to get *Memphis* positioned to take the onrushing waves safely, the court recommended that clemency be granted by the higher authorities that review convictions within the military justice system.

Secretary of the Navy Josephus Daniels signed an endorsement of the court-martial verdict in February 1917, noting that in consideration of the circumstances and of Beach's service record, the conviction would be allowed to stand, but the sentence of the court (moving Beach back twenty places on the promotion list) was reduced to moving back five places. Either punishment was of little significance—the fact that the conviction was allowed to stand meant the career in the Navy that Beach so loved would soon come to an end. An officer with a conviction would not be promoted and probably never command a ship at sea again.

While it is dangerous to speculate on what version, if any, of the circumstances surrounding the loss of *Memphis* circulated within the Navy Department, certainly the court was inclined to recommend leniency and the secretary of the Navy fully agreed, both in his initial endorsement of the court's decision and in a later review. The degree to which Admiral Pond's involvement in the incident was known in Navy circles despite a lack of testimony during the court-martial would be conjecture at this point, but there certainly had to be rumors that reached the ears of Secretary Daniels, as his later actions were to demonstrate.

[8]

Even as Secretary Daniels was signing his name to the papers that seemed to end Beach's career, the United States was severing relations with Germany over the resumption of unrestricted submarine warfare, and the infamous "Zimmermann Telegram" was released implicating Germany in a plot to entice Mexico into a war with the United States as a distraction from entering the melee in Europe. On 6 April, Congress declared a state of war existed between the United States and Germany, launching America into what would later be called the First World War.

For Beach, this was the low point of his professional life. His nation and his Navy were entering the largest conflict of his career just as he was being sidelined over the loss of *Memphis*. The needs of the expanding Navy in wartime, however, saved Beach the ignominy of an early departure from the Navy in the face of no longer being eligible for promotion. In April 1917, the Navy assigned him as inspector of ordnance at the U.S. Naval Torpedo Station at Newport, Rhode Island. Placing his feelings over the loss of *Memphis* and his conviction aside, Beach threw himself into the work at Newport, supervising the building of the torpedoes needed by a nation now at war.

Upon taking command of the torpedo station, Beach instituted a program of increased safety vigilance as the workers labored to arm torpedoes and mines that were being filled with highly explosive materials. Seeing that the base had too many of the explosives stored in too small an area, Beach arranged to have much of the dangerous substances removed to more distant storage. His farsightedness was fortunate as an accident later set off a major explosion that killed fourteen workers. Had Beach not taken the precautions he had, the presence of the removed materials would have probably killed most of the station's four thousand workers and destroyed much of the city of Newport. For his efforts, Beach was voted thanks by both houses of the Rhode Island legislature and by the City of Newport.[23] The Navy awarded him the Navy Cross and detached him from the torpedo station in order to take command of a battleship.

[9]

In April of 1918, just before his eldest son was born, Beach was ordered to command USS *New York* (BB-34), the 27,000-ton flagship of the U.S. Squadron attached to the British Grand Fleet in the North Sea. *New York*, armed with ten 14-inch guns and manned by a crew of 1,042, had been commissioned in 1914 and was immediately pressed into service as the flagship for the fleet that occupied Vera Cruz, Mexico, that same year. Given its status as flagship in the war with Germany, *New York* needed a commanding officer who had a wide range of experience in diplomatic duties, as well as the ability to run a taut ship under the direct eye of high-ranking officers.

Beach's career experiences suited the need and he at last realized one of his career dreams—commanding a line-of-battle ship in time of war.

Dignitaries from the various allies of the United States frequently visited *New York*, including King George V of Great Britain, as well as high-ranking naval officers. In his position as commanding officer of *New York*, Beach was in his element. *New York* was delegated a role in the war at sea, and toward the end of the war she was fired upon by a German submarine. All three torpedoes missed—and then *New York* took her revenge, sinking the enemy vessel.[24] The war ended with Beach still in command of *New York*, and he remained in command when the German High Seas Fleet entered the Firth of Forth, site of a major Royal Navy base at Rosyth, Scotland, to surrender. Ships of the U.S. Navy, including *New York*, were present for that surrender ceremony.

It would seem that Beach had redeemed himself. The command of *New York* and then a postwar stint as commanding officer of the Mare Island Naval Shipyard on San Francisco Bay, the major shipbuilding facility of the Navy on the West Coast, led him to believe his career had been rehabilitated. In June 1919, Secretary of the Navy Josephus Daniels issued an order rescinding all of Beach's punishment for the loss of *Memphis*.[25] With the last vestiges of *Memphis* wiped from his record, Beach began to hope that the one remaining goal of his career—achieving flag rank—was again reachable.

The major construction project at Mare Island while Beach was in command was the completion of the new battleship USS *California* (BB-44). In later life, Beach would always remark on how proud he was to have had a part in the ship's construction. When *California* was launched, Prohibition was the law of the land so, in order to have the traditional champagne with which to christen the new ship, Beach had to thwart the law by issuing a requisition for a case of "launching fluid."

Supervision of the great Navy yard was time consuming, but the senior Beach gradually came to realize that his dream of achieving flag rank was not to be as he was passed over by several promotion boards. He finally had to accept the inevitable—his career in the U.S. Navy was at an end. Believing that the pall from the loss of *Memphis* still hung over him, Beach retired from active duty in 1921. His thirty-eight-year career had seen him awarded seven medals: the Navy Cross, the Spanish Campaign Medal, the Philippine Campaign Medal, the Mexican Service Medal, the Haitian Campaign Medal, the Dominican Campaign Medal, and the Victory Medal (World War I) with Grand Fleet Clasp.

[10]

On the seventy-fifth anniversary of the loss of *Memphis*, the U.S. Navy named a building after Beach, as a tribute both to him and to the crew of the *Memphis*. The E. L. Beach Aviation Support Equipment Training Facility, located in the Naval Air Technical Training Center, Millington, Tennessee, just outside Memphis, was dedicated on 29 August 1991. The 114,000-square-foot facility contained classrooms, laboratories, and an operational trainer.

Ned participated in the dedication ceremony and donated his father's sword to the materials from *Memphis* on display in the building.[26] Other historic artifacts from the *Memphis* were moved to the facility from their previous location at the Pink Palace Museum in Memphis.[27]

[11]

Early in his naval career, Beach met and married Lucie Adelaide Quin of New York City. The couple was married on 11 May 1895, with the Reverend H. H. Clark, a Navy chaplain, performing the ceremony, which was held in the Quin home at 499 Halsey Street, Brooklyn, New York.[28] Lucie attended a training school for teachers on Nostrand Avenue in Brooklyn, but it is not known if she ever entered the teaching profession. Beach never discussed the circumstances of their meeting and courting with his children, leaving a gap in this part of his life's story. At the time of their marriage, Lucie was twenty-six and Beach was approaching his twenty-eighth birthday. Beach failed to provide much information about Lucie and their marriage in his autobiography. Ned speculated that Lucie's death left his father so heartbroken that he was incapable of writing about her, even given all the years that intervened from her death until he wrote his own life's story.

At the time of his wife's death, Beach did sit down and write a lengthy tribute to her. Written just eighteen days after her death, the heartfelt essay details their happy marriage. How Lucie played the piano while Beach played the flute, and how very much Beach enjoyed Lucie's singing for him. Beach goes on to describe how his own father's failures in business left Beach and Lucie to care for Joseph and Laura Beach in their old age, but how Lucie cheerfully accepted this task, never complaining about the small things she had to sacrifice in her own life in order to be able to provide food and shelter for Beach's parents.[29]

Lucie was one of the hundreds of thousands of women who resolutely followed their husbands in military service from one duty station to the next in those years. The marriage of Lucie and Beach remained childless, but by 1915, Lucie had contracted breast cancer. She told her husband of her disease, but kept from him the seriousness of her condition. Since he had just been promoted to captain and then assigned to command his first combatant ship, the armored cruiser *Washington*, Lucie did not want her condition to dampen Beach's joy. That his wife was seriously ill was clear to Beach, as he and Lucie talked about her condition and then she underwent surgery. Beach's mother kept him informed regarding Lucie's condition when duty called him back to his ship in the Caribbean. As Beach and *Washington* were engaged in operations in Haiti in the summer and fall of 1915, Lucie's condition grew steadily worse. Each month, Beach expected that he and the *Washington* would be relieved of duty and he could be back at Lucie's side. But the rebellion in Haiti meant both he and his ship would be in Caribbean waters indefinitely.

On 18 August 1915, Beach received a radiogram that stated, "Am still sick X When are you coming to me X Lucie."[30] Only at that last possible moment, as Lucie lay dying in a New York hospital, did Beach receive word of his wife's deteriorating condition. He arrived at Lucie's bedside in time to spend a few precious days with her before she succumbed to the ravages of the cancer on 17 September 1915. She was then buried in Boston. By all accounts, Beach was devastated by Lucie's passing, but the tyranny of the immediate issues in Haiti demanded his speedy return to *Washington* and his duties.

[12]

As another revolution terrorized the Haitian capital in July 1916, a scared and lonely Alice Fouché sought safety in a basement hiding place in the home of her uncle, with whom she lived. Later, her curiosity getting the better of her fears, Alice went to the highest window of the house to see what was happening in the city. From her lofty perch, Alice saw a massive warship coming over the horizon and into the harbor of Port-au-Prince. A warship meant the United States had sent a force so people like Alice would be protected and the violence in the streets would soon end. But that most welcome warship also brought back a handsome naval officer who so bravely came ashore to safeguard lives. The French-speaking American officer who had earned so much praise and thanks from the foreign nationals and those who feared the latest revolution's bloodletting in the Haitian capital soon found an admirer in Alice, the convent-educated young woman who spoke no English. Alice saw this American as both a protector and a savior.

As Beach went about his duties trying to negotiate a treaty, set up a democratic government, and establish a peaceful settlement between the warring factions ashore in Haiti, he was reacquainted with that charming young woman of mixed Spanish, Dominican, and French descent. At a banquet given for the officers of the American ship, the more elite members of Port-au-Prince's American and European communities gathered, including a number of attractive single women. Among them was Alice, who drew the attention of several young officers until they noted that their captain seemed to take particular interest in her. Beach was himself the subject of much attention from many of the young ladies as word spread that he had recently lost his wife and a natural sympathy made the good-looking American even more attractive. Beach's ability to speak French came to his aid again, and he soon learned that the young lady who had caught his eye also spoke fluent Spanish. So Beach requested that she teach him Spanish, and a friendship ensued.[31]

Born on 11 November 1888 in Puerto Plata, Dominican Republic (and thus twenty-one years younger than Beach), Alice was a distant relative of Joseph Fouché (1759–1820), one of the few intimates of the infamous French revolutionary Robespierre. In 1916, when Alice and Beach met, she was about to turn twenty-eight, and had no immediate family. Yellow fever had killed her parents in an 1895–1896 epidemic and her maternal grandmother had died of natural causes in 1899, leaving her dependent on the largess of her uncle, a Norwegian who had become an American citizen, and her aunt, who was of Dutch, French, and Dominican descent.[32]

Between their first casual meeting in 1916 and their marriage in 1917, Beach suffered severe personal and professional disasters with the death of his wife Lucie and the sinking of *Memphis*. The couple's growing friendship was not only plagued by the loss of *Memphis*, but also by the ensuing Navy board of inquiry and then a general court-martial. Beach's spirits were at their lowest ebb as he heard the verdict of his conviction for the loss of *Memphis*, which came less than a year after the death of his much-loved Lucie.

However, the lively Alice, who had by then moved to New York City to continue her education, soon rallied his spirits. The vivacious young woman provided an antidote for the shroud that seemed to have enveloped Beach's life—both personal and professional. The two had kept in touch and soon a romance began to blossom. On 2 April 1917, just as America prepared to enter World War I, the two were wed in New York. Later that year, even as news arrived that Alice was expecting their first child, Beach was ordered to command the U. S. Navy Torpedo Station at Newport, Rhode Island. In due course, Edward Latimer Beach Jr., arrived on 20 April 1918. No sooner had the baby boy arrived than Alice found herself living alone with her new baby in a city where she did not speak the language, and her husband was ordered to sea in command of a warship in a time of war. Alice did manage her life and that of the baby's during her husband's prolonged absence, but his return would prove to be the end of the couple's only extended period of separation. With the end of the war, Beach and his wife welcomed a new member of their family—John Blair Beach.

While life in New York with an absent husband had been tough, Alice soon found that being the wife of the commanding officer of a major naval construction base was even more taxing. English was becoming somewhat easier for Alice, but she was still having difficulty with the language and preferred to speak French at home. Alice did not learn to speak English with any ease until the family moved to Palo Alto, where she was invited to join a French club. Consisting of the wives of Stanford faculty, the members of the club sought to maintain and sharpen their French-speaking skills. In asking Alice to join, they offered to teach her English in return for her guidance in French.

[13]

As the Beach family settled into life at Mare Island, they became involved in the local community as well as the base's social life. Beach became an avid supporter of the development of sports and recreational facilities in the city of Vallejo, which was next to the Mare Island facility. His efforts and his involvement in civic affairs earned him so much respect that the city of Vallejo named a baseball field and recreation area Beach Park in his honor. According to an article in the local Vallejo newspaper, the ballpark consisted of grandstands that could seat over one thousand fans, had a completely fenced-in playing field, and was used for the town's Fourth of July, May Day, and other celebrations besides hosting baseball games.[33] That park was on the city's waterfront at the foot of Virginia Street.[34] Ironically, most people who saw or heard of Beach Park probably assumed it got its name because it is on the edge of the bay.

Beach's efforts in Vallejo were paralleled by his efforts to help the civilian workers at Mare Island. When he took command of the facilities in 1919, the workers were still being paid at mandated wartime salary levels. Price controls of food imposed during the war, however, had been lifted, creating hardships for workers whose wages were not increasing while the cost of food was recovering from those wartime price controls. In an effort to provide relief to the workers, Beach arranged to sell surplus Navy food through local stores to Navy yard workers. The Navy still made a profit off the sales, while the workers could buy food at prices below what was normally charged.[35]

In March 1921, then three-year-old Ned, and one-and-a-half year old John were joined by a sister—Alice Laura. Even as Alice arrived, Beach ended his career in the Navy and started to make plans for his family outside the naval service. After he secured a position teaching military history and naval science at Stanford University, the Beach family moved to Palo Alto, California, in the fall of 1921, eventually taking up residence first at 525 Channing Avenue, and then moving to 320 Castilleja Avenue in the 1930s.[36]

Teaching naval and military science at Stanford soon brought Beach to the realities of teaching someplace other than the Naval Academy. Instruction at the Academy was aimed at imparting knowledge within a rigid system designed to determine which students would make good officers and which would not. Teaching at other educational institutions, however, required the instructor to engage students to a greater degree so as to ensure that students were successful. When Beach gave a failing grade to Stanford football star Ernie Nevers, he soon realized some[*] important political realities of academic life outside a service academy.[1] Beach described his treatment after he "bilged" Nevers: "[T]he Assyrians came down like a wolf on the fold, ran 110 yards with me, made a touchdown, and then kicked me over the goal posts for a goal."[37] With the administrative pressure applied to give a passing grade to Nevers, who apparently seldom even attended class, Beach changed the failing grade to an "A" as a passive means of protest. This action then roused other members of the Stanford faculty to raise objections.

After three years at Stanford, Beach accepted the idea that the academic life was not his calling, so he gained appointment as city clerk and assessor for the City of Palo Alto, a position he held from 1925 to 1936.

[14]

Beach's health began to decline in the late 1930s, and he and Alice faced the proverbial empty nest as the children grew up and left home. By the time World War II began, Beach's health had steadily worsened, but he told the administrators of the Navy hospital in San Francisco that he would defer entering to seek medical assistance as long as there were wounded and injured from the war more in need of medical care.

---

[*] All-American Ernie Nevers, described by *Sports Illustrated* as the greatest college fullback of all time, played football for Stanford from 1923 to 1925. In the famous 1925 Rose Bowl game in which Stanford lost to Knute Rockne's Four Horsemen of Notre Dame, Nevers gained 114 yards rushing on thirty-four carries in spite of having been out of casts for two broken ankles for only ten days prior to the game. Nevers was eventually elected to the Rose Bowl Hall of Fame, the College Football Hall of Fame, and the Pro Football Hall of Fame.

In the last year of his life, Beach, who was also suffering from dementia (perhaps undiagnosed Alzheimer's), was able to see each of his children in spite of two of them being in uniform at a time when the world was at war. Ned was able to come home on leave from his submarine in the Pacific, and John was granted leave before going off to his first duty after he graduated from West Point. Daughter Alice was working in nearby San Francisco and was able to come home often.

Edward Latimer Beach Sr. died 20 December 1943 at Oak Knoll Naval Hospital, Oakland, California. He was buried with full military honors at Golden Gate National Cemetery, San Bruno, California.

In the years after her husband's death and the end of the war, Alice suffered from depression and began to experience paranoia. Daughter Alice and son John, who was living in Los Angeles while attending graduate school by this time, had to have their mother admitted to hospital. After several weeks of electric shock therapy, their mother was released and seemed to have made a complete recovery.[38]

With John in Los Angeles and soon on his way to West Point to take up a teaching assignment, and with Ned serving as commanding officer of USS *Amberjack* home-ported in Key West, Florida, sister Alice was the sibling living closest to their mother. Sometimes called "Alice Junior" by the family, she never married and remained in the Palo Alto area all of her life.

The bout with depression behind her, Alice (the mother) lived an active and healthy life to the age of eighty-one. The French Club where she had helped others with their French while she learned English had disbanded just a few months before her death, having met on a weekly basis for almost fifty years. At the time of her death from heart failure in 1970, she was still living alone at 1883 Park Boulevard in Palo Alto. She was still driving her own car and actively traveling, having just returned from a Caribbean cruise with her daughter. Alice was buried next to her husband in Golden Gate National Cemetery.[39]

[15]

Beach was never one to sit idle, and he had a bent for creative writing. While teaching at the Naval Academy in 1901, he set to writing a series of novels for young people about life at the Naval Academy, as well as life in the Navy in general. By 1900, the United States had passed child labor laws and instituted mandatory schooling to age sixteen, thereby creating a new social class—the adolescent. Without the modern distractions of radio, television, and other electronic entertainment devices, after the turn of the last century young people in greater and greater numbers began to fill their newly acquired hours of leisure with reading. Publishers quickly caught on to this trend and began targeting the emerging reader in the ten- to sixteen-year-old range. Books written in series were especially desirous because they brought the readers back to purchase more books from the same publisher.

This is the era to which Nancy Drew, Hardy Boys, and similar series trace their origins. Publishers hired writers—many of whom worked under several pseudonyms—who cranked out hundreds of titles with plots that all seemed vaguely similar.[40] A significant majority of these novels follow the model of the Horatio Alger stories, wherein hard work and honesty are rewarded with both personal advancement and self-satisfaction.

Beginning in 1907 with the publication of *An Annapolis Plebe*, Beach entered this world of young adult literature. Three more books, in what is known as the Annapolis series, followed in the next three years, with the final novel being released in 1910. Each novel covers one year at the Naval Academy in the life of the series' protagonist, the fictional Robert Drake. Overlapping the popular Annapolis series in publication was the Ralph Osborn series, which began in 1909 with the publication of *Ralph Osborn, Midshipman at Annapolis*. Also a four-novel series, the Ralph Osborn books cover the four years at the Naval Academy in a single volume and spend the final three volumes on the initial years of Osborn's career as an officer in the U.S. Navy. The final volume in this series was published in 1912.

Beach's third set of novels, the Roger Paulding series, began publication in 1911, with the fourth and final installment being published in 1914. These novels follow a seaman recruit from enlistment to his eventual commissioning as an officer. Like the Annapolis series, Penn Publishing Company published the Roger Paulding series in Philadelphia. H. A. Wilde Company of Boston published the Ralph Osborn series. All of Beach's novels were illustrated by Frank T. Merrill, a highly successful artist and illustrator of the period.

In 1922, the Macmillan Company of New York published *Dan Quin of the Navy*, which was to be the first installment of a projected new series. Beach had completed the second novel of the Dan Quin series by the time the first one was published, but it was never printed due to declining interest in books of that nature. In total, Beach published thirteen novels over a period of fifteen years with each running in excess of three hundred pages.

Beach's novels were highly autobiographical, unlike most of the stories then being mass produced by the writers under contract to the various publishing houses. The Ralph Osborn series includes the incident with the wife of Emilio Aguinaldo, as well as numerous events from Beach's service during the Philippine Insurrection. It is also clear in the novels that Beach is highly sympathetic to the plight of the Filipino people as they struggled for their independence.

Dan Quin of the Navy contains an accurate account of the United States' occupation of Vera Cruz in 1914, an incident in which Beach was a very active participant. The parallels between Beach's early career and parts of his novels are many—too many to be discussed here.

To be sure, the novels reflect some of the prejudices of the social and professional class to which the senior Beach belonged at the beginning of the twentieth century, but they are also decidedly understanding of the circumstances of the peoples in the Philippines and Mexico. Beach even created a fictional American minister to a Caribbean nation based on the real-life Frederick Douglass, whom Beach met while the aging Douglass was U.S. minister to Haiti. Written during the era of the denigrating Jim Crow laws of the American South, Beach's fictional character offers a picture of an educated and cultured black man who was laboring as his nation's representative in a difficult situation.

Today's reader might be put off by the style of Beach's writing. His writing was little different from the other novelists of the time, but by today's standards it would be viewed as overblown. For example, when describing graduation day at the Naval Academy in *An Annapolis First Classman*, he wrote, "Annapolis was now in ribboned and brass-buttoned glory. Proudly the brigade of midshipmen marched each afternoon for dress parade, and on the walks viewing them was much fluttering loveliness. Then, after dismissal, came pleasant, even if short, strolls through the grounds, in and about the shady walks."[41]

The novel with a youthful protagonist was a well-established genre within young-adult fiction by 1900. Beginning with Horatio Alger's *Ragged Dick* series (1867) to Mark Twain's *The Adventures of Tom Sawyer* (1876) and on to Hamlin Garland's *Boy Life on the Prairie* (1899), the reading public accepted central characters that were young.[42] Given that, by 1900, novels were being written expressly *for* the young adult, the use of young adult characters had also become de rigueur.

Today, the *Harry Potter* series is a prime example of this literary tradition still being continued. Beach's novels and those of J. K. Rowling share the commonality of young protagonists who are developing a sense of personal identity as they cope with the moral vagueness that is often part of the adult world they are soon to enter. Through courage and by upholding a sense of honor, the protagonists of such novels validate themselves and provide their young readers with models of behavior.

The novels of the senior Beach fall well within this genre, as he brought to life the U.S. Navy for a generation of young Americans. While only anecdotal evidence exists, it would not be a stretch to suggest that a good many officers who graduated from the Naval Academy in the years preceding World War II were avid readers of Beach's novels in their youth and were thus influenced to a career in the Navy as a result. Vice Adm. Thomas R. Weschler, USN (Ret.), a Naval Academy graduate (1939), who in the later part of his career was heavily involved in the Navy's Polaris missile program, has stated that, in large part, his decision to seek admission to Annapolis was the result of reading Beach's novels, along with others.[43]

The plots of Beach's novels are squarely based on what he saw and experienced. In the introduction to *An Annapolis First Classman*, Beach notes that, while the chief characters of his novels are made up, the stories are true, "countless times."[44] While at the Academy, one of his friends, Henry A. Wiley (with whom Beach daringly approached Commodore Ramsay in an effort to clear deadwood out of the Navy's officer lists) was wrongly dismissed from the Academy for hazing. Eventually, Wiley was restored. Beach later used the incident as the basis for an episode in *Ralph Osborn—Midshipman at Annapolis*.[45]

Even though his novels were set at the Naval Academy long after he had graduated, Beach also used his observations as an instructor to update his knowledge of the life of midshipmen. Chester Nimitz, later commander-in-chief in the Pacific during World War II, was a student at the Academy when Beach was teaching there. Some incidents that occurred at the Academy involving Nimitz appear as fictional events in at least one of the novels.

Several novels by Beach remain unpublished. In the files now belonging to Ingrid Beach, Ned's widow, are the following: *Bills Hartlepool, Sailor*, and *An American Sailor in a Haitian Revolution* (this was to be the second Dan Quin novel). There is also an unfinished manuscript titled *The Haitian Phoenix: A Story by E. L. Beach*. The later work is an earlier version of the Bills Hartlepool novel.

John Blair Beach (Ned's brother)

[1]

The silence was eerie as it descended across the dark forest. The deafening crescendo of exploding trees from the accurate German mortar and artillery fire ceased on a bleak mid-November day as elements of the 16th Infantry Regiment contended with well-dug-in German soldiers in the Hürtgen

Forest. When a wounded German soldier raised a white flag, 1st Lt. John B. Beach, USA, a platoon leader from Company C, walked into the open to help. The quiet was shattered as a German machine gun opened fire on Lieutenant Beach, dropping him to the ground with two bullets having passed through one of his legs. With pain from his leg wound searing in his brain, Beach anticipated imminent death. Realizing that he carried a German Lugar pistol that he had taken as a souvenir from a captured German officer and that the presence of that gun might cause the Germans to execute him, John threw the pistol as far away as he could manage given the pain in his leg. As the German who had shot him approached, machine gun at the ready, John saw that the young, blond soldier looked as scared as John felt. His hands held above his head as he lay on his back, John stared at this would-be killer. The young soldier nodded to John and then walked away.[46]

Perhaps, as he lay wounded, John recalled his older brother's advice back in 1935 to avoid the hazards of land warfare by joining the Navy. It was a sense of rebellion in not following the family tradition of naval service that led John to seek an appointment to the U.S. Military Academy at West Point, eventually placing him in the serious peril he faced on that November day in 1944.

His role as the middle child with an older brother—especially an older brother who seemed to conquer all before him—left John Beach with a desire to move from under Ned's shadow. If John ever considered following in his father's footsteps by pursuing a career in the Navy, that dream seems to have died when his older brother marched triumphantly onto the grounds at Annapolis.

John, who was named in honor of John Blair, a New York attorney and lifelong friend of the senior Beach, was sixteen when Ned left for the Academy. The distance between Palo Alto and Annapolis did not stop Ned from pouring advice on his younger brother. At the urging of his elder sibling, John became active in the Palo Alto High School student newspaper and found the one joy in his schooling—journalism. Perhaps recalling his own stumbling at casual conversation, Ned also urged his younger brother to get a radio installed in one of the family cars because they are "a great help when you're dating some babe, for it covers lapses in conversations, *etc.*[emphasis in the original]"[47]

[2]

Upon graduating from Palo Alto High School in 1936, John enrolled at San Jose State College with the intent of majoring in journalism. Ned had urged John to seek appointment to the Naval Academy, warning the younger brother that there was a war coming and that it would be better to be a naval officer than to be drafted and serve in the "trenches."[48] But it was clear that, by at least the middle of Ned's plebe year, John had clearly decided against such a course. In a home where Ned was the favored son, as well as the brilliant student who mastered all, John found his position as middle child being relegated to the role of rebel as the means to gain his father's attention. Generally disinterested in college, John attended only classes he liked, almost always journalism courses, and was willing to receive failing grades for non-attendance in the rest.[49]

During his third year at San Jose State (1939), John came to the conclusion that the United States was indeed headed toward war and he wanted to be able to do his part. An outcome of that realization was his decision to seek admission to the U.S. Military Academy at West Point. John withdrew from San Jose State and spent six months preparing for the West Point entrance exam under the tutelage of a friend of the family, a retired teacher remembered today as "Mr. Schneider."[50] His natural intellectual abilities plus study efforts were successful and he entered West Point in 1940, with a congressional appointment. Midway through his second year at West Point, the United States entered World War II, resulting in the acceleration of the programs for all the cadets.

[3]

John graduated from the Military Academy in June 1943. That December, while on leave to attend his father's funeral, John met Alison Grant, a recent Stanford University grad. Alison was born in Chicago in 1921 and grew up in River Forest, a Chicago suburb. She had attended Wellesley College in Massachusetts for a year, but disliked the climate, so she transferred to Stanford at the beginning of her sophomore year.

After graduating from Stanford in 1943, she met John's sister Alice, who was sometimes known as Alice Junior. Alison and Alice Junior became friends, so when John came home on leave that December, he was introduced to Alison, and the two were engaged within a few days. They were wed on 5 February 1944 at Camp Van Dorn, Mississippi, where John was stationed prior to being sent to fight in Europe.[51]

Newly commissioned as an officer in the U.S. Army, John attended the Tactical Infantry School at Fort Benning, Georgia, then was assigned as platoon leader in Company C, 16th Infantry Regiment, 1st Infantry Division—"the Big Red One."[52] John's platoon was designated as a replacement unit within the 16th Infantry Regiment, resulting in his arrival in Normandy, France, one day after the D-Day invasion.

Leading his platoon as the 16th Infantry Regiment fought its way across northeastern France, John was the first American to enter the town of Coeuvres-et-Valsery as it was freed from Nazi control. Having grown up speaking French as a second language, John soon discovered that the citizens of the town were not only delighted to have been liberated, but were equally pleased to find an American who spoke fluent French as their liberator. In 1994, on the fiftieth anniversary of D-Day, John returned to France and to the town of Coeuvres-et-Valsery where he was greeted by some of the same citizens who had welcomed him in 1944 and also by the French Resistance fighter with whom John had coordinated his platoon's movements half a century before.[53]

By mid-September 1944, the Allied armies' advance out of the Normandy beachhead had slowed as supply line problems and stiffening German resistance brought a new reality to the minds of the Allied soldiers who had been so euphoric after the successes of the summer. In an effort to break German resistance on their vaunted West Wall, the Ninth and First armies under the command of Gen. Omar Bradley launched a concentrated attack on a narrow front near Aachen, in the Rhineland. The 16th Infantry Regiment participated in the offensive, and John's platoon soon found itself embroiled in desperate fighting in the Hürtgen Forest.

Largely overshadowed by the Battle of the Bulge in postwar histories and popular journalism, the three-month-long Battle of Hürtgen Forest produced one of the fiercest infantry slugging matches of the European Theater. The thickly wooded forest laced with German pillboxes, barbed wire, and minefields largely neutralized the American advantages of maneuverability and firepower.

Having gone from Palo Alto to West Point and then to Normandy, 1st Lt. John Beach found himself in a German prisoner-of-war camp after he was fired upon while trying to assist a wounded German soldier waving a white flag.[54] The German who had fired on John did not move in to kill, but left John, who was later picked up by a German patrol that took him prisoner. John's own platoon had sent a newly arrived replacement infantryman to look for their "LT," but a fear of the killing zone of no-man's-land led the inexperienced young soldier to simply report that John was dead, "shot in the head." The U.S. Army considered John MIA (missing in action) pending confirmation of his death. From mid-November of 1944 to April of 1945, John was held by the Nazis and his wounds were treated, at least on a rudimentary medical level, by a captured English doctor. (For a full account of John B. Beach's service in Europe during World War II, see the article he wrote for *Bluebook*, October 1948.)

When his POW camp was liberated by Allied troops, John was eventually rehabilitated back in the United States. For his service in World War II, John was awarded two Silver Star medals—one specifically citing his gallantry in battle in the Hürtgen Forest had an oak leaf cluster attached. He was also awarded the Purple Heart, Bronze Star, Army Commendation Ribbon, and the Legion of Merit. He had a pronounced limp the rest of his life, but his career in the U.S. Army continued.

In 1949, John earned a master's degree in aeronautics and guided missiles at the University of Southern California. He then was assigned to teach chemistry at the Military Academy from 1949 to 1952. In 1956, he earned a second master's degree, this time in nuclear physics from the Naval Postgraduate School in Monterey, California. He served in South Korea for one year after the truce that ended the fighting. From 1960 to 1963, he was stationed in Japan.

John and his brother had a close relationship as they grew older, although they saw each other infrequently. When John was assigned to the Chemical Corps School at Fort McClellan in 1958, he was delegated the task of developing curricular materials for several new courses. As the Army bureaucracy failed to get him the technical information he needed to prepare the course materials, John called upon Ned, who then secured the information through his own contacts. As John's son, also John B. Beach, put it, "Ned was a very good brother to my dad."[55]

In spite of the rivalry between the Naval Academy and West Point, the Beach brothers never engaged in bantering over the sports teams of their respective schools. Neither was deeply interested in sports, so they never shared a common interest in cheering for their academies.

John retired from the U.S. Army in 1964 holding the rank of lieutenant colonel. His post-military career included work as an aerospace engineer for Pratt and Whitney and then for Ford Aerospace. For a time, he was a technical writer for Lockheed. Returning to his journalistic roots, John worked for several years as an editor for *Defense Electronics* magazine. It was while at *Defense Electronics* that he supervised the publication of three articles by his brother on the evolving role of electronics in submarine warfare.[56]

John and Alison had three daughters—Laura, Terry, and Anne—and a son, John. After John Sr. retired from the private sector, they lived in the Palo Alto area, where he died on 24 February 1999. Portions of his ashes were placed in the wall of the churchyard in Coeuvres-et Valsery, France, behind a plaque identifying him as "Liberator."

In the Beach household in the 1930s, the eldest son was his father's favorite and Alice, as the only daughter, had a special bond with her mother. Although his mother tried to compensate with extra kindness toward him, John, already the middle child, sensed the unevenness of family relations. In his own family, John strove to never allow his children to feel that same alienation, which explains why all of his own children proudly claim that each was their dad's favorite.[57]

This composite image shows John B. Beach, U.S. Army, Alice Beach, USN, and Edward L. Beach Jr., USN, during World War II.

Alice Laura Beach (Ned's sister)

[1]

Born at the Mare Island Naval Shipyard's hospital just six months before her father relinquished command as he retired from active duty, Alice spent almost all her life in or around Palo Alto. The youngest child, she strove always to be as good as, if not better than, her brothers, and to overcome the prejudice of the business world against women. Generally, Alice lived life on her own terms, not necessarily concerned with the expectations of others. Viewed in her youth as a tomboy, her older brother urged her to wear a dress more often and to lose weight. If she tried to follow Ned's nagging on these points, it never showed.

Graduating from Palo Alto High School in 1938, Alice enrolled at Reed College in Oregon; she was not content to accept the life of a housewife as her father and mother, with their Victorian values, wished for her.

Later transferring to Stanford University, Alice earned a degree in psychology, graduating in the midst of World War II. Skipping the more traditional roles for women in wartime America, Alice attempted to enlist in the WAVES (Women Accepted for Volunteer Emergency Service) of the U.S. Navy in 1944. Because she was nearsighted in one eye, she was initially rejected as not having 20/20 vision. She planned to memorize the eye chart as a means of "beating the system," but a naval officer and family friend found an exception in the regulations for her, allowing Alice to offer her service to her country. Along with 86,000 other American women, Alice helped the Navy to staff communications shore facilities, thereby releasing men for fighting roles at sea.

After being commissioned an ensign and completing communications school, Alice was assigned to the communications center of the 12th Naval District in San Francisco. She remained there until 1946 when she entered the Reserves. Called back to active duty at the beginning of the Korean War, Alice was stationed at the San Francisco Naval Shipyard in a public relations role. In 1952, she was transferred to the Great Lakes Naval Training Center in Illinois, where she remained until the end of the Korean War, eventually returning to the Reserves.[58] Her reserve service continued until 1963, when she retired at the rank of lieutenant commander. There is no record of Alice having met Ned while both were in uniform, a situation that might have required her to salute him.

[2]

Between World War II and the Korean War, she studied music in Geneva, Switzerland, using the benefits from the GI bill to fund her schooling. Before leaving, Alice built a wooden roof over her mother's patio, replacing the deteriorated canvas awning. Ned, very much the handyman, noted, "I was amazed at her ability to do this job which I would have hesitated to tackle myself."[59]

For reasons unknown, Alice gave up on her dreams of a musical career and took a position at the Los Angeles and San Diego Observatories that had offices in northern California on the Stanford campus. While employed there, Alice wrote an article detailing the technical capabilities of the Hale Telescope, which had recently been installed at Palomar Observatory. The article was published in the prestigious *Scientific American* in February 1953.

As her brothers were pursuing careers in the military, Alice remained close to home. In an ironic twist of fate, she accepted the duty of being a part-time homemaker by becoming the primary caregiver for her mother during her mother's declining years. While Alice Junior was a staunch advocate for women's rights in the workplace, she enjoyed the time she and her mother spent together, never seeming to resent being the child who was responsible for caring for her mother.

[3]

Eventually, Alice became dissatisfied with the limits placed on women where she was working, so she returned to her original field of study—psychology. Blending classroom work with practical application, Alice worked in a Veterans Administration (VA) hospital's psychiatric ward while pursuing a master's degree in psychology. Much of her work, in both a master's and then a doctoral program, focused on anxiety disorders. One research project on which Alice worked at the VA was the use of hypnosis to relieve anxiety. She reported to Ned that she had had success using the technique to help one patient overcome a fear of riding in an automobile and another patient who could not sleep, both due to anxiety.[60]

After she was awarded a master's degree from Stanford in 1962, Alice went to work as a school psychologist for the Jefferson School District, which was later part of the Santa Clara Unified School District. Just as she had done while working on her master's degree, Alice continued working full-time while furthering her education on a part-time basis. In 1966, she was awarded a PhD, again from Stanford. Eventually, she became the head of psychological services for the Santa Clara Unified School District. After twenty years with the school district, she retired to a life of travel and intellectual adventure.[61] She would always take pride in the fact that, of the three Beach children, she was the only one who earned a doctorate.[62]

[4]

Besides her professional work as a school psychologist, Alice pursued numerous hobbies and interests. In the 1950s, she developed a three-dimensional version of checkers. Using clear plastic for the three levels of the board, the game was designed for four players, either as singles or doubles.[63] In response to the craze over Rubik's Magic Cube in 1981, Alice wrote a book titled *Cube Solving for the Compleat Blockhead*, which was published privately. Not satisfied with just describing the means of solving the Rubik's Cube, the text is interspersed with short verses Alice penned:

> I thought that I had great ability
> But this cube has aroused my hostility
> My ego's destroyed
> I've become paranoid
> And I think I'm approaching senility

Travel was always a passion with Alice. She and her mother traveled extensively before the elder Alice died. After her mother's death, Alice continued her globe-trotting with her lifelong friend and next-door neighbor, Alice Mendenhall.

While in her sixties, Alice became an aficionado of the personal computer. In the last decade of her life, Alice took to volunteering at Palo Alto's public access television station. Utilizing her computer skills, she mastered the station's state-of-the-art digital imaging equipment. Drawing from the library of photographs she had taken on her world travels, she was soon the creative and technical manager for scrolling of upcoming programs and events, all set over backgrounds of her photos and classical music.[64] Alice continued in this work almost to the end of her life.

On 7 November 2003, at the age of eighty-two, Alice died peacefully in Palo Alto. Per her wishes, her ashes were scattered on the Pacific Ocean by means of a sky rocket as her family and friends looked on and toasted her life.

The Schencks (Ned's father- and mother-in-law)

[1]

Ned's mother-in-law, Inga Bergström, was the daughter of David and Ingrid Bergström. David was a leader of a liberal political reform movement in Sweden toward the end of the nineteenth century—his marriage to Ingrid was the first civil marriage performed in that nation. It was through her grandfather that Ingrid would inherit political views toward the liberal end of the spectrum. David Bergström served as the minister of defense for Sweden; he also was appointed minister (ambassador) to Finland, and then to Canada. From 1918 to 1922, he was minister to "The Orient" (meaning both Japan and China).

Inga was on a return trip from Japan to Sweden when she met her future husband while on a stop in Oakland, California, to visit friends. Her friends introduced Inga to Hugh Schenck, a young geologist, and she began telling him of her pending long train ride across the United States to catch a ship on the east coast back to Sweden. She complained how boring it would be, so he wrote her a series of letters to be read at specific times on the trip. The letters described the geology and geography of the areas through which the train traveled. The romance that had already begun was reinforced by those letters; Inga returned several months later to be married to the American geologist who wrote such charming letters.[65]

[2]

The author of the "charming" letters was Hubert Gregory "Hugh" Schenck, PhD, who taught geology for thirty-seven years at Stanford University. During World War II, he volunteered for the Army and was trained as an intelligence officer. After the war, he served in Japan for six years as chief of the Natural Resources Section of the U.S. Occupation Forces, where he supervised Japan's land reform program. As a result of his service, he was promoted to colonel. While serving in Japan, Hugh became friends with many Japanese, including the emperor, who shared his interests in microbiology and paleontology.

Following his work in Japan, Dr. Schenck served for three years as the director of the U.S. Aid Program in Taiwan. In that capacity, he supervised a large staff of scientists and bureaucrats, both American and Taiwanese. The program helped the Taiwanese develop more efficient management methods for their natural resources, just as it had done in Japan. Unfortunately, it was during this period that he contracted hepatitis B through contact with contaminated water. He died in 1960 after a long battle with the disease and was buried in Arlington National Cemetery.

Dr. Schenck had a highly successful academic career during which he published numerous papers and books on geology and paleontology. He also served as mentor and advisor to numerous Stanford graduate students working on master's and doctoral degrees.[66] His autobiography remains unpublished.

Hugh and Inga had one child, Ingrid, who later married Ned Beach.

Edward A. Beach

Ned and Ingrid's eldest son, Edward Latimer Beach III, was born in 1948, just several months before his elder sister, Inga-Marie, passed away. When the family settled in Mystic, Connecticut, Neddie—as he was then called by the family—entered Pine Point, a private elementary school that had become affordable to the family because of the royalties from *Run Silent, Run Deep*. Neddie was in fifth grade when he enrolled at Pine Point, while brother Hugh was in third. In time, all the Beach children enrolled at Pine Point School, which is in nearby Stonington, Connecticut. When the family moved to the Washington, D.C., area, all the children attended Sidwell Friends School, a Quaker prep school on Wisconsin Avenue near Georgetown.

Like most boys, Edward was keen on emulating his father, so he longed for a naval career. At age twelve Edward wrote to his father to report having finished reading, and very much enjoying, the *Bounty Trilogy*, which collectively tells of different aspects, in novel form, of the most widely known instance of mutiny in Britain's Royal Navy.[67] By this time, however, he had given up all ideas of a career in the Navy, even though he enjoyed reading sea adventure stories. While attending Pine Point School, Edward's intellectual attention had been drawn away from a naval career and on to other subjects like literature, Latin, French, biology, and especially philosophy. Through his contact with a classmate's father—a professor of philosophy at the nearby Connecticut College for Women—the seeds of interest in philosophy were planted, and would later blossom into a professional career.

After graduating from Sidwell, Edward entered Yale College, earning a Bachelor of Arts degree in 1971. Edward relates, "I then worked for a year as a book search specialist at Yale's Sterling Memorial Library, while preparing for graduate school. It was during this period that I met Diane Eaton, a divorced mother of three—Daniel, David, and Cynthia Carabello. This family became very dear to me, and I lived with them for six years. They also formed a close relationship with Ingrid and Ned, whom they came to regard as quasi-grandparents. Diane subsequently died, but I have retained ties with the children."[68]

Edward was admitted to the doctoral program at Northwestern University, completing a PhD in philosophy in 1980. The title of his dissertation: *Absolute Knowledge and the Problem of Systematic Completeness in Hegel's Philosophy*.

While at Northwestern, and anticipating a career in academe and its concurrent requirements to publish, Edward legally changed his middle name to "Allen" in an effort to distinguish his work from that of his father's and grandfather's in library catalogs. He had no particular reason for selecting "Allen" for his middle name, although it would place his works alphabetically ahead of most other Edward Beaches in bibliographies and library catalogs. The decision to change his middle name was made with the full knowledge and consent of his parents. Edward admits that, while his father understood the decision on an intellectual level, it was painful for Ned to have his son drop the middle name that both Ned and his father had so proudly borne.[69]

Upon completion of his graduate work at Northwestern, Edward was admitted to the doctoral program at Stanford University, where his maternal grandfather, Hubert Schenck taught for many, many years. In 1988, he was awarded his second PhD, this time in Religious Studies. The title of his Stanford dissertation is *Schelling's Philosophy of Mythology*.

His published works include *Dance of the Dialectic: A Dramatic Dialogue Presenting Hegel's Philosophy of Religion* (Washington,

D.C.: University Press of America, 1978) and *The Potencies of God(s): Schelling's Philosophy of Mythology* (Albany: State University of New York Press, 1994).

The eldest Beach son remains in academe—a professor in the Department of Philosophy and Religious Studies at the University of Wisconsin–Eau Claire. In 2002, Edward wed for the first time, marrying Emily Fleisher, the daughter of old friends whose association with Ingrid's family goes back four generations to when Ingrid's Swedish grandfather and Emily's American great-grandfather met in Japan, where both were living at the time.

Emily is an artist and educator whose academic and professional work is in biblical illustration and folk themes of Swedish and Jewish culture. She has recently collaborated in her husband's work by illustrating a reissued edition of his early poetic and philosophical work, *Dance of the Dialectic*. Emily has a grown child through a previous marriage, Kristoffer Fleisher-Durbin, who has become like a son to Edward. In the last year of Ned's life it was a joy to see his eldest child married, in the garden of their Georgetown home, to the daughter of close family friends.

Hugh Beach

Hubert Schenck Beach was born in 1949. Generally called Hugh by the family, he long ago abandoned any use of his birth name, preferring to be known as Hugh, even professionally. Ned characterized Hugh as the frequent winner of arguments, especially verbal ones, demonstrating that he was very quick-witted even in his youth. Edward recalls that his younger brother once argued his way out of a punishment he had coming for some infraction—a feat that very much impressed Edward.[70] A very studious child, Hugh was "always" being phoned by his classmates to get assistance with homework assignments.[71] Unlike any of the other Beach children, Hugh was interested in sports and played football on the Sidwell Friends School team during his high school years. According to Ingrid, her husband, who was generally not interested in sports, used to cheer himself hoarse at Hugh's football games where Hugh frequently scored touchdowns.[72]

While still in high school, Hugh accompanied his grandmother on one of her annual trips to Sweden. During a segment of their journey to the far north of Sweden, Hugh became intently interested in the culture of the peoples of Lapland. Through an unexpected stroke of good luck, Hugh was able to witness an annual reindeer calf-marking during which the Lapland reindeer herders marked the ears of their calves as a means of showing ownership. That interest in Lapland culture would later be channeled through his experiences in undergraduate school into a professional career.

During this period, Hugh and his brother Edward joined in serving their father as unofficial editors of his second novel, *Dust on the Sea* (1972), the sequel to *Run Silent, Run Deep*. The three Beaches enjoyed brainstorming together about the novel's characters and plot motifs, as well as about phraseology. For the two young men, this opportunity to observe and participate in their father's writing process was the experience of a lifetime. Ned later wrote in the book's acknowledgements: "Edward Beach—my son, who read and criticized the manuscript and in the process inserted much of his own philosophic, poetic nature. Hugh Beach—my other son, who also carefully went over every word and made many thoughtful comments in the knowledgeable way I have come to value so."[73]

Upon graduation from Sidwell Friends School, Hugh took a job on a Norwegian freighter and worked his way chipping rust across the Pacific Ocean to the Philippines, Japan, and then Thailand, where he left the ship to "look around." After teaching English for a period at a Buddhist temple in Bangkok, he rejoined *Themis*, the ship that had brought him to Thailand. Hugh re-crossed the Pacific, again chipping rust, while gaining a sense of the life at sea of which his father was so fond.[74]

After spending a summer working for the National Park Service at Yosemite National Park, and using his spare time to hike the entire Muir Trail, he entered Harvard College. The last of the two Beach sons to abandon any thought of a naval career, Hugh's life course was further altered by his contact during his Harvard years, on the International Honor Program's round-the-world study trip, with anthropologist Gregory Bateson. Hugh accompanied Bateson—husband of another noted anthropologist, Margaret Mead—along with twenty-five other students on a tour from Hawaii, to Japan, Hong Kong, Sri Lanka, India, and Africa. That trip cemented Hugh's desire to pursue studies in anthropology.

Not sure of where he was going with his life after graduating from Harvard in 1972, Hugh decided to take some time away from academics and return to Lapland. Ingrid was able to arrange through her contacts at the Swedish embassy in Washington for Hugh to spend a summer living with the Märak family. Johan Märak was a priest among the Saami, and a Saami himself. The Saami are one of several groups of people who inhabit the subpolar regions of northern Fennoscandia. Hugh fit in so well with the Saami, and he was enjoying the experience so much, that he decided to stay an entire year, thereby experiencing the full seasonal cycle of Saami life. After one year, he stayed on for another four years. Later, Hugh wrote of his first experiences and observations in a book titled *A Year in Lapland: Guest of the Reindeer Herders* (originally published in 1988 by Carlsson Bokförlag, and reprinted by Smithsonian Institute Press in 1993). A Swedish translation of the book was made by his wife, Annie, and was published in Sweden a few years later, while the University of Washington issued a paperback of the original English edition that is still in print.

At the end of that year, Hugh decided to remain in Sweden to pursue a doctorate in anthropology at the University of Uppsala. He completed the degree in 1981. His dissertation, *Reindeer-herd Management in Transition: The Case of Tuorpon Saameby in Northern Sweden,* was published by Almquist and Wickell in Stockholm in 1981. He remained at Uppsala as a docent (equivalent to an associate professor at an American university) in anthropology. In 2001, he was made chair of the anthropology department at Uppsala.

Some of his published works include editing *Contributions in Circumpolar Studies,* part of the University of Uppsala's Reports in Cultural Anthropology series, which was published by the university in 1986. In 1993, he co-edited, along with Ian Creery, *Polar Peoples: Native Inhabitants of the Far North,* which is part of the Minority Rights Group Reports Series. He herded reindeer for a year and a half with Inupiat herders on the Seward Peninsula of Alaska, and he has also carried out field work in northern Norway, Russia, and China.

Hugh married Annie Norell, a Swede, in 1986 in a traditional ceremony held in Lapland and officiated by the priest Johan Märak. Annie is a specialist in multicultural education for Swedish primary schools. Like his brother, Hugh has cystic fibrosis, a chronic disease which their parents were unknowingly predisposed to pass on to their children.

His cystic fibrosis having made it impossible for him to father children, Hugh and Annie turned to adoption. They first adopted a baby girl from Brazil whose mother was forced by poverty to give her up. Hugh and Annie named their new daughter Ellinor. Later, Hugh and Annie adopted Ellinor's newborn cousin, naming her Elisabeth. Ellinor was born in 1990 and Elisabeth in 1992. The fact that the girls were adopted was not kept a secret from them, and they have been back to Brazil to meet their biological mothers. Both have been raised in a bilingual home, speaking Swedish and English.

When Hugh took up permanent residence in Sweden, Ned began learning to speak a little Swedish so he would be more at ease when he and Ingrid began making regular visits to the land of Ingrid's ancestors. In 1996, Ned and Ingrid, along with son Hugh's family, purchased a summer home on the waterfront of the island of Ljusterö, in the Stockholm archipelago. Ned and Hugh then built an addition onto the house. The beautiful ocean view and the peaceful setting became a summer haven for Ned and Ingrid, as well as Hugh and his family.

Ingrid Alice Beach Robertson

The youngest of the children, Ingrid Alice was named for her mother and Ned's sister. She was born in 1952 in New London, Connecticut. Of the three children, Ingie (as she's generally called today by the family) was the one to acquire her mother's artistic interests. At Sidwell Friends School Ingie developed an interest in theatre, appearing in lead roles in several of the school's productions. With a three-year age span between herself and Hugh, Ingie remained at home with her parents for several years after Edward and Hugh had left for university. By this time, Ned was retired from active duty and had taken up duties as the staff director for the Senate Republican Policy Committee. Ingie remembers playing softball with the staff of the SRPC at one outing, and attending social occasions with her parents that were related to her father's work.[75]

Entering Tufts University after graduating from Sidwell, Ingie earned a degree in theater in 1975, having spent her third year studying theater in the United Kingdom as part of the Tufts-in-London program. Ingie recalls that her mother "visited me at one point during that time in London, and was fortunate to see me in an acting class attended by the well-known actor, Tim Curry (originator of the *Rocky Horror Show* and *Amadeus*). Mr. Curry made a special point of telling my mother how impressed he was with my acting: 'Totally convincing in her role,' were his words."[76]

Ingie then went to New York City to attempt a career on the stage, but the competitive nature of professional acting was not to her liking. Wanting to remain in the arts, she began work on a graduate degree at Columbia University, completing a degree specializing in the administration of arts programs in 1986.

While in New York, Ingie became interested in Hindu meditation and spiritual practices. She studied with an internationally recognized teacher of these subjects, Swami Muktananda, and over the next ten years spent frequent month-long periods at his ashrams (meditation communities) in South Fallsburg, New York, and Santa Monica, California. Even now, decades later, Ingie meditates regularly. Ned and Ingrid initially experienced some difficulty comprehending her interest in these esoteric topics, but ultimately they came to appreciate how much they meant to her. One of the greatest moments in Ingie's life was when her parents came to visit the South Fallsburg ashram and meet the revered swami. Ingie was somewhat nervous about how this incongruous encounter between the military officer and the meditation master would go, but both men rose to the occasion. Swami Muktananda reached out to shake hands (an uncharacteristic gesture for him) to welcome the visitors. Ingrid then spoke: "We're so happy that you've taught our daughter to be happy." With a gracious smile, the swami replied, "Well, I'm happy that you're happy that she's happy."[77]

In 1987 Ingie met a New Zealander, Bruce Robertson, who was in the United States visiting his brother. Bruce had been a spar-maker for the first New Zealand America's Cup challenge, and he has retained a lifelong interest in sailing vessels of all kinds. Ingie and Bruce married in 1988 and moved to Seattle, Washington, where they lived for eleven years. Ingie managed the New City Theater there while Bruce continued to work in the boating industry. While living in Seattle, Ingie and Bruce had two children, Jaya, born in 1991, and Ngaere, born in 1992.

The couple eventually decided to move back to Bruce's native New Zealand. They settled in the small city of Nelson on the north end of New Zealand's South Island. Bruce has a solar paneling business there, while Ingie is employed by the local town council. She works with the community to develop projects that can lead to a reduction in crime, including assisting council engineers and planners in the redesign of the inner city, seeking to ensure a safe city for the future.[78]

Ingie enjoys the beauty of New Zealand and is so glad that her father, Ned, saw her new home before he died. While touring the country in 2000, Ned turned to his son-in-law, Bruce, and said, "Now I understand why you took my daughter and grandchildren so far away. If I were a young man, I'd have done the same."[79]

Notes

Abbreviations Used

BAL: Beach Academy Letters (refers to "Letters from Midshipman Edward L. Beach, Jr.")

BP-EPL: Beach Papers at the Eisenhower Presidential Library

BP-IB: Beach Papers in the possession of Mrs. Ingrid Schenck Beach

EAB: Edward Allen Beach

ELBJ: Edward Latimer Beach Jr.

ELBS: Edward Latimer Beach Sr.

EPL: Eisenhower Presidential Library

IABR: Ingrid Alice Beach Robertson

ISB: Ingrid Schenck Beach

MPR: Military Personnel Records of Edward Latimer Beach Jr.

Preface

1. Shakespeare, *Hamlet*, in *The Living Shakespeare*, ed. Oscar Campbell (New York: Macmillan, 1949), 1.2.187–188.

Part I: 1918–1941

1. Edward L. Beach Jr., *Salt and Steel: Reflections of a Submariner* (Annapolis: Naval Institute Press, 1999), 16. (Hereinafter Edward L. "Ned" Beach Jr. will be cited as ELBJ. His father, Edward L. Beach Sr., will be cited as ELBS.)

2. Paul Stillwell, *Battleships* (New York: MetroBooks, 2001), 66.

3. ELBJ, "Letters from Midshipman Edward L. Beach, Jr.," 1:A. (Volume 1 is hereinafter referred to as BAL—Beach Academy Letters). During his four years at the Naval Academy, Ned wrote letters to his father on a very regular basis. All of the letters were kept with the intent that father and son would eventually write several novels about Academy life in the 1930s. Included to a lesser extent with these letters are letters to

Ned's mother (written in French) and a few letters to his brother and sister. The letters from Ned's first two years at the Academy are bound into two volumes and are in the possession of Ingrid Beach. Years three and four are in the Beach Papers at the Eisenhower Presidential Library, referred to here as BP-EPL.)

4. ELBJ, "Looking Backward," (senior English essay at Palo Alto High School, 1934), unpublished, BAL, 1:IIA to IIIA.

5. Ibid.

6. ELBJ, letter to ELBS, August 1935, BAL, vol. 1.

7. ELBJ, letter to ELBS, 25 August 1935, BAL, vol. 1.

8. ELBJ, BAL, 1:8.

9. John Beach Jr., letter to author, 4 April 2006.

10. "Edward L. 'Ned' Beach," *The Lucky Bag* yearbook (Annapolis: U.S. Naval Academy, 1939), 179.

11. ELBJ, letter to ELBS, 18 June 1935, BAL, vol. 1.

12. ELBJ, letter to ELBS, 26 September 1936, BAL, vol. 1.

13. Ibid.

14. The etymology for the use of "spoon" in this context is unclear. By the mid-1800s the use of "spoon" to describe a romantic relationship between a boy and a girl was common. However, to use the word with its romantic connotation to describe friendships between young men in a military setting seems unusual. Nonetheless, the word was widely used to describe such relationships.

15. ELBJ, letter to ELBS, 22 June 1935, BAL, vol. 1.

16. Ibid.

17. ELBJ, letter to ELBS, 15 February 1936, BAL, vol. 1.

18. ELBJ, letter to ELBS, 15 March 1936, BAL, vol. 1.

19. ELBJ, letter to ELBS, 29 May 1938, BP-EPL, box 1.

20. Jack Sweetman, *The U.S. Naval Academy: An Illustrated History,* revised by Thomas J. Cutter (Annapolis: Naval Institute Press, 1995), 189.

21. Ibid., 191.

22. Ibid.

23. ELBJ, letter to ELBS, 25 August 1935, BAL, vol. 1.

24. "Edward L. 'Ned' Beach," *The Lucky Bag*, 179.

25. Millard B. Frazier, "Ned Beach Leading Student at Academy," *Vallejo* (California) *Independent Press*, 5 June 1983.

26. ELBJ, letter to ELBS, 22 July 1938, BP-EPL, box 1.

27. Ibid.

28. ELBJ, letter to ELBS, 25 August 1935, BAL, vol. 1.

29. ELBJ, letter to ELBS, 26 September 1935, BAL, vol. 1.

30. "Officers Are Named to Head Midshipmen," *New York Times*, 28 August 1938.
31. ELBJ, letter to ELBS, 27 November 1938, BP-EPL, box 1.
32. ELBJ, letter to ELBS, 30 October 1938, BP-EPL, box 1.
33. Harold E. Shear, *The Reminiscences of Admiral Harold Edson Shear, USN (Ret.)*, U.S. Naval Institute Oral History Project (Annapolis: Naval Institute, 1997), 30.
34. ELBJ, letter to ELBS, 5 November 1938, BP-EPL, box 1.
35. Paul H. Backus, *The Reminiscences of Commander Paul H. Backus, USN (Ret.)*, U.S. Naval Institute Oral History Project (Annapolis: Naval Institute, 1995), 54.
36. ELBJ, letter to ELBS, 18 March 1939, BP-EPL, box 1.
37. "Program of Presentations—Dress Parade, 31 May 1939," U.S. Naval Academy, BP-EPL, box 26.
38. Ibid.
39. ELBJ, letter to ELBS, 25 February 1939, BP-EPL, box 1.
40. ELBJ, letter to ELBS, 30 April 1939, BP-EPL, box 1.
41. ELBJ, letter to ELBS, 28 January 1939, BP-EPL, box 1.
42. ELBJ, letter to ELBS, 21 July 1940, BP-EPL, box 1.
43. Navy Department, *Dictionary of American Naval Fighting Ships*, (Washington, DC: U.S. Government Printing Office, 1959–1981), 7:356–357. (*DANFS* will be used for this source in following citations.)
44. ELBJ, letter to ELBS, 21 July 1940, BP-EPL, box 1.
45. Stephen Howarth, *To Shining Sea: A History of the United States Navy* (New York: Random House, 1991), 375–376.
46. ELBJ, "Eisenhower Administration Project: Edward L. Beach," 23 August 1967, Columbia University Oral History Project (New York: Columbia University, 1971), 10–11. (Hereinafter this work will be cited as CUOHP.)
47. ELBJ, letter to ELBS, 27 June 1940, BP-EPL, box 1.
48. ELBJ, CUOHP, 2.
49. Howarth, *To Shining Sea*, 380.
50. Michael D. Hull, "Argentia Conference helped forge the grand alliance that ultimately prevailed during World War II," *WWII History* (September 2006), 16–17.
51. ELBJ, *Salt and Steel*, 58.
52. Ibid., 57.

Part II: 1941–1945

1. Hansgeorg Jentschura, Dieter Jung, and Peter Mickel, *Warships of the Imperial Japanese Navy, 1869–1945*, translated by Anthony Preston

and J. D. Brown (Annapolis: Naval Institute Press, 1977), 187–190. The first two paragraphs of this chapter contain quotes from "U.S.S. *Tirante*, Report of First War Patrol," 25 April 1945, 15.

2. ELBJ, *The United States Navy: 200 Years* (New York: Henry Holt & Company, 1985), xv.

3. Norman Friedman, *U.S. Submarines through 1945: An Illustrated Design History* (Annapolis: Naval Institute Press, 1995), 311.

4. Clay Blair Jr., *Silent Victory: The U.S. Submarine War against Japan*, (Philadelphia: J. P. Lippincott, 1975), 424.

5. ELBJ, *Submarine!* (New York: Henry Holt & Company, 1952), 4.

6. ELBJ, *Salt and Steel,* 16.

7. "Report of the Grounding of USS *Trigger* (SS-237)," 6 June 1942, 6.

8. ELBJ, Enclosure "C" of "Report of the Grounding of USS *Trigger* (SS-237)," 6 June 1942, 1.

9. "First Endorsement: to U.S.S. *Trigger* Conf. Ltr. SS237/L11-1 Serial 015 of June 7, 1942."

10. Quoted in Blair, *Silent Victory,* 267.

11. Thomas B. Buell, *Quiet Warrior: A Biography of Admiral Raymond A. Spruance*, (Annapolis: Naval Institute Press, 1987), 55.

12. Brayton Harris, *The Navy Times Book of Submarines: A Political, Social, and Military History*, ed. Walter J. Boyne (New York: Berkley Books, 1997), 262.

13. Blair, *Silent Victory,* 517.

14. ELBJ, *Submarine!,* 13–18.

15. ELBJ, "Culpable Negligence," *American Heritage*, December 1980, 41–54.

16. ELBJ, CUOHP, 30.

17. Quoted in: Dan van der Vat, *Stealth at Sea: The History of the Submarine*, (Boston: Houghton Mifflin Co., 1994), 262.

18. Blair, *Silent Victory,* 336.

19. Buell, *Quiet Warrior,* 169.

20. ELBJ, afterword to *Maru Killer: The War Patrols of the USS Seahorse*, by Dave Bouslog, 2nd ed. (Placentia, CA: R. A. Cline Publishing, 2001), 309.

21. Carl Lavo, *Slade Cutter: Submarine Warrior* (Annapolis: Naval Institute Press, 2003), 121.

22. Ibid., 138–139.

23. ELBJ, *Salt and Steel,* 143.

24. ELBJ, *Submarine!,* 66–73.

25. ISB, interview by author, Washington D.C., 11 August 2005.

26. ISB, letter to ELBJ, 31 May 1943, BP-IB.

27. ELBJ, letter to ISB, 30 June 1943, BP-IB.

28. ISB, interview by author, Washington, D.C., 16 February 2006.

29. ISB, interview by author, Washington, D.C., 11 August 2005.

30. "U.S.S. *Trigger* (SS-237)—Sixth War Patrol Report," 30 September 1943.

31. Blair, *Silent Victory*, 190–191.

32. Quoted in Blair, *Silent Victory*, 601.

33. ELBJ, *Submarine!*, 217–225; Blair, *Silent Victory*, 600–602.

34. Paul Stillwell, interview with author, Morton Grove, Illinois, 5 July 2006.

35. Quoted in Blair, *Silent Victory*, 842.

36. ELBJ, *Salt and Steel*, 154.

37. ELBJ, letter to ISB, 30 June 1943, BP-IB, 4.

38. ISB, interview by author, Washington, D.C., 11 August 2005.

39. Ibid.

40. ELBJ, *Submarine!*, 269–270.

41. Edward G. Campbell, "The Autobiography of George Campbell" (unpublished; in the private papers of Edward G. Campbell), chap. 21, 2–3.

42. Blair, *Silent Victory*, 844.

43. Ibid., 877–879.

44. ELBJ, *Submarine!*, 294.

45. Ibid., 301.

Part III: 1945–1953

1. R. T. Bond (acquisitions editor at Dodd, Mead & Company), letter to ELBJ, 20 April 1946. BP-EPL, Box 1.

2. ISB, letter to author, 15 February 2008.

3. ELBJ, *Salt and Steel*, 170.

4. Ibid., 172–173.

5. Ibid., 176.

6. Ibid., 177.

7. Norman Polmar and Thomas B. Allen, *Rickover: Controversy and Genius* (New York: Simon & Schuster, 1982), 138.

8. Ibid., 138–139.

9. Ibid.

10. John D. Alden, *The Fleet Submarine in the U.S. Navy: A Design and Construction History* (Annapolis: Naval Institute Press, 1979), 131.

11. Ibid., 131.

12. Ibid., 132.

13. Ibid.

14. Lee Bert Finley, letter to author, 30 November 2004.

15. Alden, *The Fleet Submarine*, 132.

16. Lee Bert Finley, letter to author, 30 November 2004.

17. ELBJ, *Salt and Steel*, 196.

18. Ibid., 197.

19. Frederick Wagner, *Famous Underwater Adventurers*, (New York: Dodd, Mead, 1962), 129–130.

20. ELBJ, *Salt and Steel*, 197.

21. Ibid., 198.

22. Ibid., 199.

23. ELBJ, letter to Chris and Agnes [last name unknown], 25 August 1948, BP-EPL, Box 1.

24. ISB, letter to the author, 7 June 2006.

25. Omar Bradley and Clay Blair, *A General's Life* (New York: Simon & Schuster, 1983), 511.

26. Omar Bradley, letter to Louis Denfeld, 24 August 1949, BP-EPL, box 1.

27. Michael T. Isenberg, *Shield of the Republic: The United States Navy in an Era of Cold War and Violent Peace*, vol. 2, *1945–1962* (New York: St. Martin's Press, 1993), 149, 161.

28. ELBJ, *Salt and Steel*, 214–215.

29. Ibid., 216.

30. Ibid., 218.

31. Ibid., 198–199.

32. Ibid., 221.

33. ELBJ, letter to Cdr. W. W. McCrory (personnel officer for Commander Submarines Atlantic), 2 March 1951, BP-EPL, box 2.

34. Isenberg, *Shield of the Republic*, 377.

35. ELBJ, *Salt and Steel*, 224.

36. Shear, *Reminiscences*, 128.

37. ELBJ, CUOHP, 132.

38. Ibid.

Part IV: 1953–1957

1. Dwight D. Eisenhower, Letter to the Secretary of the Navy, 14 January 1953. Papers of Sherman A. Adams, Eisenhower Presidential Library—Central Files, Official files of 72-A-2, Box 286.

2. ELBJ, CUOHP, 144.

3. Edward G. McGrath, "Ike Breaks Precedent in Picking Young Sub Hero from New London Base as his Naval Aide," *Boston Sunday Post*, 25 January 1953, 37.

4. "New Look In Aides," *Time*, 26 January 1953, 20–21.

5. William J. Crowe, telephone interview by author, 17 November 2006.

6. Ibid.

7. ELBJ, CUOHP, 288.

8. Ibid., 154.

9. Ibid., 153.

10. Ibid., 147–148.

11. David Thomson, *The New Biographical Dictionary of Film* (New York: Alfred A. Knopf, 2002), 256–257.

12. ELBJ, *Salt and Steel*, 225.

13. "New Look In Aides," *Time*, 26 January 1953, 21.

14. ELBJ, CUOHP, 172.

15. Navy Department, *DANFS*, 8:371.

16. ELBJ, CUOHP, 217.

17. Ibid., 220.

18. Ibid., 218.

19. Ibid., 245.

20. Donald J. MacDonald, "President Truman's Yacht," *Naval History*, Winter 1990, 48–49.

21. Mark I. Fox, telephone interview by author, 18 April 2006.

22. ELBJ, CUOHP, 189.

23. William J. Crowe, telephone interview by author, 17 November 2006.

24. ELBJ, CUOHP, 204.

25. William J. Crowe, telephone interview by author, 17 November 2006.

26. Ibid.

27. ELBJ, CUOHP, 274.

28. Douglas Waller, "Fumbling the Football: Now it Can Be Told," *Newsweek*, 7 October 1991, 26.

29. ELBJ, *Salt and Steel*, 235.

30. Polmar and Allen, *Rickover*, 153.

31. Isenberg, *Shield of the Republic*, 572–573.

32. Ibid., 625–626.

33. ELBJ, CUOHP, 295.

34. ELBJ, letter to Henry F. Holland, 7 December 1956, BP-EPL, Box 4.

35. "Naval Aide Replaced," *New York Times*, 25 January 1957.

36. ELBJ, CUOHP, 369.

37. Dwight D. Eisenhower, letter to Charles S. Thomas, 12 February 1957, BP-EPL, Box 4.

Part V: *Run Silent, Run Deep*

1. ELBJ, *Run Silent, Run Deep* (New York: Henry Holt & Company, 1955), 349.
2. Ruth Pirsig Wood, *Lolita in Peyton Place: Highbrow, Middlebrow, and Lowbrow Novels in the 1950s* (New York: Garland Publishing, 1995), 71.
3. ELBJ, *Run Silent, Run Deep*, 194.
4. "Mixed Fiction," *Time*, 4 April 1955, 104.
5. Herbert Mitgang, "Deep Down and Deadly," *New York Times Book Review*, 3 April 1955, 4.
6. Barbara Emerson (director of advertising at Henry Holt & Company), letter to ELBJ, 1 September 1955, BP-EPL, Box 13.
7. William E. Buckley (editor at Henry Holt & Company), letter to ELBJ, 4 December 1956, BP-EPL, Box 13.
8. "46 'Notable' Books Chosen for Year," *New York Times*, 5 February 1956, 36.
9. Alice Payne Hackett and James Henry Burke, *80 Years of Best Sellers, 1896–1975,*(New York: R. R. Bowker Co., 1977), 166–167.
10. ELBJ, letter to William E. Buckley, 31 March 1955, BP-EPL, Box 13.
11. ELBJ, letter to J. D. P. Hodapp Jr., 4 July 1960, BP-EPL, Box 9.
12. Nathan Miller, *War At Sea: A Naval History of World War II* (New York: Scribner, 1995), 319–320.
13. Quoted in: Van der Vat, *Stealth at Sea*, 291.
14. Ibid., 320n.
15. ELBJ, memo to "Chief of Information, United States Navy," 7 September 1961, 2, BP-EPL, box 11.
16. ELBJ, *Run Silent, Run Deep*, xii.
17. ELBJ, memo to "Chief of Information United States Navy," 7 September 1961, 1, BP-EPL, box 11.
18. EAB, interview by author, Washington D.C., 5 June 2006.
19. Lawrence H. Suid, *Sailing the Silver Screen: Hollywood and the U.S. Navy* (Annapolis: Naval Institute Press, 1996), 137.
20. ELBJ, letter to Jeffery Ryan, 7 July 1992, BP-IB.
21. Suid, *Sailing the Silver Screen*, 137.
22. Maurice "Mike" Rindskopf, interview by author, Annapolis, Maryland, 10 August 2006.
23. Blair, *Silent Victory*, 639.
24. Lavo, *Slade Cutter*, 173.
25. Blair, *Silent Victory*, 719.
26. ELBJ, *Dust on the Sea* (New York: Henry Holt & Company, 1972), 293.

27. Suid, *Sailing the Silver Screen*, 138.
28. Lawrence H. Suid, *Guts and Glory: The Making of the American Military Image in Film* (Lexington: University Press of Kentucky, 2002), 160.
29. Suid, *Sailing the Silver Screen*, 133.
30. "The Real Thing," press release issued by United Artists Corporation, undated, BP-EPL, box 16, 24.
31. Blair, *Silent Victory*, 379.
32. Rob Roy McGregor, introduction to *USS Sea Cat (SS-399) 1944-1968: The Boat and the Men*, by Robert Winburn (Chicago: Spectrum Press, 2001), v–vi.
33. ELBJ, letter to Max Youngstein, 10 March 1958, BP-EPL, box 7.
34. Suid, *Sailing the Silver Screen*, 138.
35. Bosley Crowther, "The Screen: Submarine Adventure," *New York Times*, 28 March 1958, 29.
36. http://www.imdb.com/title/TT0052151/awards (accessed 16 June 2006).
37. William J. Crowe, telephone interview by author, 17 November 2006.
38. ELBJ, letter to Ingrid Schenck, 8 May 1944, 3, BP-IB.
39. Roger Ebert, review of *The Hunt for Red October*, directed by John McTiernan, *Chicago Sun-Times*, 2 March 1990, http://www.suntimes.com/ebert/ebert_reviews.1990/03/554354.html (accessed 6 February 2001).
40. ELBJ, letter to Max Youngstein, 10 March 1958, BP-EPL, box 7.
41. Annie Laurie Williams, letter to ELBJ, 13 January 1960, BP-EPL, box 7.
42. ISB, letter to author, 9 October 2006.
43. "Run Silent, Run Deep," Interview with CAPT Edward L. Beach," *All Hands*, August 1999, 32, http://www.mediacen.navy.mil/pubs/allhands/aug99/pg32.htm (accessed 24 November 2004).

Part VI: 1957–1958

1. ELBJ, letter to Adm. Frank T. Watkins, 16 January 1957, BP-EPL, box 6.
2. Isenberg, *Shield of the Republic*, 444.
3. Dave Wood, letter to author, July 2004, 1.
4. Michael McAllister, letter to author, July 2004, 1.
5. ohn Lichoff, telephone interview by author, 2 June 2004.
6. Joseph Felt, letter to author, July 2004, 2.
7. ELBJ, letter to Commo. W. T. Nelson, Commander Service Force, Sixth Fleet, 26 October 1957, BP-IB.
8. Michael McAllister, letter to author, July 2004, 1.

9. Errol Flynn, letter to ELBJ, 26 June 1957, BP-EPL, box 4.

10. Michael McAllister, letter to author, July 2004, 2.

11. Louis Colbus, *The Reminiscences of Captain Louis Colbus, USN (Ret.)*, U.S. Naval Institute Oral History Project (Annapolis: Naval Institute, 2001), 61–62.

12. "To the Rescue," *All Hands*, March 1958, 34–35.

13. Joseph Felt, letter to author, July 2004, 4.

14. W. T. Nelson, Fitness Report on ELBJ, 9 December 1957, Military Personnel Records of ELBJ (hereinafter cited as MPR).

15. "Newport-Based Sailor Given Navy Medal for his Bravery," *Newport* (Rhode Island) *Daily News*, 23 December 1957, 1.

16. Ibid.

17. IABR, e-mail to author, 13 July 2006.

18. Hugh Beach, e-mail to author, 21 January 2007.

19. Edward A. Beach, "Eulogy by Edward Allen Beach.," Naval Academy Chapel, 14 January 2003.

20. Edward A. Beach, interview by author, Washington, D.C., 5 June 2006.

21. Ibid.

22. Hugh Beach, e-mail to author, 21 January 2007, 1.

23. "Mystic Homes Open June 10," *The Day* (New London, CT), 2 June 2000, F-24.

24. Roy S. Benson, *Reminiscences of Rear Admiral Roy S. Benson, USN (Ret.)*, vol. 2, U.S. Naval Institute Oral History Project (Annapolis: Naval Institute, 1980), 795.

25. Ibid.

26. "Mystic Homes Open June 10."

27. IABR, "Eulogy by Ingrid Alice Beach," Naval Academy Chapel, 14 January 2003.

28. ELBJ, letter "To All Households Abutting the Same Alley We Do," 13 May 1994, 1, BP-IB.

29. Ibid., 2.

30. Dave Davenport, letter to ELBJ, 11 April 1994, BP-IB, "Ship models" file.

Part VII: 1958–1961—*Triton*

1. "*Log of the USS* Triton, *16 February 1960 to 10 May 1960*," B-138. This chapter tells the story of *Triton*'s submerged circumnavigation of the globe. However, most of what is told here relates to events leading up to and after the voyage. Anyone wishing a more detailed account of the actual voyage should see Ned's *Around the World Submerged: The*

Voyage of the Triton ((New York: Holt, Rinehart and Winston, 1962), now available from the Naval Institute Press in paperback.

2. ELBJ, letter to ISB, 19 May 1947, BP-IB.

3. "Atoms and Prophets," *Newsweek*, 6 June 1955, 56.

4. Lewis L. Strauss, *Men and Decisions* (Garden City, NY: Doubleday, 1962), 344.

5. Jimmy Carter, *Why Not the Best? Why One Man is Optimistic about America's Third Century* (Nashville, TN: Broadman Press, 1975).

6. Will Mont Adams Jr., interview by author, Washington, D.C., 7 June 2006.

7. ELBJ, CUOHP, 52.

8. Ibid., 50.

9. ISB, interview by author, Washington, D.C., 11 August 2004.

10. Isenberg, *Shield of the Republic*, 415.

11. Ibid.

12. Hyman G. Rickover, Fitness Report on ELBJ, 5 September 1958, MPR.

13. Paul Stillwell, interview by author, Morton Grove, Illinois, 5 July 2006.

14. Francis Duncan, *Rickover: The Struggle for Excellence* (Annapolis: Naval Institute Press, 2001), 157–158.

15. Ibid., 152.

16. Edith Hamilton, *Mythology* (Boston: Little, Brown and Company, 1942), 42.

17. ELBJ, letter to Rear Adm. Frank T. Watkins, 16 January 1957, BP-EPL, box 6.

18. S. P. Moncure, letter to ELBJ, 16 August 1957, with attached undated memorandum from Hyman G. Rickover to James L. Holloway, BP-EPL, box 5.

19. Navy Department, Division of Naval History (Op-29), Ship's History Section, "History of USS *Triton* (SS-201)," 22 July 1958, 6, BP-EPL, box 24.

20. Navy Department, "*Triton*," in *DANFS*, 7:296–298.

21. Norman Friedman, *U.S. Submarines since 1945: An Illustrated Design History* (Annapolis: Naval Institute Press, 1994), 87–99.

22. ELBJ, *Around the World Submerged*, 4.

23. Duncan, *Rickover*, 170.

24. Polmar and Allen, *Rickover*, 302.

25. Will Mont Adams Jr., interview by author, Washington, D.C., 7 June 2006.

26. Ibid.

27. ELBJ, commissioning speech for USS *Triton*—handwritten text, BP-EPL, box 25.

28. Marion D. Williams, *Submarines under Ice: The U.S. Navy's Polar Operations*, (Annapolis: Naval Institute Press, 1998), 103.

29. E. P. Aurand, memorandum to Chief of Naval Operations Arleigh Burke, 6 January 1960, Papers of Evan P. Aurand, EPL, box 25.

30. Ibid.

31. Arleigh Burke, memorandum to E. P. Aurand, 18 January 1960, Papers of Evan P. Aurand, EPL, box 25.

32. E. P. Aurand, memorandum to James Hagerty, 26 January 1960, Papers of James Hagerty, EPL, box 10.

33. ELBJ, *Around the World*, 42–43.

34. ELBJ, "*Triton* Follows Magellan's Wake," *National Geographic*, November 1960, 586.

35. ISB, interview by author, Washington, D.C., 11 August 2004.

36. Jessie Ash Arndt, "Navy Wife Serves With Courage, Too," *Christian Science Monitor*, 24 May 1960, 6.

37. Alan Villiers, *Men, Ships, and the Sea*, new edition (Washington, DC: National Geographic Society, 1973), 107.

38. Ibid., 48–49.

39. Will Mont Adams Jr., letter to author, 30 November 2006.

40. Ibid.

41. ELBJ, *Around the World*, 92.

42. Ibid., 150–151.

43. Will Mont Adams Jr., interview by author, Washington, D.C., 7 June 2006.

44. Ibid.

45. ISB, letter to author, 23 September 2006.

46. ISB, letter to ELBJ, 4 October 1960, 1, BP-EPL, Box 25.

47. Villiers, *Men, Ships, and the Sea*, 109.

48. Jack Sweetman, *American Naval History: An Illustrated Chronology of the U. S. Navy and Marine Corps, 1775–Present*, 3rd ed. (Annapolis: Naval Institute Press, 2002), 180.

49. "Only One Saw Sub, and He Got Scared," *Charleston* (West Virginia) *Gazette*, 11 November 1960, 16 .

50. ELBJ, *Around the World Submerged*, 291–292.

51. The paragraph is a summary of numerous letters found in the Beach files held by Ingrid Schenck Beach.

52. Allen Steele, interview by author, San Diego, California, 1 July 2004.

53. Ibid.

54. ELBJ, *Around the World Submerged*, 255–256.

55. "2,000 Welcome Triton on Return to Home Port," *New York Herald Tribune*, 12 May 1960, 2.

56. Walter R. Tkach, letter to ELBJ, 16 September 1960, BP-EPL, box 9.

57. Villiers, *Men, Ships, and the Sea*, 110–111.

58. ELBJ, letter to Nora Zah, 23 April 1993, original in author's files.

59. David Halberstam, *The Fifties* (New York: Villard Books, 1993), 710–711.

60. "Legion of Merit Citation for Edward L. Beach, Jr.," White House, 10 May 1960, BP-IB.

61. Michael R. Beschloss, *Mayday: Eisenhower, Khrushchev, and the U-2 Affair* (New York: Harper & Row, 1986), 250–251.

62. ELBJ, *Around the World Submerged*, 280.

63. Ibid., 281.

64. T. H. Henry, Fitness Report on ELBJ, 31 August 1960, MPR.

65. T. H. Henry, Fitness Report on ELBJ, 4 March 1961, MPR.

66. ELBJ, *Around the World Submerged*, 293.

67. *KAPL Employee's Headliner*, 17 May 1960, 1, BP-EPL, box 8.

68. Press release, Office of Information, Department of the Navy, 10 May 1960, Papers of James Hagerty, EPL, box 10.

69. Press release, Office of U.S. Senator Prescott Bush (R-CT.), 19 May 1960, BP-EPL, box 8.

70. Carol (no surname given), letter to ELBJ, 26 October 1960, BP-EPL, box 9.

71. ELBJ, letter to George Avakian (Director of Artists and Repertoire, Warner Brothers Records), 13 June 1960, BP-EPL, box 8.

72. Allen Steele, interview by author, San Diego, California, 1 July 2004.

73. Commencement program, American International College, June 1961, BP-EPL.

74. News release, Office of News Services, U.S. Department of Defense, 17 October 1960, BP-EPL, box 9.

75. Edward C. Whitman, "U.S. Radar Picket Submarines: Cold War Curiosities," *Undersea Warfare*, Winter/Spring 2002.

76. Friedman, *U.S. Submarines since 1945*, 243.

77. Samuel Loring Morison (compiler), "U.S. Naval Battle Force Changes, 1 January 2007–31 December 2007," U.S. Naval Institute *Proceedings*, May 2008, 102.

78. "*Log of the USS* Triton, *16 February 1960 to 10 May 1960,*" B-138.

Part VIII: 1961–1966

1. Paul H. Nitze, memorandum to ELBJ, 11 May 1965, BP-IB.
2. Chief of Naval Operations, memorandum to ELBJ, 30 March 1965, BP-IP.
3. EAB, e-mail to author, 1 August 2009.
4. Ibid.
5. EAB, interview by author, Washington, D.C., 5 June 2006.
6. Ibid.
7. Ibid.
8. ISB, e-mail to author, 21 February 2007.
9. Blair, *Silent Victory*, 883.
10. Maurice Rindskopf, e-mail to author, 2 September 2006.
11. ELBJ, *Salt and Steel*, 240.
12. William Tuohy, *The Bravest Man: The Story of Richard O'Kane and U.S. Submariners in the Pacific War* (Stroud, Gloucestershire, UK: Sutton Publishing Limited, 2001), 400.
13. Francis D. Walker, Fitness Report on ELBJ, 5 July 1961, MPR.
14. Robert B. Moore, Fitness Report on ELBJ, 11 July 1962, MPR.
15. H. A. Renken, Fitness Reports on ELBJ, 2 April 1964, 9 April 1965, 11 June 1965, MPR.
16. Paul Masterton, Fitness Report on ELBJ, 12 April 1966 and 13 August 1966, MPR.
17. ELBJ, telephone interview by author, 29 July 1995.
18. Ibid.
19. ELBJ, *Salt and Steel*, 240.
20. ISB, letter to author, 5 October 2006.
21. Corwin Mendenhall, telephone interview by author, 25 July 1995.
22. ELBJ, *Salt and Steel*, 240.
23. Arleigh Burke, letter to ELBJ, 26 January 1949, BP-EPL, box 1.
24. ISB, letter to author, 5 October 2006.
25. Slade D. Cutter, *The Reminiscences of Captain Slade D. Cutter, USN (Ret.)*, U.S. Naval Institute Oral History Program (Annapolis: Naval Institute, 1985), 1:104–105.
26. Isenberg, *Shield of the Republic*, 576.
27. ISB, letter to author, 5 October 2006.
28. ELBJ, CUOHP, 357.
29. ELBJ, letter to ELBS, 25 August 1935, BAL, vol. 1.
30. Ibid., 132.
31. ELBJ, letter to ISB, 18 May 1964, 3, BP-IB.
32. Ibid.

33. Isenberg, 444–445.

34. Fred G. Bennett, Fitness Report on ELBJ, 22 December 1966, MPR.

Part IX: 1966–2002

1. ELBJ, quoted in a press release from Holt, Rinehart and Winston upon the publication of *Dust on the Sea*, October 1972, 2.

2. Ibid.

3. Edward L. Schapsmeier, and Frederick H. Schapsmeier, *Dirksen of Illinois: Senatorial Statesman* (Urbana: University of Illinois Press, 1985), 233.

4. George F. Will, telephone interview by author, 28 February 2006.

5. Ibid.

6. Ibid.

7. Donald E. deKieffer, interview by author, Washington, D.C., 18 February 2006.

8. Ibid.

9 Ibid.

10. Beachley Edwards, "Mission: 1956," *Esquire,* August 1950, 26–27.

11. "Eisenhower's Naval Aide Adds Chapter to Career," *New York Times,* 21 January 1953, 22.

12. Doc Abbot, summary of meeting held 4 April 1981 in Birmingham to determine the reasons for complaints, BP-IB, "Denton" file.

13. Howard H. Baker Jr., letter to ELBJ, 16 December 1980, BP-IP, "Howard Baker Campaign" file.

14. Jeremiah A. Denton Jr., letter to ELBJ, 17 April 1981, 2, BP-IB, "Denton" file.

15. Jeremiah A. Denton Jr., e-mail to author, 21 September 2006.

16. ELBJ, memorandum to Republican administrative assistants, 10 April 1981, BP-IB, "Denton" file.

17. "'Run Silent, Run Deep,' Interview with CAPT Edward L. Beach," *All Hands*, 34–35.

18. ISB, letter to ELBJ, 15 February 1961, 2, BP-EPL, box 10.

19. ELBJ, letter to Louis [no last name provided], 18 October 1960, BP-ELB, box 9.

20. Ibid.

21. ISB, interview by author, Washington, D.C., 16 February 2006.

22. ELBJ, *The United States Navy: 200 Years*, xii.

23. Jan Snouck-Hurgraonje, letter to ELBJ, 30 August 1974, BP-IB.

24. ELBJ, *The United States Navy: 200 Years*, xiii.

25. Ibid., xv.

26. Paul Stillwell, telephone interview by author, 19 July 1995.

27. ELBJ, interview conducted by Edward A. Beach, 2000, on four VHS tapes, BP-IB.

28. Ibid.

29. ELBJ, *The United States Navy: 200 Years*, 113–114.

30. Ibid., 450.

31. ELBJ, letter to William D. Wilkinson, 24 February 1994, BP-IB, "Naval History Advisory Committee" File.

32. Fred Borch and Daniel Martinez, *Kimmel, Short, and Pearl Harbor: The Final Report Revealed* (Annapolis: Naval Institute Press, 2005), 8.

33. Ken Ringle, "Pearl Harbor's Last Casualty," *Washington Post*, 2 December 1994, F1, F7.

34. ELBJ, *Scapegoats: A Defense of Kimmel and Short at Pearl Harbor* (Annapolis: Naval Institute Press, 1995), 5–6.

35. ELBJ, telephone interview by author, 26 July 1995. For an account of the role of the Roberts Commission Report, which was the first investigation of the Pearl Harbor attack to be made public, see: Martin V. Melosi, *The Shadow of Pearl Harbor: Political Controversy over the Surprise Attack, 1941–1946* (College Station: Texas A&M University Press, 1977).

36. Roy Des Horn, "Navy Blue and Gold" (music by J. W. Crosley), reprinted in *The Book of Navy Songs*, collected and edited by the Trident Society of the U.S. Naval Academy (Annapolis: Naval Institute Press, 1955), 10.

37. Paul Stillwell, "Looking Back," *Naval History*, February 2003, 4.

38. Carol Mason, "Beach Hall: 'Living, Breathing Memorial,'" *Shipmate*, July/August 1999.

Epilogue

1. V. T. Boatwright, Letter to ELBJ, 29 July 1953, BP-EPL, Box 3.

2. ELBJ, Telephone interview by author, 26 July 1995.

3. Horn, "Navy Blue and Gold," 10.

Appendix III: Brief Biographies of Beach Family Members

1. Hartwell Osborn, and others, *Trials and Triumphs: The Record of the Fifty-fifth Ohio Volunteer Infantry*. (Chicago: A. C. McClurg & Co., 1904).

2. Navy Department, *DANFS*, 6:325.

3. ELBS, *From Annapolis to Scapa Flow* (Annapolis: Naval Institute Press, 2003), 43.

4. Ibid., 87–98.

5. Brian McAllister Linn, *The Philippine War: 1899–1902* (Lawrence, KS: University Press of Kansas, 2000), xiii.

6. Navy Department, *DANFS*, 4:423.

7. John S. D. Eisenhower, *Intervention! The United States and the Mexican Revolution, 1913–1917* (New York: W. W. Norton, 1993), 109–138.

8. Biddle Porter, letter to ELBS, 13 August 1914, BP-EPL, box 2.

9. David Healy, *Gunboat Diplomacy in the Wilson Era: The U.S. Navy in Haiti, 1915–1916* (Madison: University of Wisconsin Press, 1976), 5.

10. Philippe Dartiguenave, letter to ELBS, 4 October 1916, translated from the original French by the Office of Naval Intelligence, BP-EPL, box 1.

11. Healy, *Gunboat Diplomacy*, 4–5.

12. Ibid., 18.

13. ELBS, "Admiral Caperton in Haiti," National Archives Record Group 45, Subject File ZWA-7, "Allied Countries: Haiti," 1919.

14. Healy, *Gunboat Diplomacy*, 259.

15. See: Robert D. Heinl and Nancy G. Heinl, *Written in Blood: The Story of the Haitian People, 1492–1995*, 2nd ed. (Lanham, MD: University Press of America, 1996), and Ivan Musicant, *The Banana Wars: A History of United States Military Intervention in Latin America from the Spanish-American War to the Invasion of Panama* (New York: Macmillan, 1990).

16. ELBS, *From Annapolis to Scapa Flow*, 244.

17. EAB, interview by author, Washington, D.C., 5 June 2006.

18. ELBS, letter to Laura Beach, 6 September 1916, BP-IP, "Beach, Schneider, Slade Family Photos" file.

19. Ibid.

20. ELBJ, *The Wreck of the* Memphis (New York: Henry Holt & Company, 1966), 283.

21. "The Loss of the U.S.S. *Memphis*," *Scientific American* 115 (25 November 1916), 477.

22. ELBJ, *The Wreck of the* Memphis, 290.

23. "Death Ends Career of Capt. Beach," *Palo Alto* (California) *Times*, 27 December 1943.

24. ELBS, letter to John Lee Beach (ELBS' nephew), 22 November 1916, in the papers of John B. Beach Jr.

25. Josephus Daniels, "Memorandum from Josephus Daniels, Secretary of the Navy to the Chief of Bureau of Navigation," 27 June 1919, BP-EPL, box 13.

26. "Beach key participant in dedication ceremony," *The Millington* (Tennessee) *Star*, 4 September 1991, page 1.

27. "Bearings—Valiant efforts of *Memphis* captain and crew remembered," *All Hands*, June 1992, 44; "New AS school dedicated and named after former captain of USS *Memphis*," *Bluejacket*, 5 September 1991, 25.

28. "Beach-Quin," *Brooklyn* (NY) *Daily Eagle*, 15 May 1895, 7.

29. ELBS, "Lucie Quin Beach," 5 October 1915, 1, unpublished, original in the files of John B. Beach Jr.

30. Ibid., 3

31. John B. Beach Jr., letter to author, 4 April 2006.

32. "Alice Beach, city clerk's widow, dies," *Palo Alto* (California) *Times*, 14 March 1970.

33. "It's Rich," clipping from an unknown newspaper dated 5 August 1976, BP-IB, "Mare Island" file.

34. Millard B. Frazier, "Capt. Beach Aided Family Food Plight," *Vallejo* (California) *Independent Press*, 27 May 1983.

35. Ibid.

36. ELBJ, letters to ELBS, BP-EPL, Box 1.

37. ELBS, letter to George H. Whistler, 6 October 1939, BP-EPL, box 26.

38. John B. Beach Sr., letter to ELBJ, 27 May 1949, BP-EPL, box 1.

39. "Alice Beach, city clerk's widow, dies," *Palo Alto* (California) *Times*, 14 March 1970.

40. Bruce Watson, "Tom Swift, Nancy Drew, and Pals All had the Same Dad," *Smithsonian* 22 (7 October 1991), 56.

41. ELBS, *An Annapolis First Classman* (Philadelphia: Penn Publishing, 1910), 237.

42. Marcia Jacobson, *Being a Boy Again: Autobiography and the American Boy Book* (Tuscaloosa: University of Alabama Press, 1994), 2.

43. Thomas R. Weschler, *The Reminiscences of Vice Admiral Thomas R. Weschler, USN (Ret.)*, U.S. Naval Institute Oral History Project (Annapolis: Naval Institute, 1995), 1:12.

44. ELBS, *An Annapolis First Classman*, 4.

45. ELBS, *From Annapolis to Scapa Flow*, 22–23. See also: ELBS, *Ralph Osborn, Midshipman at Annapolis* (Boston: W. A. Wilde Company, 1909), chapters XXV to XXVII.

46. John B. Beach Jr., interview by author, 7 May 2006.

47. Ibid.

48. Ibid.

49. John B. Beach Jr., letter to author, 4 April 2006.

50. John B. Beach Jr., e-mail to author, 25 May 2006.

51. George W. Cullum, *Biographical Register of the Officers of the U. S. Military Academy*, Supplement, vol.9, 1940–1950, part 2, ed. Charles N. Branham (West Point, NY: Association of Graduates of the U.S. Military Academy, 1950), 1267.

52. "Lt. Col. John Beach, World War II hero," *Palo Alto* (California) *Weekly*, 17 March 1999.

53. ELBJ, letter to Thomas Parker, 10 October 1946, BP-EPL, box 2.

54. John B. Beach Jr., interview by author, 7 May 2006.

55. See Appendix II for a list of the articles written by ELBJ for *Defense Electronics*.

56. "John Beach, 79, Army colonel," *Palo Alto* (California) *Daily News*, 6 March 1999.

57. Millard B. Frazier, "M.I.-Born Alice Beach Has Long Navy Career," *Vallejo* (California) *Independent Press*, 13 July 1983.

58. ELBJ, letter to Thomas Parker, 10 October 1946, BP-EPL, box 2.

59. Alice L. Beach, letter to ELBJ, undated, BP-ELB, box 7.

60. "Alice Beach," *Palo Alto* (California) *Weekly*, 19 November 2003.

61. Alice L. Beach, letter to ELBJ, 3 February 1953, BP-EPL, box 12.

62. John B. Beach Jr., interview by author, 7 May 2006.

63. Ibid.

64. "Alice Beach," *Palo Alto* (California) *Weekly*, 19 November 2003.

65. Ibid.

66. Ibid.

67. EAB, letter to ELBJ, 29 September 1960, BP-EPL, box 25.

68. EAB, e-mail to author, 5 August 2009.

69. Ibid.

70. EAB, interview by author, 5 June 2006.

71. ISB, letter to ELBJ, 2 October 1960, BP-EPL, box 25.

72. ISB, interview by author, 11 August 2005.

73. ELBJ, *Dust on the Sea*, vii.

74. Hugh Beach, e-mail to author, 21 January 2007.

75. IABR, e-mail to author, 20 October 1998.

76. IABR, e-mail to author, 5 August 2009.

77. Ibid.

78. Ibid.

79. Ibid.

Bibliography

General Note on the Papers of Edward L. Beach Jr.

The papers of Edward L. Beach Jr. are located in several collections, while significant portions are still held by Mrs. Ingrid Beach. Among the valuable sources of information in the papers held by Mrs. Beach are an almost complete set of letters sent by Beach to his fiancé/wife during World War II.

The Dwight D. Eisenhower Presidential Library in Abilene, Kansas, has most of the papers from Beach's Navy career until he retired from active duty. At the present time, regretfully, Beach's letters home during his years as a midshipman are divided, with Mrs. Beach in possession of the first two years' worth (bound in two volumes), while the Eisenhower Presidential Library has the letters from Beach's last two years at the Academy (unbound).

The Submarine Force Museum, Groton, Connecticut, has early drafts of Beach's novels, as well as drafts of the stories that were first published in *Blue Book*, and were then eventually accumulated in the book *Submarine!* Beach donated eleven boxes of papers to the Naval Institute before his death, but since the Institute at the time lacked the expert staff and facilities to process and care for such materials, they were transferred to the archive collection of the Nimitz Library of the U.S. Naval Academy. The Nimitz Library was also not really equipped as an archival facility and lacked the necessary staff to process such a large influx of material, so the Beach papers in its possession remain closed to researchers at the time of this writing.

Books

Alden, John D. *The Fleet Submarine in the U.S. Navy: A Design and Construction History*. Annapolis: Naval Institute Press, 1979.

———. *U.S. Submarine Attacks During World War II: Including Allied Submarine Attacks in the Pacific Theater*. Annapolis: Naval Institute Press, 1989.

Anderson, Charles R. *Day of Lightning, Years of Scorn*. Annapolis: Naval Institute Press, 2005.

Beach, Edward L., Jr. Afterword. In *Maru Killer: The War Patrols of the USS Seahorse*, by Dave Bouslog, 308–317. 2nd ed. Placentia, CA: R. A. Cline Publishers, 2001.

Beach, Edward L., Sr. *An Annapolis First Classman*. Philadelphia: Penn Publishing, 1910.

———. *An Annapolis Plebe*. Philadelphia: Penn Publishing, 1907.

———. *An Annapolis Second Classman*. Philadelphia: Penn Publishing, 1909.

———. *An Annapolis Youngster*. Philadelphia: Penn Publishing, 1908.

———. *Dan Quin of the Navy*. New York: The Macmillan Company, 1922.

———. *Ensign Ralph Osborn*. Boston: W. A. Wilde Company, 1911.

———. *Lieutenant Ralph Osborn Aboard a Torpedo Boat Destroyer*. Boston: W. A. Wilde Company, 1912.

———. *Midshipman Ralph Osborn at Sea*. Boston: W. A. Wilde Company, 1910.

———. *Ralph Osborn, Midshipman at Annapolis*. Boston: W. A. Wilde Company, 1909.

———. *Roger Paulding: Apprentice Seaman*. Philadelphia: Penn Publishing, 1911.

———. *Roger Paulding: Ensign*. Philadelphia: Penn Publishing, 1914.

———. *Roger Paulding: Gunner*. Philadelphia: Penn Publishing, 1913.

———. *Roger Paulding: Gunner's Mate*. Philadelphia: Penn Publishing, 1912.

Beach, Elmer Taylor. *Beach in America*. Kalamazoo, MI: Quintin Publications, 1923.

Becker, Beril. *Captain Edward L. Beach: Around the World Under Water*. Chicago: Kingston House, 1961.

Beschloss, Michael R. *May-Day: Eisenhower, Khrushchev, and the U-2 Affair*. New York: Harper and Row, 1986.

Blair, Clay, Jr. *Silent Victory: The U.S. Submarine War against Japan*. Philadelphia: J. B. Lippincott, 1975.

Borch, Fred, and Daniel Martinez. *Kimmel, Short, and Pearl Harbor: The Final Report Revealed*. Annapolis: Naval Institute Press, 2005.

Bradley, Omar, and Clay Blair. *A General's Life*. New York: Simon and Schuster, 1983.

Buell, Thomas B. *Quiet Warrior: A Biography of Admiral Raymond A. Spruance*. Boston: Little, Brown and Company, 1974. Reprint, Annapolis: Naval Institute Press, 1987. Page references are to the 1987 edition.

Calvert, James F. *Silent Running: My Years on a World War II Attack Submarine*. New York: John Wiley and Sons, 1995.

Carter, Jimmy. *Why Not the Best? Why One Man is Optimistic about America's Third Century*. Nashville, TN: Broadman Press, 1975.

Connolly, Francis X. *A Rhetoric Casebook*. New York: Harcourt, Brace and Company, 1953.

Cullum, George W. *Biographical Register of the Officers of the U.S. Military Academy*. Edited by Charles N. Branham. Supplement, vol. 9, part 2, 1940–1950. West Point, NY: Association of Graduates of the U.S. Military Academy, 1950.

Dull, Paul S. *A Battle History of the Imperial Japanese Navy (1941–1945)*. Annapolis: Naval Institute Press, 1978.

Duncan, Francis. *Rickover: The Struggle for Excellence*. Annapolis: Naval Institute Press, 2001.

———. *Rickover and the Nuclear Navy: The Discipline of Technology*. Annapolis: Naval Institute Press, 1990.

Eisenhower, John S. D. *Intervention! The United States and the Mexican Revolution, 1913–1917*. New York: W.W. Norton, 1993.

Evans, Thomas. *Sea of Thunder: Four Commanders and the Last Great Naval Campaign, 1941–1945*. New York: Simon and Schuster, 2006.

Fernandez, Ronald. *Cruising the Caribbean: U.S. Influence and Intervention in the Twentieth Century*. Monroe, ME: Common Courage Press, 1994.

Fluckey, Eugene B. *Thunder Below!* Urbana: University of Illinois Press, 1992.

Friedman, Norman. *U.S. Submarines since 1945: An Illustrated Design History*. Annapolis: Naval Institute Press, 1994.

———. *U.S. Submarines through 1945: An Illustrated Design History*. Annapolis: Naval Institute Press, 1995.

Gannon, Robert. *Hellions of the Deep: The Development of American Torpedoes in World War II*. University Park, PA: Pennsylvania State University Press, 1996.

Hackett, Alice Payne, and James Henry Burke. *80 Years of Best Sellers, 1896–1975*. New York: R. R. Bowker, 1977.

Hagan, Kenneth J. *This People's Navy: The Making of American Sea Power*. New York: The Free Press, 1991.

Halberstam, David. *The Fifties*. New York: Villard Books, 1993.

Hamilton, Edith. *Mythology*. Boston: Little, Brown and Company, 1942.

Harris, Brayton. *The Navy Times Book of Submarines: A Political, Social, and Military History*. Edited by Walter J. Boyne. New York: Berkley Books, 1997.

Healy, David. *Gunboat Diplomacy in the Wilson Era: The U.S. Navy in Haiti, 1915–1916*. Madison: University of Wisconsin Press, 1976.

Heinl, Robert D., and Nancy G. Heinl. *Written in Blood: The Story of the Haitian People, 1492– 1995*. 2nd ed. Lanham, MD: University Press of America, 1996.

Howarth, Stephen. *To Shining Sea: A History of the United States Navy*. New York: Random House, 1991.

Isenberg, Michael. *Shield of the Republic: The United States Navy in an Era of Cold War and Violent Peace*. Vol. 1, *1945–1962*. New York: St. Martin's Press, 1993.

Izod, John. *Hollywood and the Box Office, 1895–1986*. New York: Columbia University Press, 1988.

Jacobson, Marcia. *Being a Boy Again: Autobiography and the American Boy Book*. Tuscaloosa: University of Alabama Press, 1994.

Jeans, Peter D. *Ship to Shore: A Dictionary of Everyday Words and Phrases Derived from the Sea*. Santa Barbara, CA: ABC-CLIO, 1993.

Jentschura, Hansgeorg, Dieter Jung, and Peter Mickel. *Warships of the Imperial Japanese Navy, 1869–1945*. Translated by Anthony Preston and J. D. Brown. Annapolis: Naval Institute Press, 1977.

Lavo, Carl. *Slade Cutter: Submarine Warrior*. Annapolis: Naval Institute Press, 2003.

Linn, Brian McAllister. *The Philippine War: 1899–1902*. Lawrence: University Press of Kansas, 2000.

McGregor, Rob Roy. Introduction. *USS Sea Cat (SS-399), 1944–1968: The Boat and the Men*, by Robert Winburn, v–vi. Chicago: Spectrum Press, 2001.

Melosi, Martin V. *The Shadow of Pearl Harbor: Political Controversy over the Surprise Attack*. College Station: Texas A&M University Press, 1977.

Mendenhall, Corwin. *Submarine Diary*. Chapel Hill, NC: Algonquin Books of Chapel Hill, 1991.

Miller, Nathan. *War at Sea: A Naval History of World War II*. New York: Scribner, 1995.

Morison, Samuel Eliot. *History of United States Naval Operations in World War II*. 15 vols. Boston: Little, Brown and Company, 1947–1962.

Musicant, Ivan. *The Banana Wars: A History of the United States Military Intervention in Latin America from the Spanish-American War to the Invasion of Panama*. New York: Macmillan, 1990.

Navy Department. *Dictionary of American Naval Fighting Ships*. 8 vols. Washington, D.C.: U.S. Government Printing Office, 1959–1981.

O'Kane, Richard H. *Clear the Bridge! The War Patrols of the U.S.S. Tang*. Chicago: Rand McNally, 1977.

Osborn, Hartwell, and others. *Trials and Triumphs: The Record of the Fifty-fifth Ohio Volunteer Infantry*. Chicago: A. C. McClurg & Company, 1904.

Polmar, Norman, and Thomas B. Allen. *Rickover: Controversy and Genius*. New York: Simon and Schuster, 1982.

Puryear, Edgar F. *American Admiralship: The Moral Imperatives of Naval Command*. Annapolis: Naval Institute Press, 2005.

Rindskopf, M. H., and Richard Knowles Morris. *Steel Boats, Iron Men*. Paducah, KY: Turner Publishing Company, 1994.

Roscoe, Theodore. *United States Submarine Operations in World War II*. Annapolis: Naval Institute Press, 1949.

Schapsmeier, Edward L., and Frederick H. Schapsmeier. *Dirksen of Illinois: Senatorial Statesman*. Urbana: University of Illinois Press, 1985.

Scoggins, Margaret, ed. *Battle Stations: True Stories of Men in War*. New York: Alfred A. Knopf, 1953.

Shakespeare, William. *Hamlet*. In *The Living Shakespeare*, edited by Oscar Campbell. New York: Macmillan, 1949.

Shenk, Robert, ed. *Authors at Sea: Modern American Writers Remember Their Naval Service*. Annapolis: Naval Institute Press, 1997.

Spectorsky, A. C., ed. *The Book of the Sea: Being a Collection of Writings about the Sea in all its Aspects*. New York: Appleton-Century-Crofts, 1954.

Stillwell, Paul. *Battleships*. New York: MetroBooks, 2001.

Strauss, Lewis L. *Men and Decisions*. Garden City, NY: Doubleday, 1962.

Suid, Lawrence. *Guts and Glory: The Making of the American Military Image in Film*. Lexington: University Press of Kentucky, 2002.

———. *Sailing the Silver Screen: Hollywood and the U.S. Navy*. Annapolis: Naval Institute Press, 1996.

Sweetman, Jack. *American Naval History: An Illustrated Chronology of the U.S. Navy and Marine Corps, 1775–Present*. 3rd ed. Annapolis: Naval Institute Press, 2002.

———. *The Naval Academy: An Illustrated History*. 2nd ed. Edited by Thomas J. Cutler. Annapolis: Naval Institute Press, 1995.

Thomson, David. *The New Biographical Dictionary of Film*. New York: Alfred A. Knopf, 2002.

Trident Society of the U.S. Naval Academy. *The Book of Navy Songs*. Annapolis: Naval Institute Press, 1955.

Tuohy, William. *The Bravest Man: The Story of Richard O'Kane and U.S. Submariners in the Pacific War*. Stroud, Gloucestershire, UK: Sutton Publishing Limited, 2001.

Van der Vat, Dan. *Stealth at Sea: The History of Submarines*. New York: Houghton Mifflin Co., 1994.

Villiers, Alan. *Men, Ships, and the Sea*. New edition. Washington, DC: National Geographic Society, 1973.

Wagner, Frederick. *Famous Underwater Adventurers*. New York: Dodd, Mead, 1962.

Ward, John. *Submarines in World War II*. St. Paul, MN: MBI Publishing, 2001.

Williams, Marion D. *Submarines under Ice: The U.S. Navy's Polar Operations*. Annapolis: Naval Institute Press, 1998.

Wood, Ruth Pirsig. *Lolita in Peyton Place: Highbrow, Middlebrow, and Lowbrow Novels in the 1950s*. New York: Garland Publishing, 1995.

Oral Histories

Anderson, George W. Jr. *Reminiscences of Admiral George W. Anderson, USN (Ret.)*. U.S. Naval Institute Oral History Project. Annapolis: Naval Institute, 1983.

Backus, Paul H. *Reminiscences of Commander Paul H. Backus, USN (Ret.)*. U.S. Naval Institute Oral History Project. Annapolis: Naval Institute, 1995.

Beach, Edward L., Jr. "Eisenhower Administration Project: Edward L. Beach." Columbia University Oral History Project. New York: Columbia University, 1971.

Benson, Roy S. *Reminiscences of Rear Admiral Roy S. Benson, USN (Ret.)*. U.S. Naval Institute Oral History Project. Annapolis: Naval Institute, 1980.

Burke, Julian T. *Reminiscences of Rear Admiral Julian T. Burke, USN (Ret.)*. U.S. Naval Institute Oral History Project. Annapolis: Naval Institute, 2003.

Colbus, Louis. *Reminiscences of Captain Louis Colbus, USN (Ret.)*. U.S. Naval Institute Oral History Project. Annapolis: Naval Institute, 2001.

Cutter, Slade D. *Reminiscences of Captain Slade D. Cutter, USN (Ret.)*. 2 vols. U.S. Naval Institute Oral History Project. Annapolis: Naval Institute, 1985.

Davison, John F. *Reminiscences of Rear Admiral John F. Davison, USN (Ret.)*. U.S. Naval Institute Oral History Project. Annapolis: Naval Institute, 1986.

Shear, Harold E. *Reminiscences of Admiral Harold E. Shear, USN (Ret.)*. U.S. Naval Institute Oral History Project. Annapolis: Naval Institute, 1997.

Weschler, Thomas R. *Reminiscences of Vice Admiral Thomas R. Weschler, USN (Ret.)*. U.S. Naval Institute Oral History Project. Annapolis: Naval Institute, 1995.

Periodicals

"Atoms and Prophets." *Newsweek*, 6 June 1955, 56.

Baker, A. D., III. "Historic Fleets." *Naval History*, June 2005, 12–13.

"Bearings—Valiant Efforts of *Memphis* captain and crew remembered." *All Hands*, June 1992, 44.

Benson, Roy S. "Lucky Bag of Books." *Shipmate*, March 1980, 32.

Buell, Thomas A. "Memorandum for the Deputy Secretary of Defense: 'Advancement of Rear Admiral Kimmel and Major General Short' (Review)." U.S. Naval Institute *Proceedings*, April 1966, 98–100.

Conaty, Barbara. "Fiction." *Library Journal*, 15 October 1978, 2132.

"The Davy Jones War." *Time*, 9 June 1952. http://www.time.com/time/printout/0,8816,806494.html (accessed 9 December 2009).

"Denfeld, Louis E(mil)," *Current Biography*, 1947 annual, 159–161.

Hayward, Edward B. "History." *Library Journal*, 1 September 1966, 3935–3936.

Hessman, James D. "'Keepers of the Sea:' A Stunning Achievement." *Sea Power*, October 1983, 42.

"History of a Family Flag." *Life*, 13 June 1960, 48, 91.

Howard, Lawrence. "Beach, Edward L." *Best Sellers*, February 1979, 335.

Hull, Michael D. "Argentia Conference helped forge the grand alliance that ultimately prevailed during World War II." *WWII History*, September 2006, 16–17.

Kirkus Reviews, 15 August 1972, 966.

Kirkus Reviews, 15 August 1978, 887.

"The Loss of the U.S.S. Memphis." *Scientific American*, 25 November 1916, 477.

MacDonald, Donald J. "President Truman's Yacht." *Naval History*, Winter 1990, 48–49.

Maguire, Clinton J. "Non-Fiction," *Best Sellers*, 1 October 1966, 242–243.

Mason, Carol. "Beach Hall: 'Living, Breathing Memorial,'" *Shipmate*, July/August 1999.

"Mixed Fiction." *Time*, 4 April 1955, 104.

Morison, Samuel Loring. (Compiler.) "U.S. Naval Battle Force Changes, 1 January 2007–31 December 2007." U.S. Naval Institute *Proceedings*, May 2008.

"Navy League News." *Sea Power*, June 2000, 60.

"New AS school dedicated and named after former captain of USS Memphis." *Bluejacket*, 5 September 1991, 25.

"New Look in Aides." *Time*, 26 January 1953, 20–21.

Peterson, Gordon I. "The Pen and the Sword." *Sea Power*, July 1999, 1.

"'Run Silent, Run Deep,' Interview with CAPT Edward L. Beach." *All Hands*, August 1999, 32–37. http://www.mediacen.navy.mil/pubs/allhands/aug99/pg32.htm (accessed 24 November 2004).

Ryan, William F. "The Genesis of the Techno-thriller." *Virginia Quarterly Review*, Fall 1992.

Stavridis, James. "Book Reviews." *Naval War College Review*, August 2003, 180–182.

Stevens, Karen. *Library Journal*, 15 February 1973, 659.

Stillwell, Paul. "Looking Back." *Naval History*, February 2003, 4.

Thurber, James G. "The Unicorn in the Garden." *New Yorker*, 21 October 1939, 24.

"To the Rescue." *All Hands*, March 1958, 34–35.

Waller, Douglas. "Fumbling the Football: Now It Can Be Told." *Newsweek*, 7 October 1991, 26.

Watson, Bruce. "Tom Swift, Nancy Drew, and Pals All had the Same Dad." *Smithsonian*, 22 (7 October 1991), 56.

Whitman, Edward C. "U.S. Radar Picket Submarines: Cold War Curiosities." *Undersea Warfare*, Winter/Spring 2002.

Newspaper Articles

"46 'Notable' Books Chosen for Year." *New York Times*, 5 February 1956, 36.

"2,000 Welcome Triton on Return to Home Port." *New York Herald Tribune*, 12 May 1960, 2.

"Alice Beach." *Palo Alto* (California) *Weekly*, 19 November 2003.

"Alice Beach, city clerk's widow, dies." *Palo Alto* (California) *Times*, 14 March 1970.

Arndt, Jessie Ash. "Navy Wife Serves with Courage, Too." *Christian Science Monitor*, 24 May 1960, 6.

Barkman, John. "Underwater Thriller." *San Francisco Chronicle*, 17 October 1978.

"Beach key participant in dedication ceremony." *The Millington* (Tennessee) *Star*, 4 September 1991, 1.

"Beach-Quin." *Brooklyn* (NY) *Daily Eagle*, 15 May 1895, 7.

Blackwell, Morton C. "Quickly Noted." *The Right Report*, January 1977, 3.

Bodi, Alexander. "A note for her friends." *Palo Alto Times*, 5 July 1976, 16.

Buell, Thomas B. "Of Ships and the Men Who Sail Them." *Washington Post Book World*, 3 August 1986.

Crowther, Bosley. "The Screen: Submarine Adventure" *New York Times*, 25 July 1958, 29. http://www.imdb.com/title/TT0052151/awards (accessed 16 June 2006).

Dalton, Stephen. "Film Choices." *The Times* (London), 9 May 2006, Television section, 27.

"Death Ends Career of Capt. Beach." *Palo Alto* (California) *Times*, 27 December 1943.

Ebert, Roger. Review of *The Hunt for Red October*. Directed by John McTiernan. *Chicago Sun-Times*, 2 March 1990. http://www.sun-times.com/ebert/ebert_reviews.1990/03/554354.html (accessed 6 February 2001)

"Eisenhower's Naval Aide Adds Chapter to Career." *New York Times*, 21 January 1953, 22.

Faber, Harold. "Books of the Times." *New York Times*, 8 October 1966, 29.

"Fiction: War under the Sea." *Christian Science Monitor*, 29 November 1972, 22.

Frazier, Millard B. "Capt. Beach Aided Family Food Plight." *Vallejo* (California) *Independent Press*, 27 May 1983.

———. "M.I.-Born Alice Beach Has Long Navy Career." *Vallejo* (California) *Independent Press*, 13 July 1983.

———. "Ned Beach Leading Student at Academy." *Vallejo* (California) *Independent Press*, 5 June 1983.

Fredericks, Pierce G. "The Ship and the Wave." *New York Times Book Review*, 16 October 1966, 4.

Hamilton, Robert A. "Admiral Harold E. Shear dies at 80." *The Day* (New London, CT), 7 February 1999. http://www.ussvi.org/names/admshear.htm.

"It's Rich." Clipping from an unknown newspaper dated 5 August 1976. BP-IB, "Mare Island" file.

"John Beach, 79, Army colonel." *Palo Alto* (California) *Daily News*, 6 March 1999.

Lane, Richard. "U.S. Navy: 200 Years of Its Ups and Downs." *The Washington Times Magazine*, 11 August 1986.

Levin, Martin. "New and Novel." *New York Times Book Review*, 22 October 1977, 46.

"Lt. Col. John Beach, World War II hero." *Palo Alto* (California) *Weekly*, 17 March 1999.

McGrath, Edward G. "Ike Breaks Precedent in Picking Young Sub Hero from New London Base as his Naval Aide." *Boston Sunday Post*, 25 January 1953, 37.

Mitgang, Herbert. "Deep Down and Deadly." *New York Times Book Review*, 3 April 1955, 4.

"Mixed Fiction." *Time*, 4 April 1955, 104.

"Mystic Homes Open June 10." *The Day* (New London, CT), 2 June 2000, F24.

"Naval Aide Replaced." *New York Times*, 25 January 1957.

"Newport-Based Sailor Given Navy Medal for his Bravery." *Newport* (Rhode Island) *Daily News*, 23 December 1957, 1.

"Officers Are Named to Head Midshipmen." *New York Times*, 28 August 1938, 34.

"Only One Saw Sub, and He Got Scared." *Charleston* (West Virginia) *Gazette*, 11 November 1960, 16 .

Potter, E. B. "In the Wake of Magellan." *New York Times*, 28 October 1962.

Pryor, Thomas M. "Film Deal Signed by United Artists." *New York Times*, 25 July 1957, 28.

Ringle, Ken. "Pearl Harbor's Last Casualty." *Washington Post*, 2 December 1994, F1, F7.

Spencer, Rich. "New Staff, Mission for GOP Policy Unit." *Washington Post*, 1 January 1977, A4.

Stillwell, Paul. "New Submarine Story Mingles Fact and Fiction." *Navy Times*, 5 February 1979.

"Tower Accused of Purge." *Texas News Summary*, 8 December 1976.

Van Riper, Frank. "Sen. Tower Firing Panel Staff." *New York Daily News*, 8 December 1976.

Weigley, Russell F. "Organization Sailor." *New York Times Book Review*, 31 August 1986, 11.

"With Congress." *Roll Call*, week ending 6 January 1977, 9.

Wood, Percy. "A Questionable Court Martial." *Chicago Tribune Book Review*, 25 September 1966, 4.

Sound Recordings

Newhart, Bob. "The Cruise of the U.S.S. Codfish." *The Button-Down Mind of Bob Newhart*. Warner Archives Compact Disc 2-45690, 24 January 1995. (Originally issued 10 February 1960.)

Sahl, Mort. *The Hungry i*. Verve MGVS 15012, 1960. Vinyl record.

Manuscript Collections and Other Unpublished Sources

Adams, Sherman A. Papers. Dwight D. Eisenhower Presidential Library, Abilene, Kansas.

Aurand, Evan P. Papers. Dwight D. Eisenhower Presidential Library, Abilene, Kansas.

Beach, Edward L., Jr. "Letters from Midshipman Edward L. Beach, Jr." 2 vols. Private Collection of Mrs. Ingrid Schenck Beach.

———. Military Personnel Records. National Personnel Records Center, St. Louis, MO.

———. Papers. Dwight D. Eisenhower Presidential Library, Abilene, Kansas.

———. Papers. Private collection of Mrs. Ingrid Schenck Beach.

Beach, Edward L., Sr. "Admiral Caperton in Haiti." National Archives Record Group 45, Subject File ZWA-7, "Allied Countries: Haiti," 1919.

———. "Lucie Quin Beach." (Eulogy to his wife.) In the private papers of John Blair Beach Jr.

Beach, Joseph Lane. "Civil War Account of Joseph Lane Beach." In the private papers of John Blair Beach Jr.

Campbell, Edward G. "The Autobiography of George Campbell." Chapter 21. In the private papers of Edward G. Campbell.

Hagerty, James. Papers. Dwight D. Eisenhower Presidential Library, Abilene, Kansas.

USS *Piper* (SS-409). Third War Patrol Report, 19 July 1945–9 September 1945. National Archives, Washington, D.C.

USS *Tirante* (SS-420). First War Patrol Report, 25 April 1945–3 May 1945. National Archives, Washington, D.C.

USS *Trigger* (SS-237). "Report of the Grounding of USS *Trigger*," 6 June 1942.[*] National Archives, Washington, D.C.

---

[*] Because USS *Trigger*'s first war patrol resulted in the accidental grounding of the submarine, the numbers of the boat's war patrol reports are all one digit off the actual patrol numbers. For example, what is listed in the National Archives as *Trigger*'s "First War Patrol Report" is actually for her second war patrol.

————. First War Patrol Report, 26 June 1942–10 August 1942. National Archives, Washington, D.C.

————. Third War Patrol Report, 3 December 1942–22 January 1943. National Archives, Washington, D.C.

————. Fifth War Patrol Report, 30 April 1943–22 June 1943. National Archives, Washington, D.C.

————. Sixth War Patrol Report, 1 September 1943–30 September 1943. National Archives, Washington, D.C.

————. Seventh War Patrol Report, 22 October 1943–8 December 1943. National Archives, Washington, D.C.

Navy Department. "Log of the USS *Triton*, 16 February 1960 to 10 May 1960." U. S. Naval Institute Archives, Annapolis, MD. (Author's note: The National Archives reports this log as "missing," but somehow it came into the possession of the U.S. Naval Institute, and that is where it is currently located.)

Index

A

Adams, Sherman A., 59
Adams, Will Mont, Jr., 100, 101, 107–8, 113, 115, 116
Aguinaldo, Emilio, 185
Air Force, creation of, 47
aircraft carriers, 47
Aleman, Miguel, 66
Alfred A. Knopf, 45–46
Alfred Thayer Mahan Award for Literary Achievement, 157
All Hands magazine, 88, 158
Allott, Gordon, 152, 153
Amberjack (SS-522), 50
American Library Association, 79
Argosy magazine, 130
Arkansas (BB-33), 11
Armed Forces: postwar restructuring of, 47–48; presidential military aides and, 60–61; service unification and, 54. *See also specific services*
Army Air Corps, 47
Around the World Submerged: The Voyage of the Triton (Beach), 132
Atlantic Conference, 18
Atomic Defense Section. *See* Op-36

atomic weapons delivery, 47–48
Augusta (CA-31), 18
Aurand, Evan P., 74, 110
Authors at Sea: Modern American Writers Remember Their Naval Service, 45

B

B-36 strategic bomber, 55
Backus, Paul H., 13
Baker, Howard, 157
Balaguer, Joaquin, 3
Balboa, Vasco, 111
Barb (SS-220), 41
Baring, Rufino, 124
Bateson, Gregory, 215
battery storage capacity, submarine, 50–51
Battle of Chapultepec, 11
Battle of Hürtgen Forest, 206
Battle of Leyte Gulf, 123
Battle of Manila Bay, 184
Battle of Midway, 23, 163
Battle Stations: True Stories of Men in War (Scroggin, ed.), 45–46
Beach, Alice Laura (sister), 3, 32, 170, 208–11
Beach, Alice (mother), 2, 31, 196–200

Beach, Alison (sister-in-law), 205

Beach, Annie Norell (daughter-in-law), 216

Beach, Edward A. (son), 49, 94, 137–38, 170, 212–14

Beach, Edward L. "Ned," Jr.: bibliography of published works, 177–79; childhood of, 3–4; chronology of life, 173–76; death of, 170; engagement to Ingrid Schenck, 31–32; as high school journalist, 5; home-improvement schemes of, 96–98; on honor, 162; Kimmel case and, 161–65, 171; on Sen. Denton staff, 156–57; Senate Republican Policy Committee and, 151–55; ship model collection of, 98; speaking engagements, 131–32; writing methods of, 158–60

Beach, Edward L. "Ned," Jr. (naval assignments): to *Amberjack,* 50; on JCS staff, 54–56; to *Lea,* 15; to Op-36, 47; to Op-90A, 135–36; as presidential naval aide, 59; to *Salamonie,* 89; to *Tirante,* 39; to *Trigger,* 22–23; to *Trigger II,* 57; to *Triton,* 99

Beach, Edward L. "Ned," Jr. (naval career): as Academy regimental commander, 12; in civil defense planning, 68–70; Eisenhower on, 74; fitness reports of, 93, 141, 148; on Hyman Rickover, 101; leadership style of, 90–91; *Lucky Bag* entry on, 7; on Midway Island, 28; military awards of, 148; Naval Academy appointment, 7; in nuclear-powered submarine development, 48–49; promotion and, 140–47; retirement of, 148; on role of wartime navy, 20–21; on Slade Cutter, 28; on torpedo defects, 26–27; on *Trigger* grounding, 24; on *Triton* commissioning, 109; in "war of the worlds," 13; on war's end, 43

Beach, Edward L., Sr. (father), 99; death of, 32, 200; Haitian occupation and, 186–89; literary career of, 4, 200–203; marriages of, 3, 195; military awards of, 194; at Naval Academy, 182–83; Philippine Insurrection and, 184–86; post-naval career of, 3; at Stanford University, 199; wreck of the *Memphis* and, 99, 134, 150–51, 165, 190–92, 194; writings on Haiti, 189

Beach, Elisabeth (granddaughter), 216

Beach, Ellinor (granddaughter), 216

Beach, Emily Fleisher (daughter-in-law), 214

Beach, Hugh (son), 56, 94, 96, 138, 170, 214–17

Beach, Inga-Marie (daughter), 44, 53

Beach, Ingrid Alice (daughter). *See* Robertson, Ingrid Alice Beach

Beach, Ingrid (wife), 56, 170; early marriage and, 37–39; engagement to Beach, 31–32; at Foreign Language Institute,

137; as husband's editor,
158–59; on Hyman Rickover,
101; influence on children's
development, 96; Project
Magellan and, 113, 122; on
promotion process, 145

Beach, John Blair (brother), 3, 32,
203–8

Beach, Joseph Lane (grandfather),
181–82

Beach, Lucie (first wife of Edward
Beach Sr.), 3, 195–96

Beach family life, 94–96

Beach Hall dedication, 165–67

Beach Park, Vallejo, California, 198

Beakley, Wallace M., 111

Beckhaus, Lawrence W., 93–94,
130

Bennett, Fred G., 148

Benson, Mrs. Roy S., 57

Benson, Roy S., 24–25, 32, 161

Bergström, David, 211

Bergström, Ingrid, 211

Beyond Magellan (documentary),
115

bildungsromans, 78

Bismarck (Germany), 17–18

Blair, John, 191, 204

Blue Book magazine, 45, 206

Bodsworth, Fred, 79

bomb shelters: Beach family, 96–
97; White House, 69–70

*Book of the Sea: Being a Collection of
Writings about the Sea in All its
Aspects* (Spectorsky, ed.), 46

Bowman, Frank L. "Skip," 170

Bradley, Omar, 53–54, 55

Brennecke, Jochen, 80–81

Broach, Fred, 161

Brooke, Edward W., 152

Broussard, Clarence, 18

budget and oversight hearings,
135–37

Buell, Thomas, 25, 28

Bulmer, Robert W., 113, 117

Burke, Arleigh, 73, 144, 161

Bush, George H.W., 163

Bush, Prescott, 130–31

"Button-Down Mind of Bob
Newhart, The" (record
album), 131

C

California (BB-44), 2, 23, 194

Camp David presidential retreat,
67, 68

Campbell, Edward G., 39

Carney, Robert B., 73

Carter, Jimmy, 100

Carter administration, 156

Cassell Military Paperback Series,
79

Cheney, Richard, 163

Chesapeake/Leopard affair, 163

Chester (CA-27), 15

Chief of Naval Operations, 73

children's literature, 4, 200–203

Chisolm, Hugh J., 65

Churchill, Winston, 18, 66

civil defense planning, 68–70

Civil War, 181–82

Clancy, Tom, 87, 155, 170

class ranking system, at Naval
Academy, 9–10

Classics of Naval Literature series,
79

Clifton, Chester V., 55–56

Clinton, Bill, 164

Colbus, Louis, 93

Cold is the Sea (Beach), 155, 159

Coleridge, Samuel Taylor, 77

Colonial Williamsburg, Virginia, 66

Columbus, Christopher, 111
Columbus (German passenger liner), 15–16
congressional budget and oversight hearings, 135–36
Connole, David, 40
Connolly, Francis X., 45
Council of Twenty-one American States Treaty, 73–74
Court-Martial of George Armstrong Custer, The (film), 83
Cox, William, 163
Crane, Stephen, 78
Cravat, Nick, 87
Crowe, William A., Jr., 61, 69, 85
Crowther, Bosley, 85
Currie, Charles, 90
Cutler, Thomas, 170
Cutter, Slade, 11, 28, 29, 83, 145, 161

D
Dalton, John, 161, 164
Daniel, John C., 94
Daniels, Josephus, 151, 192, 194
Dartiguenave, Philippe, 188
Daspit, L.R., 111
Davenport, Dave, 98
Daves, Delmar, 82
Dealy, Sam, 45, 83–84
Defense Department, 47
Defense Posture Hearings (1965), 136
deKieffer, Donald, 153, 154
demobilization process, 46
Denfeld, Louis E., 46, 54, 144
Dennison, Robert Lee, 60, 67
Denton, Jeremiah A., 156, 157
depth charges, 22
Destroyers for Bases Agreement, 17

Deutch, John, 161
Dewey, George, 184
Dirksen, Everett McKinley, 152
Dodd, Mead and Company, 44
Dönitz, Karl, 81
Dornin, Robert E. "Dusty," 29, 32–35, 161
Douglass, Frederick, 202
down-the-throat shot, 34, 83
"drags," 9
Draper, William G., 62
Dulles, Allen, 127
Duncan, Francis, 104
Dunford, James M., 10
Dunne, Irene, 63
Durant, Mary Beth, 97
Durant, Peter, 97
Dust on the Sea (Beach), 78, 84, 151–52

E
E-1B "Tracer," 133
Eagle Scout Recognition Dinner, 131–32
Eaton, Diane, 213
Ebert, Roger, 87
Eck, Heinz-Wilhelm, 81
Edwards, Beachley. *See* Beach, Edward L. "Ned," Jr.
Ehrlich, Max, 79
Eisenhower, Dwight D., 59, 163; on Beach, 74; in Beach's assignment to *Triton*, 99–100; inauguration ceremony of, 63; military aides and, 60–61; Navy's attitude toward, 72–73; presidential yacht and, 65; on Project Magellan, 126; U-2 incident and, 129
Eisenhower, Mamie: in launch of *Nautilus*, 71–72, 103;

presidential yacht and, 66
E.L. Beach Aviation Support
    Equipment Training Facility,
    195
El Salvador, 154
Esquire magazine, 155

F
Face the Nation, 130
*Fall Laconia, Der: Ein hohes Ied
    der U-boot-Waffe* (Brennecke),
    80–81
fathometer, 120–21
Faulkner, "Pop," 92
Fechteler, William M., 59, 73
Felt, Joseph, 90, 93
Finley, Bert, 51–52
First Train to Babylon (Ehrlich), 79
Fleisher-Durbin, Kristoffer, 212
Fluckey, Eugene B., 41
Flynn, Errol, 92
Fong, Hiram L., 154
Foreign Language Institute, 137
Forester, C.S., 80
Forrestal, James V., 49
Fouché, Alice. *See* Beach, Alice
Fouché, Joseph, 3, 197
Fox, Mark I., 68
Franke, William B., 126
frequency-modulated (FM) sonar
    set, 42
*From Annapolis to Scapa Flow: The
    Autobiography of Edward L.
    Beach Sr.* (Beach), 167–68
From Here to Eternity (film), 86

G
Gable, Clark, 86
Gato-class submarine, 21
Gay, John, 83
Gearing (DD-710), 92

General Dynamics, 71, 107
"Giant of Adventure" award, 130
Golden Laurel Awards, 85
Goldwater, Barry, 152
Good Shepherd, The (Forester), 80
Gordon, Mary, 160
Gordon, Vance, 160
graduate education, 135
Grenfell, Elton W., 49, 141
Grouper (SS-214), 84
"Guppy II" submarine, 50–51

H
Hagan, Kenneth J., 160
Hagerty, James, 104, 110, 129
Haitian occupation, 186–89
Hamilton, Edith, 104
"*Harder*" (Beach), 46
Harder (SS-257), 45, 83
Harder (SS-568), 58
Harlan, Russell, 85
Harlfinger, Frederick Joseph
    "Fritz," III, 24, 35
Harry Potter (Rowling), 202
Hart, Thomas C., 10
Hawthorne, William G., 12
Hay, James C., 170
hazing practices, 8
Hazlett, Everett "Swede," 59–60
Hecht, Hill, and Lancaster, 84
Henry, T.H., 129
Henry Holt and Company, 45, 79,
    80, 132, 151, 155, 160
Heureaux, Ulises, 3
"Hit 'em Again, *Harder*" (Beach),
    45
Hiyo (Japan), 29
Holland, Henry F., 74
Honduras, 154
Hopkins, John Jay, 71
Horatio Hornblower series, 80

Howarth, Stephen, 160
Hunt for Red October, The
    (Clancy), 87

I
inaugural parades, 63
Isenberg, Michael, 57, 102, 146

J
Japan: surrender of, 42; U.S.
    submarine strategy against, 27
Japanese-American reparations,
    163
Japanese operational codes, 40–41
Javits, Jacob K., 152
Joe Blunt (fictional character), 142
John W. Weeks (DD-701), 127
Johnson, Hiram, 7
Johnson, Louis, 55
Joint Chiefs of Staff, 54, 73
Joint Congressional and Special
    Material Division (Op-90A),
    135
Jones, James, 86
Juzan Maru (Japan), 41

K
Keepers of the Sea (Beach), 158,
    168
Kennicott, Donald, 45
Khrushchev, Nikita, 110, 127–28
Kimmel, Husband E., 161
Kimmel, Short, and Pearl Harbor:
    The Final Report Revealed
    (Broach and Martinze), 161
Kimmel case, 161–65, 171
King, Ernest, 35
Kiyotada Maru (Japan), 40
Koch, Howard, 12
Korean War, 55

L
Laconia Order, 81
Laconia sinking, 80–81
Lancaster, Burt, 86–87
Langello, Charles J., 85
Last of the Curlews (Bodsworth),
    79
Lay, Beirne, Jr., 46
Lea (DD-118), 15–19
Lebanon operations, 91
Lewis, Harrison, 81
Lewis, J.H., 23, 24
Lichoff, John, 90
Lockwood, Charles, 22, 45
Long, Russell, 154
Lowndes, Edward R., 9
Lowndes, William R. "Bill," 9
Luce, Stephen B., 150
Lucky Bag, The (Naval Academy
    yearbook), 7

M
MacDonald, Donald J., 68
Macon (CA-132), 118–20
Magellan Bay, 123
Magellan's voyages, 111, 113–14,
    120, 123, 126
Mahan, Alfred Thayer, 146
man-overboard rescue, 92–93
Märak, Johan, 215
Mare Island Navy Yard, 2, 194
Marjorie Morningstar (Wouk), 79,
    80
Marshall, William J., 113, 117
Martin, Harlan F., 125
Martinze, Daniel, 161
Masterton, Paul, 141
May, Andrew Jackson, 22
McAdoo, William G., 189
McAllister, Michael, 90, 91, 92
McDonald, David L., 135–36

McGregor, Rob Roy, 84–85
Meadows, Earnest R., 115
Medal of Honor, 41
medical evacuation, at-sea, 118–20
Memphis (ACR-10), 99, 134, 150–51, 190–92, 194
Mendenhall, Corwin G., 13, 144
Mercury Theatre on the Air, 12
Mexican-American War, 11, 186–87
Midway Island, 28
military awards, 148
Miller, Nathan, 81
minelaying operations, 27
"Mission in 1956" (Edwards), 155
Mitgang, Herbert, 78–79
Mitscher, Marc, 161
Montanaro, Lou, 98
Moore, Gary, 130
Moore, Johnnie, 43
Moore, Robert R., 141
Moran, Stanley P., 134
Mortimer, Philip P., Jr., 122
Morton, Dudley Walter "Mush," 25
Morton-O'Kane technique, 25–26, 35
motor patrol torpedo (PT) boats, 69
music pirating, 154
Mutiny on the Bounty (film), 83

N
National Geographic magazine, 124, 130
National Reactor Testing Station, 107, 108
National War College, 135
NATO exercises (1960), 131, 132
Nautilus (SSN-571), 50, 71–72, 105

Naval Academy: academic innovations at, 10; children's books set at, 201–3; class ranking system at, 9–10; dedication of Beach Hall at, 165–67; entrance examinations for, 6–7; hazing practices at, 8; regimental commander position at, 12; in "war of the worlds," 12–13
naval aide. *See* Office of the Naval Aide
Naval Historical Foundation, 170–71
Naval History Prize, 170–71
Naval History Symposium, 164
Naval Institute, 79, 166–67
Naval Institute *Proceedings,* 56, 186
Naval Terms Dictionary, The (Beach and Noel, eds.), 151, 168
Naval War College, 150
Naval War College Review, 150
Navy: budget and oversight hearings for, 135–37; cooperation of, in filming of *Run Silent, Run Deep,* 84; Eisenhower's attitude toward, 72–73; nuclear submarine program and, 48–50; officer promotion process in, 139–40, 162; officer rotations in, 102; Revolt of the Admirals, 54–55, 73; ship naming policy, 89; strategic role of, 47; White House functions funded by, 67–68
Navy Cross, 41
Navy League of the United States, 157

Navy yard overhaul, 31
Nedam, Curtis, 117, 119
Nelson, W.T., 93
neutrality patrols, 16
Nevers, Ernie, 199
New York (BB-34), 2, 193–94
New York Times, 78
New York Times best-seller list,
    79–80
New York Times crossword puzzle,
    170
Newhart, Bob, 131
night attack tactics, 26, 41
Nimitz, Chester, 23, 28, 49, 81,
    101, 163
Nishimura, Shoji, 123
Nitze, Paul H., 136
Nixon administration, 153
Noel, John V., Jr., 151
"Notes on *Run Silent, Run Deep*"
    (Daves), 82
nuclear defense, 68–70
nuclear football, 70
Nuclear Powered Ship and
    Submarine Recycling Program,
    133
nuclear-powered submarines:
    Beach's selection for service
    on, 101–4; development of,
    48–49; launch of *Nautilus,*
    71–72; navigational fixes
    and, 117; officer selection for
    service on, 100–101; officer
    training for service on, 102;
    public perception of, 103. *See
    also* submarines and submarine
    warfare
nuclear reactor operator training,
    107–8
nuclear weapon delivery systems,
    47–48

O
O'Brien, Tim, 78
Office of the Naval Aide: Beach's
    assignment as, 59; duties of,
    63–65; presidential yacht and,
    65–67; White House functions
    managed by, 67–68
officer promotion process, 139–40,
    162
O'Kane, Richard Hetherington,
    25, 140
Oldendorf, Jesse B., 123
Op-36, 47
Op-90A, 135–36
Operation Pacific (film), 82
Organization of American States,
    154
Osborn, Hartwell, 182

P
Palo Alto High School, 4–5
Paris Summit (1960), 110
Parsons, William S. "Deak," 48
Peabody, Endicott "Chubb" II, 39
Pearl Harbor attack, 23, 161–63
periscope liberty, 123
Philippine Insurrection, 184–86
Piper (SS-409), 42, 44, 46
Pluto and the Little Chickens
    (cartoon), 95
Pocket Books, 79
Polaris submarine program, 103,
    130–31
Pond, Charles Fremont, 190,
    191–92
Poole, J.R., 118
Potomac (AG-25), 65
Povich, Shirley, 12
Powers, Francis Gary, 127, 131
Pratt, Albert, 74
"Presidential Football," 70

presidential military aides, 60–61
presidential yacht. *See Williamsburg* (AGC-369)
Preston, Ruth, 5
Prettyman, Courtney, 17
Project Magellan: historical precedence for, 110–12; hydraulic system failure during, 125–26; media coverage of, 130–32; medical evacuation during, 118–20; navigational methods, 117; photographic records of, 115; plaque commemorating, 127; psychological studies conducted during, 121–22; route selected for, 113–14, 120, 123; scientific projects in, 115; secrecy surrounding, 112–13; voyage statistics, 130
promotion board procedures, 139–40, 162
Prospective Commanding Officer School, 36
Pyle, Howard, 95

Q
Quelpart anchorage, 20, 41

R
radar picket platform, 106–7, 133
Ramsay, Francis M., 183–84
Reader's Digest Condensed Books series, 79
Reagan, Ronald, 156, 163
Reagan Revolution, 156
Red Badge of Courage, The (Crane), 78
Renken, H.A., 141
Republican Policy Committee, 151–55

Revolt of the Admirals, 54–55, 73
Rhetoric Casebook, The (Connolly, ed.), 45
Rickover, Hyman G., 48, 49, 72, 108, 166; animosity toward, 103–4; Beach on, 101; interview techniques of, 100–101; selection of *Triton* commander by, 101–4
Rime of the Ancient Mariner, The (Coleridge), 77
Rindskopf, Maurice "Mike," 83, 140, 161
Roberts, J. Baylor, 115, 130
Roberts Commission Report, 165
Robertson, Bruce (son-in-law), 218
Robertson, Ingrid Alice Beach (daughter), 63, 94, 97, 217–18
Robertson, Jaya (granddaughter), 218
Robertson, Ngaere (granddaughter), 218
Rochefort, Joseph John, 163
Roddis, Louis H., Jr., 10
Roosevelt, Franklin D., 16, 18, 63
Roosevelt Naval History Prize, 157
Rowling, J.K., 202
Royal Hawaiian Hotel, 28
Royal Navy, neutrality rules and, 16–17
Run Silent, Run Deep (Beach), 75; allegations concerning incident in, 80–82; reviews of, 78–79; sequels to, 151–52, 155; success of, 79–80; themes in, 76–78
Run Silent, Run Deep (film): Beach's involvement in, 87–88; casting of, 85–87; in

submarine film genre, 82–85
Russell, James, 103–4

S
S-32 (SS-137), 35
Saami people, 215–16
Sahl, Mort, 131
Sailing the Silver Screen: Hollywood and the U.S. Navy (Suid), 82
Salamonie (AO-26), 87; in Lebanon operations, 91; man-overboard emergency and, 92–93; physical condition of, 90; wartime service of, 89
Salt and Steel: Reflections of a Submariner (Beach), 144, 167
Sand Pebbles, The (film), 85
Santee (training ship), 183
Saturday Evening Post, 130
Scapegoats: A Defense of Kimmel and Short at Pearl Harbor (Beach), 164
Schack, George D., 92
Schenck, Hubert Gregory "Hugh," 211, 212
Schenck, Inga, 31, 211–12
Schenck, Ingrid. *See* Beach, Ingrid
Schiff, John J. "Jack," 167
Schulz, Robert L., 62
Scroggin, Margaret C., 45–46
Sea Cat (SS-399), 84
Seahorse (SS-304), 28
Selective Service System, 137–38
Sellers, David F., 10
Senate Republican Policy Committee, 151–55
Shear, Harold, 13, 58
Shepherd, Johnny, 37
ship launching traditions, 70–72
ship model collection, 98
Ship's Inertial Navigation System (SINS), 114–15
Short, Walter C., 162
Sidwell Friends School, 137, 212, 217
Silent Service (television series), 46
Smith, Bernard Brussel, 79
snorkel development, 51
Soccer War (1969), 154
social aides, 64–65
Soviet Union: technology race with, 109–10; U-2 incident and, 127–29
Spanish-American War, 184–85
Spectorsky, A.C., 46
Spong, William, 154
Spruance, Edward Dean, 38
Spruance, Raymond, 25
Sputnik, 109–10
Stanford University, 6, 199
Stark, James E., 118
Steele, Allen, 124–26, 131–32
steep angle maneuvers, 51–52
Steinhaus, Gary, 159
Stillwell, Paul, 36, 102, 162, 170
Story of King Arthur and His Knights, The (Pyle), 95
strategic bombing, 47
Strauss, Lewis L., 100
Street, George L., III, 20, 36, 39, 41, 46
Submarine! (Beach), 30, 43, 45
submarine film genre, 82–83
submarine officer advancement, 89, 139–40
Submarine Operational History of the United States Navy in the Second World War (unpublished), 26–27
Submarine Squadron Eight, 135
submarine tactics: battery capacity and, 50–51; down-the-throat

shot, 34, 83; Morton-O'Kane technique, 25–26, 35; night attacks, 26, 41; steep angle maneuvers, 51–52; Wolf packs, 40

submariner casualties, 42

submarines, nuclear-powered. *See* nuclear-powered submarines

submarines and submarine warfare: attack on Quelpart anchorage and, 20–21; depth charges and, 22; early problems with, 25; minelaying operations, 27; as radar picket platforms, 106–7, 133; success of, in WWII, 41–42; in U.S. strategy, 27, 48; weapons and, 21–22

Suid, Lawrence, 82, 83

Sullivan, John L., 49

Swami Muktananda, 218

Sword of the Class of 1897, 13–14

T

Talk of the Nation (radio show), 131

Tanamont, Del, 170

Tang-class submarine, 57–58

Texas (BB-35), 11

Things They Carried, The (O'Brien), 78

This People's Navy: The Making of American Sea Power (Hagan), 160

Thomas, Charles S., 74

Thurber, James, 122

Thurmond, Strom, 161

Time magazine, 78

"*Tirante*" (Beach), 46

Tirante (SS-420): in attack on Quelpart anchorage, 20, 41; officers of, 39; public relations

mission of, 39–40

Tkach, Walter R., 126

To Shining Sea: A History of the United States Navy 1775-1991 (Howarth), 160

tomb-stone promotions, 162

torpedo defects, 26–27

torpedoes, 21, 39–40

Tower, John, 152, 154–55

"*Trigger* Fights Her War, The" (Beach), 45

Trigger II (SS-566), 57–58, 146

Trigger (SS-237): in attack on *Hiyo*, 29–30; in attack on Japanese convoy, 35–36; Beach's assignment to, 22–23; Beach's stories about, 44; in East China Sea operations, 33–35; grounding of, 23–24; in minelaying operations, 27; Robert Dornin assignment to, 32–33; sinking of, 37, 40

Triton namesakes, 105

Triton (SSR[N]-586), 1; Beach as PCO of, 104; commissioning of, 109; Eisenhower in Beach's assignment to, 99–100; fate of, 133; nuclear reactor arrangement on, 105–6; as radar picket platform, 106–7; Rickover in Beach's assignment to, 101–4. *See also* Project Magellan

Truman, Harry S., 65

Tuohy, William, 140

Tuscaloosa (CA-37), 16

U

U-156 (Germany), 81

U-2 incident, 127–29, 131

underway refueling, 92

"Unicorn in the Garden, The"
(Thurber), 122
United Artists, 88
United States Navy, The: 200 Years
(Beach), 20, 159, 160–61, 167

V
Vera Cruz occupation, 186–87
Verrill, Dena, 170
Vietnam War, 137–38
Vinson, Carl, 55

W
Wahoo (SS-238), 25
Walker, Francis D., 141
Wall Street Journal, 170
War of the Worlds, The (Welles), 12
Washington (ACR-11), 187
Washington Post, 164
Wayne, John, 85, 86
Welles, Orson, 12
Weschler, Thomas R., 203
West Point, 12
Weybrew, Benjamin, 114, 121–22
What's My Line? (television show),
130
White House bomb shelter, 69–70
White House Mess, 67–68
White House motor patrol torpedo
(PT) boats, 69
White House naval aide. *See* Office
of the Naval Aide
White House Office of Military
Affairs, 68
Wiley, Henry A., 2, 183, 203

Wilkinson, Eugene P. "Dennis,"
50, 72
Wilkinson, Janice, 72
Will, George F., 152
Williams, Annie Laurie, 88
Williamsburg (AGC-369), 63,
65–67
Wilson, Walter Pye, 36–37, 57
Wilson administration, 188
Wise, Robert, 85
wolf packs, 40
Wood, Dave, 90
World War I, 193–94
World War II: Alice Laura Beach's
service in, 209; demobilization
process following, 46; John
Beach's service in, 203–7;
Kimmel case in context of,
165; military restructuring
following, 47–48; neutrality
rules preceding, 15–17;
submarine warfare role in,
41–42
Worth, Sam, 134
Wouk, Herman, 79
Wreck of the Memphis, The (Beach),
150–51, 159, 191

Y
Yaddo retreat, 159
yard overhauls, 31
Yasunobu, Takeo, 29n

Z
Zebra Books, 79

About the Author

Holding a doctorate in history education, Edward Finch retired in 2004 after teaching for thirty years at Freeport (Illinois) High School. He is now director of the Stephenson County History Museum and resides in Freeport with his wife Cathy and their dog Addie, a Pembroke Welsh Corgi named for Addison and Clark streets in Chicago—home of the Cubs.

The Naval Institute Press is the book-publishing arm of the U.S. Naval Institute, a private, nonprofit, membership society for sea service professionals and others who share an interest in naval and maritime affairs. Established in 1873 at the U.S. Naval Academy in Annapolis, Maryland, where its offices remain today, the Naval Institute has members worldwide.

Members of the Naval Institute support the education programs of the society and receive the influential monthly magazine *Proceedings* or the colorful bimonthly magazine *Naval History* and discounts on fine nautical prints and on ship and aircraft photos. They also have access to the transcripts of the Institute's Oral History Program and get discounted admission to any of the Institute-sponsored seminars offered around the country.

The Naval Institute's book-publishing program, begun in 1898 with basic guides to naval practices, has broadened its scope to include books of more general interest. Now the Naval Institute Press publishes about seventy titles each year, ranging from how-to books on boating and navigation to battle histories, biographies, ship and aircraft guides, and novels. Institute members receive significant discounts on the Press's more than eight hundred books in print.

Full-time students are eligible for special half-price membership rates. Life memberships are also available.

For a free catalog describing Naval Institute Press books currently available, and for further information about joining the U.S. Naval Institute, please write to:

Member Services
U.S. Naval Institute
291 Wood Road
Annapolis, MD 21402-5034
Telephone: (800) 233-8764
Fax: (410) 571-1703
Web address: www.usni.org